GCE English Language

A study and revision course for O Level

Elizabeth A. Cripps
and Caroline Footman

CAMBRIDGE
UNIVERSITY PRESS

PUBLISHED BY THE PRESS SYNDICATE OF THE UNIVERSITY OF CAMBRIDGE
The Pitt Building, Trumpington Street, Cambridge, United Kingdom

CAMBRIDGE UNIVERSITY PRESS
The Edinburgh Building, Cambridge CB2 2RU, UK
40 West 20th Street, New York, NY 10011-4211, USA
477 Williamstown Road, Port Melbourne, VIC 3207, Australia
Ruiz de Alarcón 13, 28014 Madrid, Spain
Dock House, The Waterfront, Cape Town 8001, South Africa

http://www.cambridge.org

First published 2002
Fourth printing 2004

Printed in the United Kingdom at the University Press, Cambridge

Typeface Minion 11pt/15pt *System* QuarkXpress®
Design and illustration by Hardlines Ltd, Charlbury, Oxford

A catalogue record for this book is available from the British Library

ISBN 0 521 00989 8 paperback

Contents

Acknowledgements

The authors would like to thank the following: English Language examination candidates worldwide for providing inspiration and material for the book; students from the American Intercontinental University, London; John S. Gammon.

The publisher has used its best endeavours to ensure that the URLs for external websites referred to in this book are correct and active at the time of going to press. However, the publisher has no responsibility for the websites and can make no guarantee that a site will remain live or that the content is or will remain appropriate.

With thanks to the following for permission to reproduce copyright material in this book: Alfred Hitchcock Mystery Magazine p32, Arrow Books p143, BBC Worldwide p139, BUAV p125, Carel Press p28, 29, Dorling Kindersley p15, Edexcel p13, Edinburgh Health Club p38, 39 40, Emap elan p67, Fraser and Dunlop p23, Goldenjoy Holidays p131, 132, 133, Guardian Newspapers p20, 76, 78, 151, 152, 153, 157, 158, 159 202, 203, 204, Hamish Hamilton p147, Independent Newspapers p47, Lifespan Collective p16, London Zoo p108, Macmillan Publishers p58, Newsweek International p128, Orion Publishing Group p17, Oxford University Press p23, Penguin p202, Sanyo p9, Secker and Warburg p33, 54, 55, Times Newspapers p35, 115, Tower Bridge p88, 89, Tower of London p96, Virago Press p27, World Wildlife Fund p107

Picture Credits
Associated Press p160, Corbis p96, Robert Harding p132, Popperfoto p156, Pete Postlewaith p35, RSPCA p107, 108, 125, Stone p67, 131, 132, 133, 173, Troika Photos p204

Cover image by © Kurt Stier/CORBIS

Introduction: the syllabus and the examination

Who will find this book useful?

This book is aimed mainly at students who are taking a course leading to the GCE O' Level in English Language. They may be studying English just for this exam, or using it as a first or second language or as a medium for education or employment. Teachers and parents may also find it interesting and supportive. It could also be useful for other readers with a wider interest in improving their skills in understanding and writing English for a range of purposes.

Why is there a need for a new syllabus?

At the time of writing the O' Level syllabus offered by Edexcel has been revised, and this book is intended to accompany the new syllabus. It is felt that the expansion of the media, changes in styles and methods of communication, and the increasing use of the English language for cultural activities and entertainment have created new demands for education and employment.

We hope that this book reflects these changes and will enable you to communicate more clearly and effectively using English as an international language.

This examination, to be taken for the first time in May/June 2003, is intended for all candidates for whom English is to be the language of education or employment, whether or not English is their first language.

You may need a qualification in English for further or higher education, for employment or promotion, to further your career aims or for personal satisfaction. Whatever your motivation, we wish you enjoyment and a sense of achievement both in working through the book and tackling the exam.

We hope that you find the structure, examples and guidance helpful and stimulating, and that you will gain confidence as you work towards your goal.

What is covered in the syllabus?

The syllabus comprises three sections:
- Section A (30%) Questions are set on the language and content of the stimulus material. This may include a comparison, or justification for a choice or preference.
- Section B (35%) Candidates are asked to produce a summary, based on material in the paper, which is clearly defined in terms of purpose, context, audience and length.

- Section C (35%) This is a single writing task from a choice of topics and styles, based on ideas related to the stimulus material.

Why is it a 'themed' paper?

How often in everyday life are you asked to make connections between various sources of information? It might be in a group research project at school or college, with each member investigating a different aspect before meeting to share resources and select the most relevant material for a presentation to the class. It would be really boring, and show a lack of initiative, if each of the groups merely read parts of one source.

This also happens in the work situation, where as an individual or as part of a team you have to access up-to-date or archived information in order to make a written or oral report to a committee, prepare a proposal or explain a problem and suggest solutions. It could also be for a leisure or recreational purpose, such as collecting and comparing information before planning a purchase or a holiday, or preparing for an event.

Whatever the situation or purpose, the ability to examine a number of different sources and types of material, to question and understand the information, to select the relevant and discard the less important and to re-present the key points for a new audience and situation are skills which show a sense of purpose and direction. To do all this in a language that is not your main one shows an ability to use and understand the language over and above the ability to translate.

The examination for which you are preparing will therefore contain a number of extracts which are linked or themed in content, but come from a variety of sources, including fiction or factual prose sourced from books, newspapers or magazines, advertisements, letters, web pages – in fact any type of material which can be reproduced on a printed page. The material will probably be more varied than in papers you have looked at for English before, but it should be interesting and realistic, and will allow you to show a range of skills.

Aims

Following a course for this examination should enable you to:
- read material from a range of sources, including literary and non-literary material and media;
- read with understanding and enjoyment for a variety of purposes;
- use the standard forms of written English for a variety of purposes, such as persuasion, arguments, etc., with care for content, appropriateness and quality of expression.

How the syllabus is assessed

The following grid shows the assessment objectives for the examination.

	Section A	Section B	Section C
AO1 read with understanding texts of various kinds in standard English	✔	✔	
AO2 select, order and present in writing, information, ideas and opinions from the texts provided		✔	
AO3 use and adapt forms and types of writing for specific purposes, effects and audiences		✔	✔
AO4 write using the standard forms of English with accurate spelling and punctuation		✔	✔
AO5 adopt appropriate styles, exercising care for clarity and quality of expression		✔	✔

As you can see, different skills will be emphasised in the three sections of the paper, but you will need to read with understanding, show this in your writing and express your own ideas clearly and accurately.

There is one three-hour written paper, with a selection of themed stimulus material. This may include reading or graphical material, including copies of leaflets and other realistic items, as well as literary or non-literary texts.

Sections A and B are directly related to this stimulus material. Section C asks you to develop the theme of the material in one of a variety of ways. It is therefore very important that you should spend time (about 15 minutes is suggested) reading the texts, to familiarise yourself with the content and ideas.

Section A   (30%)

There will be four to seven questions in this section, on the language and content of the stimulus material. You are advised to spend about 40 minutes on these questions, all of which should be answered. The number of marks for each question is shown, and should be used as a guide to the length and detail expected. The questions are designed to assess your understanding of, and response to, the stimulus material. They focus on aspects of content, meaning and style. Understanding of both significant detail and broader implications is needed. Some questions may ask for the selection of information to be presented in a given format, such as numbered points or a short paragraph.

Marks are given in this section primarily for content and understanding, but sufficient care must be taken with clarity and accuracy for these to be recognised. Some questions will ask for the information to be presented in your own words; some may ask for a comparison between pieces of text.

Section B (35%)

In this section you are asked to use some of the material in the paper to produce writing directed in terms of purpose, context and audience. This is a test of understanding, selection and summary skills and the ability to adapt material to produce a new piece. The task may be to inform or instruct, to advise or persuade or to express attitudes, in a recognised format, such as a talk, an article for a newspaper or magazine, a letter or a report, or two short pieces. The length required will vary according to the task set and will be clearly stated on the paper. You will receive no credit for points beyond the stated **word limit**.

This section will be assessed for selection of relevant information, appropriateness of style and format, and quality and accuracy of expression. Direct copying from the original text(s) will be penalised in the expression and accuracy mark. About one hour should be spent on this section.

Section C (35%)

You are given a choice of tasks related to the stimulus material and should complete one of them. This could be a narrative, descriptive, argumentative or discursive piece of writing. There will be opportunities for imaginative and personal responses to the themes and topics studied for the previous sections. You should spend about an hour on this section, writing between 350 and 400 words.

You should allow up to ten minutes to check your work and make any necessary corrections.

Standard English

The syllabus assesses reading and writing in the internationally recognised forms of standard English: either British or American standard forms are acceptable in your writing. Spelling must, however, be consistent. For instance, 're' or 'er' endings, such as *centre* or *center* are each considered correct, but not both; similarly, you should use either 'our' or 'or' endings, as in *favour* or *favor*. Some words, however, may have different meanings according to the spelling. An example is *program*, which has various meanings in America; however, in British English *program* and *programme* have different meanings.

Grade criteria

This is an indication of the ability level needed to achieve certain grades overall; as mentioned above, certain skills are emphasised in different sections of the paper.

Grade A

You will be able to:

- show a good level of understanding of the theme of a text, both explicit and implicit;
- read with clear understanding of specific items of vocabulary;
- select accurately main and supporting points of argument;
- differentiate between fact and opinion;
- present the selected material relevantly, clearly and coherently;
- write in a variety of styles and forms for given purposes;
- show audience awareness;
- use standard grammatical forms and idioms of English;
- use a variety of sentence structures with confidence and organise writing with skill;
- write with an impressive range of appropriate vocabulary, expressing ideas with precision;
- show advanced accuracy in spelling and punctuation;
- show skill in a range of writing styles, fitting your writing to the tasks required;
- show control, clarity and consistency in each piece of writing.

Grade C

You will be able to:

- show reasonable understanding of the theme of a text;
- show fair understanding of explicit meaning and occasional understanding of inferential meaning;
- show understanding of some vocabulary items;
- select some major points of argument and some supporting points;
- show some ability to present the material selected clearly;
- write in several styles and forms for given purposes;
- recognise the intended audience;
- write reasonable standard English;
- use some variety of sentence structure and vocabulary;
- spell and punctuate fairly accurately;
- show some ability to sustain a theme and consistent style in a piece of writing.

Grade E

You will be able to:
- show some grasp of the theme of a text;
- understand some explicit meaning;
- select one or two points of argument;
- present selected material so that a reader can follow it;
- write simply for a given purpose;
- attempt to fit form to purpose;
- write at a level of basic coherence in standard English;
- write simple sentences;
- show a basic understanding of the conventions of spelling and punctuation;
- write at a basic level in a suitable style.

Those of you who are familiar with the previous syllabus will note that there are basic similarities – the length, number of sections, types of writing and reading tasks required and the need for standard English and accuracy. The paper will still be themed in content.

There are important changes, however, and we hope that this book will take you through the skills required to meet the demands of the new syllabus, with ideas of how to improve your range of styles, your fluency and technical accuracy. You will be able to see how other students have responded to tasks and how examiners would grade their efforts.

New aspects of the syllabus

Section A Comprehension

The stimulus material is taken from a wider range of types of writing and may include real documents in the form of leaflets, brochures, handouts, letters, with pictures or diagrams, tables or graphs, as well as written text. There is a list of possible types of source material in the full syllabus.

There are fewer questions than previously, but you still need to show your understanding of content and language and the themes of the pieces. This could be in the form of choosing words or phrases, writing a short piece in response to a set task, and/or comparing the style, impact or purpose of the documents. You will be given guidance in each question about the type of response the examiners are looking for and the length of answer needed, as well as the marks for each question.

Section B Summary and directed writing

This is similar to the previous syllabus, but as indicated above, the material on which the tasks are based will be more varied. You will be asked to produce a piece of written work using ideas from the passage or passages, in your own words as far as possible, for a new purpose and audience. You will be given ideas about how to structure the task and where to find relevant ideas and other ways to focus your answer. The maximum number of words will be given and will be important. You will need a balance between making valid points from the material and changing tone and style for the new document. This will involve expressing ideas mainly in your own words.

Section C Essay

There will be a choice of three titles. You will be asked for one piece of writing, which will have a clear link with the theme of the material for the previous sections. There will be no additional pictures for this section, but you will have a choice of types of response, such as personal writing, an argument, a description or a discussion of ideas raised in the stimulus material, which may include illustrations. The length required will be 350 to 400 words.

Your writing will be marked on the relevance and quality of the content and how you organise your ideas; how well you express them, with variety of vocabulary and sentence structures; and how accurately you use English.

The skills examiners will be looking for in marking your answers will be very similar to those for previous syllabus, but the ways you are asked to show these skills may be different. We have included an exemplar paper in Appendix A to help you to prepare for the examination.

This book aims to help you to match your skills to the demands of the exam, to increase your confidence and therefore, your chances of success. Good luck!

Reading a variety of texts for explicit meaning

How often do you need to interpret information, show understanding of details, follow instructions? When you are taking an exam, the first test of your understanding is reading the instructions and filling in the front page of your answer book, before you have even been told to open your paper (see pages 12–13)! Throughout your life you are constantly showing that you understand what you hear, see and read, even if you don't always agree with it.

Showing understanding could be needed in real life when explaining how something works, reporting on an incident or using a piece of equipment. In the exam, the assessment of your understanding will often involve rephrasing original information in your own words, so you will need to:

- understand the original;
- follow any sequence in the text;
- find information throughout a passage or document;
- re-express words or phrases.

You may also need to compare two or more items in different styles to establish whether the information in them varies.

Reading for precise meaning: instruction texts

Instruction manuals which come with electrical equipment often contain a wide range of types of information, including abbreviations, subject-specific terms, warnings, operating instructions, troubleshooting advice and guarantee details, each of which has its own style and layout. The language is usually very concise and specific, and the writer has to be very careful to make it clear because of possible dangers and to prevent damage.

Let us examine a page from an instruction manual to see how you can best show your factual understanding. Study the page carefully, then look at the questions, answers and comments on pages 10–11.

1

INTRODUCTION

GB

Only cassettes marked **VHS** can be used with this VCR

PRECAUTIONS

Safety precautions

DANGER:
This VCR contains live parts. Do not remove the cabinet.

WARNING:
To prevent fire or shock hazard, do not expose this product to rain or moisture.

CAUTION:
Do not put your hand or other objects in the cassette loading slot because of the risk of injury or an accident. Be sure to keep small children away from the VCR.

Caution concerning condensation

Be careful of condensation

Condensation can form inside a VCR when it is suddenly moved from a cold place to a warm, humid one, or when a heater has been turned on to quickly heat the room.

Do not insert a video cassette if you use this VCR in areas subject to condensation.
Wait for $1\frac{1}{2}$ to 2 hours to completely eliminate condensation before using the VCR.

Operating precautions

• Place the VCR on a flat, stable, level surface. Never subject it to violent shaking or any other shock or impact.

• Do not expose the unit to high temperatures. Excessive heat (heat sources such as heaters, ovens, closed cars on hot days, etc.) may damage the unit.

• Be sure to use this VCR only in a temperature range of 5°C to 40°C (41˚F to 105˚F) and at less than 80% humidity.

• Do not use the unit under the following conditions:
- in locations with high humidity
- in presence of excessive dirt or dust
- in areas subject to strong vibrations
- near strong magnetic fields (e.g. transmitting antennas, motors, fluorescent lights, etc.)

• Do not stack anything on top of your VCR, or block the air vents, to prevent damaging or overheating.

• Do not place anything, except VHS video cassette tapes, in the unit.

• Do not allow rain, steam, dew, salt water, sand, oily smoke, metal objects, etc. to enter the unit.

• Clean with a dry and soft cloth, or a soft cloth slightly moistened with a mild detergent solution.

• Do not use any type of solvent, such as alcohol or benzine.

Adapted from Sanyo instruction manual.

The manual uses the abbreviation VCR. What is this short for?

Video Cassette Recorder

The answer seems straightforward, and you may well have known this already. If not, there are three illustrations and the term 'video cassette' is used in the text.

Define a VCR in your own words.

A piece of electrical equipment which captures moving images and sound from a television or camera and transfers them onto a tape for playback. It can also be used to copy other tapes.

This question is more challenging, as you need to show your understanding and the breadth and precision of your vocabulary. See how the explanation has avoided the root of each of the original words, including changing 'record' to 'copy' or 'capture'. An electrical engineer might give a more elaborate or technical definition; a dictionary might have a shorter one, but the answer above would gain full marks in an English exam!

What is the name for a piece of equipment which records sounds but not images?

A tape recorder, an audio tape machine, a telephone answering machine, or a cassette recorder.

This is a different type of question, because the information is not in the text, and there are several possible answers. The question could also have been asked in reverse: 'What is the essential difference between an audio recorder and a VCR?' This would have been a way of testing whether you knew the difference between 'audio' and 'video' rather than the names of items of equipment. It is very important to know what sort of information each question is looking for in order to maximise your marks.

Under the heading 'Safety precautions' there are three sections, labelled
'DANGER', 'WARNING' and 'CAUTION'. Can you explain the difference
between these words?

*'Danger' is the strongest, suggesting risk to life. 'Warning' suggests possible
damage to equipment or people. 'Caution' suggests less serious consequences
but still inconvenience or pain.*

This question is asking you to distinguish between three similar words, in this
case with differing degrees of force, so you are being tested on your ability to
interpret and explain them. It would be wrong here to use one of the words
in the explanation of either of the others, such as 'Danger is a warning.'

Give four examples of dry materials which should be kept out of the unit?

Dirt, dust, sand, metal objects.

This question requires you to differentiate between wet or damp and dry
materials and to find information in more than one section of the text. You
also need to work out that advice to avoid dirty or dusty areas suggests that
the machine could be damaged there.

Based on the advice in the booklet, would you recommend using the VCR in
any of the following places?
  a) near a beach
  b) on the slopes of a volcano
  c) in a caravan
  d) in an indoor sports arena
  e) on a boat

The answer to each of the choices is no.

The venues are not listed in the text, but you are advised to avoid sand,
excessive heat or vibrations, fluorescent lights and salt water, each of which is
likely to be present in one of the places listed.

Why would it be sensible not to spray the machine with a cleaning agent?

*You are advised to use a dry or slightly damp cloth, and to avoid solvent which
might contain alcohol.*

The mark scheme for such a question would have at least two marks, which
would be an indication that the answer should contain two ideas.

Some of these questions are more straightforward than others, but they all refer to information which is stated in the text, or relates very closely to it. There are some responses which require you to make links and use your judgement, but not to search for a viewpoint or opinion or a hidden agenda. It would be strange if an instruction booklet did contain any of these attitudes, as factual writing should be clear, unambiguous, helpful and objective.

If you were to look in a reference source, such as an encyclopaedia, website or textbook, you would expect to find facts, definitions and information of varying levels of complexity, rather than opinions, debate or persuasion. It is important to be able to distinguish between fact and opinion, both in source material and in your own responses. If, for example, you had used a VCR on a boat without problems, this should not affect your response to Question 6, which asks you to use the text from the booklet to find the answer. (After all, if the VCR had broken down while being used in this situation, the manufacturers would probably deny liability, as their advice would have been ignored.)

Reading the exam paper

You can help yourself to feel confident, save time and approach the paper more calmly if you are familiar with the **rubric** for the whole paper and for each section. Of course, you will still need to study the texts and questions, but you will have a better idea of what to expect and how to tackle it and organise your time.

Let's look at the instructions on the front of a typical exam paper on page 13. It is possible that nerves or anxiety may affect your ability to follow instructions; some students seem confused by what seems clear to others. Rest assured that your paper will be marked even if you haven't filled in the information in the right boxes, but you will feel more confident, and it will be easier for the marker, if you are sure what to do.

The points on the front page appear under **sub-headings**, in order of importance. If you have a chance to study practice papers you should familiarise yourself with the rubric. When you study the question paper itself, you will also notice the use of capitals, bold print, an indication of marks, asterisks and maybe footnotes. It will be important to take note of each of these, as they will help you to understand what examiners are looking for and what you need to do to gain credit for your answers.

Some instructions are in bold or capitals, to emphasise their importance, for example, **'Answer ALL questions in Sections A and B and ONE question from Section C.'** In some other subjects you may have a different number of sections or choice of questions.

The phrasing of other points alters the tone and degree of compulsion, for example, 'You should pull out the passages and spend 15 minutes reading these texts before answering the questions' is advice rather than an edict. It appears in a section headed 'Information for Candidates'. This is just meant as a helpful suggestion; your teacher may have given you different guidance,

Paper Reference(s)

7161

London Examinations GCE

English Language
Ordinary Level

Specimen Paper

First examination June 2003

Time: 3 hours

Materials required for examination	Items included with question papers
Answer book (AB16)	Nil

Instructions to Candidates

Answer ALL questions in Sections A and B and ONE question from Section C.

In the boxes on the answer book, write the name of the examining body (London Examinations), your centre number, candidate number, the subject title (English Language), the paper reference (7161), your surname, other names and signature.

Answer your questions in the answer book. Use supplementary answer sheets if necessary.

Information for Candidates

The total mark for this paper is 100. The marks for parts of questions are shown in round brackets: e.g. (2).

The questions in this paper are based on the two texts inserted with this paper. You should spend 15 minutes reading these texts before answering the questions.

Advice to Candidates

Write your answers neatly and legibly.

and it is unlikely that anyone will check whether you have followed it to the letter. 'Use supplementary answer sheets if necessary' is also guidance, but must be followed if you need more paper, so is included in the Instructions section. 'Write your answers clearly and legibly' could appear on the front page of any exam paper. We hope that candidates will follow this advice, but if you make mistakes or have to cross out work, as long as your answers are legible, they will be marked.

Reading a variety of texts for explicit meaning

Comparing: instruction texts

If you wanted to cook a particular dish, you might well look in several recipe books to compare recipes, maybe to find the one which matched most closely the ingredients in your cupboard or your preferences for flavour or cooking method. You might want to combine recipes to make up your own version.

Look at the following recipes for making pizza bases and complete the tasks that follow.

Text A

Pizza base

(Makes one 30cm (12in) round pizza base
or four 15cm (6in) bases.)

INGREDIENTS
175g (6oz) plain strong white flour
175g (6oz) plain strong wholemeal flour
1/2 tsp* salt
15g ($\frac{1}{2}$oz) fresh yeast or 2 tsp dried yeast
1 tsp sugar
200ml (7fl oz) tepid water
45ml (3 tbsp*) olive oil
butter or oil to grease the baking sheet

Preparation

1   Tip the flours and salt into a large bowl, mix roughly together with your fingers and leave in a warm place until warm (not hot) to the touch.
2   If using fresh yeast, crumble into a small bowl with the sugar and pour in the tepid water. If using dried yeast, put the water and sugar into the bowl first, then sprinkle the yeast on top and stir.
3   Leave the yeast until it has frothed up like the head on a glass of beer: about five minutes.
4   Add the oil to the flour, and pour in the yeast. Mix to a dough that leaves the sides of the bowl clean, then turn it out on to a clean work surface and knead for 5–10 minutes or until the dough feels soft and silky. If sticky, add more flour.
5   Return the dough to the bowl and cover with clingfilm or a clean tea towel wrung out in hot water. Leave in a warm place until the dough has almost doubled in size: 30 minutes to an hour.
6   Lightly grease a pizza plate or baking sheet with butter or olive oil.
7   Punch down the dough with your fist, remove it from the bowl and knead it briefly. Flatten it into a circle 30cm (12in) in diameter or, to make individual pizzas, divide the dough into four pieces and flatten these into circles. Place on the plate or baking sheet.
8   Arrange topping of choice.
9   Bake for 10–15 minutes for individual pizzas, 20 minutes for a large one.

* tsp = teaspoon;
tbsp = tablespoon

Adapted from Classic Vegetarian *by Rose Elliot.*

Pizza

For the bread dough:
12oz wholewheat flour
1oz fresh yeast or $\frac{1}{2}$ oz dried yeast
2 tbsp oil
$\frac{1}{4}$–$\frac{1}{2}$ pt warm water
1 tsp salt
1 tsp sugar or honey

Cream the yeast with the sugar in a cup and blend it with the warm water. Put the cup in a warm place until the yeast mixture is frothy. Meanwhile, put the flour and salt in a bowl somewhere warm. When the yeast mixture is active and frothy, mix it with the oil into the flour and salt until a soft dough is formed. Add more water if necessary (flours vary enormously in the amount of water they need). The dough should not be too sticky, but should feel soft and silky. Knead it well. A low surface is essential to get a good amount of pressure and strength behind your kneading. The more you knead, the better your dough will be. Then place your dough in an oiled container which is big enough to allow it to double its size. Brush the top with oil, cover the container with a damp cloth and put it in a warm place until doubled in bulk (45 minutes–1 $\frac{1}{4}$ hours).

Preheat the oven to 190°C, gas mark 5. When the dough has risen, knead again, then place on an oiled baking tray and flatten to about $\frac{1}{8}$ inch thick. The base can be the shape of the baking tray, a circle on a bigger tray or little circles for individual pizzas, whichever you prefer. Pour on the topping. Leave in a warm place to rise for 30–40 minutes. Bake in the oven for 30 minutes or until the bread base is cooked. Serve with a salad.

Adapted from Full of Beans *by Lifespan Collective Ltd.*

Pizza

When it comes to making bread and pizza doughs, I prefer to remain as old-fashioned and traditional as possible. There is no dried yeast and no food processor for me. I like the frothiness and unmistakable smell of fresh yeast and the kneading and stretching and general thumping of the dough. But I admit that this is pure romanticism and you could halve the preparation time by resorting to labour-saving devices.

This recipe makes six 10cm/4in pizzas. I prefer my pizza bases thin and crisp so don't allow for a second rising. If you prefer a thicker, more focaccia-like* base, you must allow the dough to rise for a further 20 minutes after rolling it out.

* focaccia = Italian bread

Reading a variety of texts for explicit meaning

INGREDIENTS

For the dough
15g/ $\frac{1}{2}$oz fresh yeast
$\frac{1}{2}$ tsp caster sugar
150ml/6fl oz hand-hot water
300g/10oz strong white flour
1 heaped tsp salt
1 tbsp virgin olive oil

METHOD

Dissolve the fresh yeast with the sugar in a little of the water and set aside for about 10 minutes until a froth appears on the surface. Place the flour mixed with the salt in a mound on your worktop or simply in a bowl and make a shallow well in the centre. Put the warm liquid into the well and mix with the flour. Then add the olive oil and the rest of the water. It is difficult to give an exact quantity of water so if the dough is too sticky, simply sprinkle a little more flour into it and if it is too dry and does not hold together properly, add a little more water until the dough comes away cleanly from the work surface or bowl. Knead the dough on a lightly floured surface for 8–10 minutes until it is smooth and elastic.

Place in a lightly floured bowl and make an incision across the top with a knife, which will help it rise. Sprinkle a little more flour on top, cover loosely with a tea towel and place in a warm, draught-free spot to rise until doubled in volume. This may take as little as 45 minutes or as long as three hours, depending on the temperature.

Knock back the dough, adding a little flour if necessary, then knead it briefly – a couple of minutes will do. Divide the dough into even-sized lumps and roll each into a rough circle. The dough should not be thicker than 2.5mm / $\frac{1}{8}$ in thick when rolled out.
Preheat the oven to 200ºC.

Prick each of the pizza bases with a fork; brush generously with topping. Drizzle olive oil lightly over the top. Place on a lightly floured baking tray and bake for 15 minutes until the pizza dough is crisped and lightly browned around the edges.

Adapted from The New Cranks Recipe Book *by Nadine Abensur.*

You will have immediately noticed differences between these recipes, in length, layout, units of measurement and other features. To start, however, let's look at the basic similarities, taking the ingredients first.

Task 1

If you were assembling the ingredients to make pizza for your friends, what would you need for the base? In spite of the minor differences in adjectives, quantities and order, could you list the six vital ingredients?

The answer is flour, yeast, oil, water, salt, sweetener (sugar or honey). These may be common ingredients, but there are still differences in the quantities and types used.

Task 2

Complete a grid to show the differences.

	Recipe A	Recipe B	Recipe C
Flour	175g (6oz) plain strong white; 175g (6oz) plain strong wholemeal	12oz wholewheat flour	10oz strong white flour
Yeast			
Oil			
Water			
Salt			
Sweetener			

You can clearly see that there are differences in quantities and types of flour, the single largest ingredient.

Now look at the methods. The easiest way to compare them might be to make three lists of numbered points, in the form of a summary or notes. This will show both whether you have understood the recipes and if there are any major differences. You could start with Text A as it is already laid out as numbered points.

Text A
1 Put salt and flour, mixed, in large bowl in warm place until warm.
2 Fresh yeast, crumble into small bowl, add sugar and tepid* water.
   Dried yeast, add to water and sugar.
3 Leave yeast till frothy (about 5 minutes).
4 Add yeast and oil to flour. Mix until sides of bowl are clean,
   then knead** on clean surface until soft and silky (5–10 minutes).
   Add more flour if sticky.

*Did you understand 'tepid'? You could look in the other recipes for clues. They refer to 'warm' and 'hand-hot' water; a dictionary gives 'slightly' warm or 'lukewarm'.

**Did you understand 'knead'? This is a technical term which appears in all three recipes, so it is obviously important and subject-specific. Can you work it out from the context? Have a go before you check in a dictionary! See page 19 for the answer.

Reading a variety of texts for explicit meaning

Task 3

Can you continue these points for this recipe? Try making a list of points for the other recipes as well. We'll start you off.

Text B
1 Put the flour and salt in a bowl in a warm place. (Notice we've altered the order here, to make comparison easier.)
2 Cream fresh yeast with sugar (no mention of honey) in a cup, blend with water.
3 Leave yeast mixture in a warm place until frothy.
4 Add yeast with oil to flour and salt; mix until soft dough has formed. Add more water if needed; dough should be soft and silky, not sticky. Knead well. (Note that Texts A and B both use the term 'soft and silky'.)

Text C
1 Place flour with salt mixed in on worktop or in bowl (no mention of pre-warming).
2 Dissolve yeast and sugar in a little water.
3 Leave for 10 minutes until frothy.
4 Make a well in the flour and salt mix. Add yeast mixture, oil and rest of water.

When you have completed the lists of points for each of the three recipes, you can see the basic recipe outline and decide which one you wish to follow. This is a practical example of understanding, comparing and summarising texts, during which you have practised skills that you will need in the exam. Maybe you will also want to try to make a pizza!

(** To knead = to work and press a soft substance, such as a bread dough, into a uniform mixture with the hands.)

Summarising: argument texts

In the exam, understanding of information is also tested in summary and directed writing questions, which require you to identify points, to select and organise them according to the task set, and to try to express them in your own words.

Look at the following article, with contributions from a panel of writers.

The Panel

The Question: Madonna has vetoed Guy Ritchie's idea of his'n'hers Harley-Davidsons on the grounds that riding a motorbike is irresponsible behaviour for parents. So what kind of risk is acceptable for mums and dads who still want to get their kicks?

Jack O'Sullivan

Fathers Direct

There are two issues with risky behaviour when you become a parent. The first is about making sure you don't die; the second is about setting a good example to your child. Becoming a father made me less of a risk-taker because I felt that I had a duty to survive. I had parachuted before my daughter was born and I would do it again because it feels safe, but I wouldn't go bungee-jumping or ride a motorbike because that doesn't feel safe. I think you should tell the truth to a child if you've been reckless in the past, but it doesn't mean you have to carry on that way once you become a parent.

Verdict: Parachuting

Eric Walton

Motorcyclist, father of two

Unlike Madonna, I ride a motorbike. But I didn't get on one until I was 40 and had had lots of experience driving a car first. My bike is the apple of my eye, but I wouldn't encourage my children on to it. I don't think bikes are a good idea when you have no road experience and haven't got your hormones under control. I think there are various activities that are for adults and various ones that are for children. It's important to explain to them there are things that accrue to you at a certain stage of your life. If you try to protect your children from everything, it creates a joyless and restricted life.

Verdict: Mature motorbiking

Sheila Wolfendale

Professor of educational psychology and grandmother

Parenthood bring responsibilities. It means that decision-making in all aspects of life has to be more considered. I know from experience what conflict there can be between the hedonistic impulse to do something you have always done and the equal and opposite impulse to duty. I wouldn't be surprised if even Madonna had a few seconds of doubt before deciding not to buy a motorbike. I think that every decision that a parent makes – whether it is to go off trekking in the South American rainforest or the smaller everyday matters – is weighed up much more carefully once children arrive.

Verdict: No trekking

Jane Brewer

Trekker, mother of one

For the first few years of my son's life I calmed down a bit, but now he's five I feel back to how I was before. He and I travelled around India for six weeks at Easter. It was something I had always wanted to do and I didn't see a problem with taking him along. Everyone thought I was mad to take a child to India and my mum wouldn't speak to me the night before we left. I've come to realise that when I'm happy, he's happy: it's important not to be put off doing things just beacuse you're a parent. If you want to do it all when you become a parent, you have to do it all.

Verdict: Passage to India

Lindis Percy

Activist, midwife and mother

As a parent, you have to strike a balance between what you want to do and what the family needs. But if you do believe very strongly in something – as I do in the elimination of weapons of mass destruction – you have to resist a lot of family pressures. I went to prison for the first time for my activism when the children were teenagers. I have always felt that what I'm doing in campaigning for peace is for the children and the next generation anyway. There has been conflict in the family but I don't think that's unhealthy. The trick is to manage it successfully.

Verdict: Protest and survive

From The Guardian.

Task 1

Complete the grid below for each of the five panellists to show
  a) the activities;
  b) the degree of risk involved;
  c) whether parents should tackle them, and why.
The first line is completed for you.

	ACTIVITY	RISK	YES/NO	COMMENTS
Panellist 1	Parachuting Motorcycling	Low	Yes	Feels safe
Panellist 2				
Panellist 3				
Panellist 4				
Panellist 5				

This activity has asked you to identify, classify and summarise, and the grid reveals varied views. You are not asked for your opinion, but to present the information in the article in a different format. In order to complete the grid you have to understand the article. A further task, asking you to comment on what the article revealed about the personalities of the contributors, would deal with implicit information, which is covered in the next chapter. An article about the lives of children of risk-taking parents would also need you to change your terms of reference and look beneath the information presented.

Task 2

Use the grid you have completed to make notes for a debate on responsible parenthood. You are not sure which side you will take, so you need to prepare points for and against parents of young children taking unnecessary risks. Make a list of points on each side of the argument, under two headings. Again, the list is started for you. Motorcycling may cause you a problem, so you need to think carefully about conflicting views amongst the panel.

RISKS WORTH TAKING	RISKS NOT TO BE TAKEN
Parachuting – feels safe	Bungee jumping – doesn't feel safe
Motorcycling – OK if you have lots of road experience	Motorcycling – doesn't feel safe

Task 3

Prepare a debating speech to propose the motion that parents should not take unnecessary risks because of their responsibilities towards their children.

Decide which side of the argument you support and, using your notes from Task 2 and referring back to the article, select the points which would fit your side. They might start something like this:

1 Two main issues – stay alive; be a good role model.
2 What feels/is safe?
3 Parenthood changes your attitude to risk-taking.
4 Difference between safety for adults and children.
5 Give them something to look forward to.

Once you have completed the list of points, you need to organise them, avoiding unnecessary repetition and structuring them in the most effective way.

You might decide to deal with the conflicting views by acknowledging them both; on the other hand you could ignore them, but then you risk missing the opportunity of countering one of the opposing side's points. This could weaken your argument.

This whole exercise demonstrates the importance of identifying, understanding and organising arguments, before you can select what is most appropriate for the new purpose and format.

Comprehension: literary texts

Often in a piece of descriptive writing there are contextual clues which will help you to make intelligent guesses as to the meanings of new words. These may include synonyms, giving alternative words for the same meaning; multiple adjectives to build up a picture; words from the same language root; or other pointers. In a comprehension, especially in vocabulary questions, you need to study words in context to make sure you are not misled.

Check that the meaning you choose for a word is the one which fits in the passage, as many words in English have more than one meaning. Think of 'fits' in the previous sentence. In one English dictionary the verb 'fit' has eight meanings, the adjective has eight and the noun has a further six. Some of the meanings are similar, but it is vital to check back that the definition you have chosen is the correct one for the sense in the text.

Read the following description, which includes some words which may be **ambiguous**.

A Pair of Yellow Lilies

Ruth Rendell

A famous designer, young still, who first became well known when she made a princess's wedding dress, was coming to speak to the women's group of which Bridget Thomas was secretary. She would be the second speaker in the autumn program, which was devoted to success and how women had achieved it.

Bridget had a precarious job in a small and not very prosperous bookshop. In her mid-thirties, with a rather pretty face that often looked worried and worn, she thought that she might learn something from this current series of talks. Secrets of success might be imparted, blueprints for achievements, even shortcuts to prosperity. She never had enough money, never knew security, could not have aspired to a designer ready-to-wear even when such a garment had been twice marked down in a sale. Clothes, anyway, were hardly a priority, coming a long way down the list of essentials which was headed by rent, fares, and food, in that order.

In the library, where she had gone to research the speaker, she was not noticeable. She was not, in any case and anywhere, the kind of woman on whom second glances are bestowed. On this Wednesday evening, when the shop closed at its normal time and the library later than usual, she could be seen by those few who cared to look wearing a long black skirt with a dusty appearance, a T-shirt of a slightly different shade of black – it had been washed fifty times at least – and a waistcoat in dark striped cotton. Her shoes were black-velvet Chinese slippers with instep straps and there was a hole she didn't know about in her turquoise-blue tights, low down on the left calf. Bridget's hair was wispy, long and fair, worn in loops. She was carrying an enormous black-leather bag, capacious and heavy, and full of unnecessary things. Herself the first to admit this, she often said she meant to make changes in the matter of this bag but she never got around to it.

This evening the bag contained a number of crumpled tissues, some pink, some white, a spray bottle of cologne, three ballpoint pens, a pair of nail scissors, a pair of nail clippers, a London tube pass, a phone-card, an address book, a mascara in a shade called After-Midnight Blue, a chequebook, a notebook, a postcard from a friend on holiday in France, a calculator, a paperback she had always meant to read but was not getting on very fast with, a container of nasal spray, a bunch of keys, a book of matches, a silver ring with a green stone, probably onyx, a pheasant's feather picked up while staying for the weekend in someone's cottage in Somerset, three quarters of a bar of milk chocolate, a pair of sunglasses, and her wallet – which contained the single credit card she possessed, her bank-cheque card, her library card, her never-needed driving licence, and seventy pounds, give or take a little, in five- and ten-pound notes. There was also about four pounds in change.

From A Pair of Yellow Lilies *by Ruth Rendell.*

Now answer the following questions. Some ideas to help you are given below each question.

Question 1

What was Bridget Thomas's paid job?

In the passage, the answer to Question 2 is given first. The paid job is the one in the bookshop, as a shop assistant.

Question 2

What was her unpaid post?

The unpaid post is secretary of the women's group. Do not assume that the questions will necessarily follow the order of the passage.

Question 3

Why was her job described as 'precarious'?

Look for the sentence where her job is called 'precarious'. Read the rest of the sentence: 'in a small and not very prosperous bookshop'. The fact that the bookshop is small is not in itself a reason for the job insecurity suggested by 'precarious', but combined with 'not very prosperous' (i.e. not making much profit) and the fact that she was an employee rather than the owner, her position is vulnerable or precarious.

Question 4

Where did clothes come in her list of priorities?

We are told that clothes came 'a long way down the list of essentials', so all we know for sure is that they come after 'rent, fares, and food', not how many other items come in between them.

Question 5

Why did she go to the library on Wednesdays?

Look at the sentence in the second paragraph which mentions the library. We are told that the shop (that is, the bookshop where Bridget worked) 'closed at its normal time and the library [closed] later than usual.' We can therefore work out that she could only go to the library when it was open late, at a time when she was not working in the shop.

What evidence is there in the passage that her bag was 'capacious'?

You can work out the meaning of 'capacious' both by its similarity to 'capacity' and by the lengthy paragraph which describes the contents of the handbag. It is therefore likely that a bag which holds so many items is large, but a more precise meaning would be 'capable of holding a great deal, roomy, spacious'. The answer would need to show both an understanding of the word 'capacious' and give the evidence, that is the number of items, some bulky, that it contained.

How would you describe her financial position?

We are given information about her poor financial position in several places in the passage. This question requires you to take note of both the direct references ('never had enough money', 'precarious job', 'never knew security') and the indirect ones about her clothes, the contents of her handbag, etc.

Give three reasons for your answer to Question 7.

Question 7 could be answered 'always short of money' or 'not very secure' or 'always worrying about juggling her finances' or 'of limited means'.

The evidence for Question 8 is varied, and includes the points in the previous paragraph. Her clothes did not match and her T-shirt had been washed many times. The fact that her tights had a hole in them could, however, be evidence of a lack of awareness rather than poverty, so you need to take care here. The contents of her wallet are indicative of a limited lifestyle, in that she possessed only one credit card and did not need her driving licence (presumably because she did not own a car). The detail about the cash might suggest wealth, but could also suggest a keen awareness of how much she had. Can you see how you must take great care to read both the passage and the question in order to identify the correct information for a question like this? Guessing, or writing down the first three points you read, might lose you marks.

Give another word or phrase (maximum 5 words) for each of the following, as used in the passage:

devoted   worn   current   shortcuts   calf

These words have been deliberately chosen because each of them could have more than one meaning or definition, so beware!

'Devoted' can mean 'feeling loyalty or devotion', 'ardent', 'devout', 'dedicated' or 'consecrated'. Look carefully at the passage to help you decide which meaning best fits here. There is no sense of religious fervour in the context, so the meaning is unlikely to be 'devout' or 'consecrated'. 'Feeling loyalty or devotion' does not fit either, as the topic is not personal. 'Dedicated' conveys the meaning of a program on a single theme, so 'dedicated' or 'assigned' would fit here.

'Worn' might make you think of the past of 'to wear' as later in the paragraph there is mention of clothes. It can therefore mean affected by long use (as in 'worn-out clothes'), but a better definition when applied to a face would be 'haggard', 'drawn' or 'weary'.

'Current' is unlikely to refer to a flow of water or air or electricity here; you can choose between 'of the immediate present', 'in progress' or even 'contemporary'. Each would gain credit in an exam.

'Shortcuts' is used metaphorically here. The concrete meaning would be a route that is shorter than the usual one, so you could define this use as 'time- or effort-saving methods', which just fits the five-word limit.

'Calf' is unlikely to mean a young cow here. Context should tell you that it is part of the body on which tights are worn, and probably visible under her long skirt. 'Lower leg' or 'leg above the ankle' would be precise enough.

Your turn

Now try some questions for yourself. The next example is part of an account of local entertainment in the Caribbean.

I was about to witness goat racing. A little later there would be crab racing. I was fighting my way through ice-cream vans, hordes of people, food stalls and hot music singeing my eardrums. Even though the general movement was towards the racecourse, I elbowed my way through the crowds in an effort to get a good pitch. An area had been cordoned off to make a course for the competitors, not quite on a par with the traditional racing scale but on a parallel assumption that spectators were to line either side of a stretch of ground along which the participants would travel.

Some people take this event very seriously. "The goats are looking frisky." I wish I could have used that expression to describe what I saw. The glazed preoccupation of the goats as they stood chewing their cuds made them look anything but 'frisky'. You will not find jockeys seated on their mounts here. Good job too! An attempt was made to keep a handful of select goats in order. No mean achievement when dealing with an animal fabled to eat almost anything it can lay its mouth to. At the end of each rope was a man holding a stick.

And they were off! I soon got the idea. It was how quickly you and your quadruped could race the other men and theirs to the finishing line. Bare feet and hooves pounded stones further into the ground. The humans were moving as if their lives depended on it. The goats were probably certain their lives did. Curried goat is a delicacy on the islands. First one across the line got cooked? Or was it the last one to cross who went into the pot? Either way, it would be best to play safe and stay close to the middle. The tension on the rope was nail-biting. There always is one. There is always one soul who remains oblivious to ruin. The hooves of one billy* were thudding on the quaking earth as if his life would begin when he reached the finishing line. His minder looked a worried man. He had reason. His feet had hardly touched the ground since the race began. He was hanging on to the end of the rope with both hands and being tugged to the finishing line. He was declared the winner. Rumour had it the goat ended up in the pot, anyway. They had to throttle it to get it to stop running. The minder responded to everyone who congratulated him with the same surprised, bewildered smile.

From Sequins for a Ragged Hen *by Amryl Johnson.*

* billy = a male goat

1 In your own words, explain why the writer needed to push her way through the crowds.

2 Explain how the area had been 'cordoned off'.

3 Can you explain the pun intended by the use of 'parallel' in the last sentence of the first paragraph?

4 Why is the music described as 'singeing' the eardrums?

5 Why was it 'best to play safe and stay close to the middle'?

6 Describe the two facial expressions of the winning owner in your own words.

7 What happened to the winning goat? (There are two things to mention here.)

Sample exam questions and answers

We shall now move to some exam-type questions, looking at sample answers and examiner responses.

Study these texts and answer the following questions based on them. Remember that starred (*) questions should be answered in your own words. As these questions do not represent a complete exam section, the total number of marks available is less than the 30 marks allotted to a complete Section A in the exam.

Text A

Hearing damage on the dance floor

Can clubbing seriously damage your health? Two new studies have found a link between dancing and deafness...

Now that your work place, your cars and just about everything else are subject to noise restriction regulations, nightclubs are probably the most dangerous places for your ears. Two new studies have shown that not only are more people exposed to high levels of noise at clubs than ever before, but that the act of dancing increases your chances of hearing damage.

German scientist Dr Helmut Ising found that higher levels of damage occurred in the hearing of animals who'd been exercising before being bombarded with noise compared with those which had been relaxing before the test. Ising noted that exercise used up the experimental mice's reserves of magnesium – an element thought not only to increase blood supply to the ears but also to protect hearing.

Similar experiments have been carried out on soldiers. Before arduous manoeuvres a group of soldiers was given magnesium supplements while others were not. The former group's hearing was far less affected by battle noise than the other soldiers.

Research is at an early stage and its relevance to everyday life is uncertain. "The links between noise, exercise and hearing loss are not fully understood," says Dr Deepak Prasher of University College London. "Magnesium depletion is almost certain to be a factor, but as the moment it's impossible to say."

More certain is the link between our increasing exposure to social noise – nightclubs, gigs, personal stereos – and hearing damage. In a study of 18- to 25-year-olds, the Medical Research Council found that the number of people exposed to loud noise at work had halved over the past 10 years, but the number listening to loud social noise had quadrupled.

"Sources of noise have changed since the 1980s," said Professor Adrian Davis, who conducted the MRC research.

"We found that 35 per cent of men in the age group are now exposed to noise greater than 97 decibels [considered dangerous], compared to seven per

35 per cent of men are now exposed to noise levels considered dangerous

cent in the earlier studies."

Nightclubs are the main source of noise – twice as many people listen to potentially dangerous levels of sound there than on their personal stereo. Significant numbers also listened to their hi-fis at 97dB-plus levels. Rock concerts are not on the danger scale – they are relatively short and, for most people, infrequent.

Are nightclubs making people deaf? "There is still no

direct link between noise level and the after-effects," says Dr Prasher. "One person can listen to 100dB for hours every day of his life and not be damaged. Another can listen to it for one hour and get tinnitus.*

"If you listen in moderation – say 80dB for two hours per day – then you'll be OK. If you listen to over 100dB for over two hours – you could get tinnitus. Ten per cent of people tested in the MRC study complained they could not hear speech in noisy environments, which indicates they have a hearing problem. The best thing to do is give your hearing time to recover – going to nightclubs four times a week is asking for trouble."

From Essential Articles 5.

*tinnitus = disturbing noises in the ear.

Text B

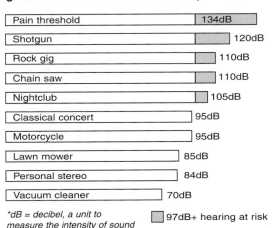

How loud is loud?
There may not appear to be a big difference, but watch out: a 3dB increase doubles the volume (e.g. 95dB* is twice as loud as 92dB).

Pain threshold	134dB
Shotgun	120dB
Rock gig	110dB
Chain saw	110dB
Nightclub	105dB
Classical concert	95dB
Motorcycle	95dB
Lawn mower	85dB
Personal stereo	84dB
Vacuum cleaner	70dB

*dB = decibel, a unit to measure the intensity of sound

▢ 97dB+ hearing at risk

From Essential Articles 5.

Text C

The Focus test: are you going deaf?

- Do you flinch at doors slamming or cutlery dropping? Hypersensitivity to loud, and especially high-pitched, noise could mean your brain is straining just to hear ordinary noises. This means that when a loud one arrives it creates a disproportionate surprise.

- Do you struggle to hear what someone's saying when you're in a loud environment like a pub or club? If so, it could mean that the part of your brain dedicated to filtering out unimportant noise is on the decline.

- Ringing in the ears and a dulled sense of hearing is normal if you've just been exposed to high noise levels. But it should disappear after a couple of hours. If it lasts longer than that, you've damaged your ears.

From Essential Articles 5.

Question 1

Give two reasons from the passage for potential hearing loss for nightclub users. **(2 marks)**

The level of noise in nightclubs has increased; dancing, or any exercise, reduces the body's supply of magnesium.

This answer uses information from the first two paragraphs, showing understanding of how dancing damages hearing.

Question 2

In your own words, why is magnesium important for our hearing?* **(2 marks)**

Magnesium helps carry blood to the ears and prevents damage to hearing.

This answer rephrases the facts from the passage, but does not waste words trying to find synonyms for 'ears' and 'hearing'.

Question 3

Explain the effects on the hearing of the soldiers not given magnesium supplements before training. **(2 marks)**

The hearing of the group not given magnesium supplements was affected by the sounds of fighting.

This question requires you to work out the reverse of the facts given, as the passage refers to those given supplements.

Question 4

How many more young people are now listening to loud music for entertainment? **(1 mark)**

Three times as many young people.

There are a number of figures given in the passage; the answer is not given as a number, but a word: 'quadrupled'.

Reading a variety of texts for explicit meaning

Question 5

What is considered the danger level of noise? Give three examples from the passage of noise this loud. **(4 marks)**

More than 97 decibels; some hi-fis, a nightclub and a chain saw.

This needed some care, to notice the 'greater than' and 'plus'. Other answers could have been a rock concert (gig) and a shotgun. The pain threshold is not a sound but a level at which noise inflicts pain.

Question 6

List in your own words three symptoms of hearing damage.* **(3 marks)**

Difficulty in understanding speech in a noisy place; being very sensitive to sudden loud noises; reduced ability to distinguish sound which persists for more than two hours.

The first point is made twice, in Text A and as the second bullet point in Text C; the other two points are summarised from bullet points in Text C; all show some effort to use own words.

Question 7

Using ideas from all the texts, write a list of points to help 18- to 25-year-olds to avoid hearing loss. **(4 marks)**

- *Take magnesium supplements before taking part in noisy activity.*
- *Limit your visits to nightclubs.*

These are explicit; the next two are implicit or inferential.

- *Turn down your personal stereo and hi-fi.*
- *Wear ear protectors if working in a noisy place.*

It is very important to be able to distinguish fact from opinion, reality from fiction, news coverage from comment or persuasion. In other parts of this book you will need to be aware of these distinctions, to identify techniques in the writings of others and to be able to use them yourself. If you can be more confident in your ability to understand, organise and explain explicit information and to distinguish between various versions of the same material, you are well on the way to recognising implicit information and explaining meaning and purpose. The next chapter looks at implied meaning in a range of texts.

2

Reading a variety of texts for implied meaning

> **In this chapter you will practise:**
> - reading intensively, reflectively and inferentially
> - reading report, persuasive, rhetorical and literary texts for implied meaning
> - recognising how persuasive texts achieve their aims
> - looking at some features of rhetorical texts

As you have read in Chapter 1, some meaning is spelled out perfectly explicitly.

Sometimes, though, the reader has to work harder: meaning is partly in the text, but readers have to use their own understanding of the subject, and sometimes of life generally, to complete the sense. This is known as **inference** in reading comprehension.

Let us take a basic example. This is a short crime story.

"Officer, I did see the robbery. I was in the High Street, looking at the fashions in GAP. I particularly liked the way the wall of mirrors gave depth to the whole display, so I stood there for a few minutes, while the incident happened."

"Yes, yes. You said all this before, didn't you? You saw three men in a black station wagon, licence plate 3900I, heading east. Well, we checked it out. That vehicle is on the other side of the country and it is owned by a high court judge, no less."

"Well, this time I've brought the photo I took of the display. Look!"

The sergeant took the photo, then threw it down, after a casual glance. He sighed and went over to the coffee machine. Suddenly, he turned back and snatched up the picture.

"Constable," he called, "take this to the lab. and get an enlargement – NOW."

Half an hour and two cups of coffee later, the sergeant was given the enlargements. He called urgently down the phone, "That's right. A black station wagon, licence I00PE, heading west." As he put the phone down, he mumbled something about a mirror.

Based on Reflective Witness *by Pat Popelier.*

You will not have much difficulty deciding what the sergeant mumbled. How do you know the answer? It is not in the text. You know because your experience of mirrors tells you that images are reversed in reflections.

Read the second example and try to work it out yourself. It is the opening of a student's essay:

> *How would you like to spend countless hours in one small room? How could you cope with not being able to turn around, not being able to stretch, not being able to walk? How would you like to live with no sunshine, like many others – imprisoned? How could you stand not being able to control when you want to eat, sleep, or just rest? It would be hell wouldn't it? And yet millions are forced to live in this hell. They will spend their lives like this. So what is this Hell? It is called ....*

No doubt, as an experienced reader, your mind is at first engaging in **explicit comprehension**. The circumstantial details given seem to add up to a scene of imprisonment: endless time spent in cramped conditions, shut away from the warmth of the sun. The word 'imprisoned' seems to confirm your reading so far. As you read on, this seems to be the worst kind of imprisonment. The prisoners have to endure a strict regime for eating, sleeping, resting. They seem to be utterly helpless. To the ordinary person, it does indeed sound like hell. But, is it true that millions are forced to live like this? Perhaps universally there are many thousands, but the account does seem to be exaggerated. We begin to suspect that the writer is really discussing something else, and that suspicion is confirmed when we read, 'So what is this Hell?' Why ask the question if the answer is so obvious? There is definitely another level of meaning. We must add to all the information in the text our knowledge of life. Did you fill in the two-word gap at the end? The answer is 'factory farming'.

This third example shows how deep and complex meaning can be conveyed very simply through inference. Here is a short fable. The words are simple and so are the sentence structures. At first thought, it seems to be a story you could read to quite a young child, though the ending surprises. The child would get the explicit meaning, but you would find something totally different in it because you are more mature, with greater knowledge of life.

> "Alas," said the mouse, "the world is growing smaller every day. At first it was so wide that I was afraid. I ran and was glad when at last I saw in the distance walls to the right and left; but these long walls are hurrying so quickly towards one another that I am already in the last room, and there in the corner stands the trap into which I am running."
>
> "You have only to change direction," said the cat – and ate it up.

From 'A Little Fable' by Franz Kafka.

The meaning here is universal. Everyone's life starts with hopes and expectations. Gradually, experience tells most of us that we have a more limited path to follow. As we progress, we find – no matter what route we take or what advice we follow or ignore – that we all reach the same end.

Reading for implied meaning

In the examination you need to be alert for inference in reading comprehension. Usually, sets of questions on a text begin with some direct, explicit questions, to lead the candidate to answer confidently. You may later be asked to trace an argument, summarise in your own words and also answer questions about indirect meaning.

To do this work well you need to read quite carefully. At the start, your gaze glances along the lines to get a general sense of what you read. This is **skimming**.

Once you have taken in the main ideas of the text, you need to slow down to steadier reading. You will have looked at the questions and maybe found that you do not know enough to answer them. There may be particular details you need to refer to in your own words, or quote exactly, so you read carefully, looking for points that will help you to answer the set questions. This is **intensive reading**.

Later, you reach questions where the answer cannot be quoted from the text, nor is it detail you can write out in your own words, keeping close to the text (known as **paraphrase**). You need to think about it, puzzle it out, make a judgement. All this takes a little more time, so you read again, thoughtfully, maybe pausing to look up from the text now and again, as your mind processes what you have read, matches it with past experiences and reaches a conclusion. This is **reflective reading**.

Finally, there may be questions where there is no detail in the text that will give you an answer you can be sure about. There may well be hints and parallel ideas, but there is a gap you need to fill in yourself. This is **inferential reading**.

Reading report texts

Report texts give us the facts about particular events, but sometimes there is more to the story than the mere facts. To get the most from a report, we need to use the reading skills described above.

The following is a newspaper article. You might well have picked it up, been intrigued by the title and glanced at it. Read it through quickly, skimming the text.

Shy prodigy 'stretching her wings'

THE missing Oxford prodigy Sufiah Yusof may just be "stretching her wings" after a gruelling three-year mathematics degree, her college head said yesterday.

Sufiah, 15, one of Oxford's youngest-ever undergraduates, was last seen by her father after her final maths examination on June 21.

Despite appeals from her distraught family to get in touch, there was no word yesterday from Sufiah, whose results will be posted up at the university today or tomorrow.

She was due to attend a lunch with tutors that day but failed to arrive, although a young woman claiming to be Sufiah telephoned the college, St Hilda's, to say: "I am OK. I am with friends."

Elizabeth Llewellyn-Smith, the college Principal, said yesterday that there was no evidence that Sufiah had been suffering from stress. The call showed that the girl "needed

Sufiah Yusof: "She has vanished into thin air"

space" and may want to "stretch her wings" after the academic year, she said.

Ms Llewellyn-Smith added: "I have absolutely no reason to think she was worried about her work. As far as her tutor is concerned there was no risk of her failing her exam.

"I do not think it is the pressure. She has been here for three years with no sign of suffering from pressure of that sort. If it was going to happen it would probably have been in her first or second term, not her third year.

"We made a very careful assessment before she came of the sort of special arrangements that should be made, as we would for someone with special needs. The basic decision was that she should remain under her family's care in a family flat and not just be thrown into student residences."

However, fellow students talked about the pressures she was under at the university. Jo Charman, 21, who is in the same year, said: "She found it difficult. She was really shy and because she wasn't really living in college she did not get the social life the rest of us get."

"She used to come around for tea and we could sense she was under quite a lot of pressure to do well. She would get more worked up than we did if she wasn't getting it."

Another St Hilda's undergraduate who knew Sufiah, Zoë Hodges, 22, said: "She was very shy and she was not surrounded by her peers.

She did not appear to be very relaxed in her environment. If I was her parent I would not have sent her to university at that age."

Sufiah joined St Hilda's at 13, equalling the record of the child prodigy Ruth Lawrence.

The police denied suggestions that Sufiah's last known telephone message was a hoax, saying that they did not yet know where the call was made from.

They have checked more than 400 e-mail messages which she deleted from her computer, but which were retrieved by the university's back-up tapes.

Farooq Yusof, 43, Sufiah's father, renewed his appeal for the "naive and innocent" girl to make contact.

"We are all desperately worried at the moment and feel so helpless," he said. "We are concerned she is in some sort of danger. I would implore her to make some form of contact with us to let us all know that she is safe and well. I cannot reassure her enough that she will not be in any trouble."

Mr Yusof, who is comforting his wife Halimaheon, 44, and his four other children, added: "She is conscientious and diligent. She gets up at 4am each morning to pray and now we are all praying for her."

Sergeant Jim Sudworth, of Oxford police, said: "She had seemingly vanished into thin air. Every lead we follow comes up with nothing. It is a complete and utter mystery."

From The Times.

Now look at the first two questions and try to answer them. Your answers will be something like those in the handwritten script.

Question 1

What is this report about?

The report is about a fifteen-year-old girl, just graduated, who is missing from her college.

Question 2

Why is this incident newsworthy?

It is newsworthy because she is unusual – a prodigy, or very young to be an undergraduate student. Her sudden disappearance is a mystery.

There is more to the passage than this general, literal meaning, though. The next question asks you to gather more details, again by literal comprehension. Answer it for yourself, then compare your answer with the one in handwritten script.

Question 3

What do her fellow students suggest might be the reason for her disappearance?

They agree about 'the pressures she was under at the university'. They say she found it hard to fit in with the others because she was shy, very quiet. They say she got upset if she wasn't doing well in her studies. They say she had no one else of her own age to be friendly with; she did not seem to be at ease. They suggest it may have been a mistake to send her to university so young (as she has graduated aged fifteen, she must have started the course when she was only thirteen).

To get all this detail, you will have had to read more slowly and carefully, maybe underlining the parts of texts where you located the information.

Now go on to Questions 4 and 5, which ask you to probe more deeply into the meaning of the passage. Some of the ideas you should cover are given in the commentary.

Question 4

Why might she be at risk in her present situation?

The answer to this question will have already been building up in your mind. Adding all these details together and matching them with your knowledge of the world, you will be aware of the following: a shy, young girl, not socially confident or streetwise, coming from a sheltered environment, lacking the money to support herself, with no known place to stay and possibly emotionally upset, is in danger.

Question 5

What do you think could be the explanation for her disappearance?

You could agree with any of the points which were made by Sufiah's fellow students (see Question 3) but you have scope to add new ideas of your own which are not in the text. You may be the same age as Sufiah – think about your general experience of relationships with people of your own age and with adults. Sufiah may have been afraid to get the final results of the degree, since success mattered so much to her. She might have just run off, straight after taking the examination. She could have felt the need to go somewhere relaxing, to unwind, do something entirely different from studying.

Do you agree that to answer both Questions 4 and 5 you have to do some reflective reading?

Now try the final question. Is your answer something like the one shown in handwritten script?

Question 6

What does the title suggest is the reason for her disappearance?

The title has the image of a bird, a fledgling just ready to learn to fly and to leave the nest. Sufiah may have just reached the stage in life when she needs to taste her freedom, actually by running away from her college and her home. We sometimes use the expression 'to take flight' from something. Behind it is a metaphor: moving on suddenly from a secure, known set of circumstances to a wider, unknown situation, as a young bird does.

You will have reached this conclusion by inferential reading.

Reading persuasive texts
Advertising

A successful book about advertising had the title *The Hidden Persuaders*. The effect of the language of advertisements is indirect. Advertisements are all around us – on hoardings in the street, in our newspapers and on television. The main purpose behind advertisements is to persuade us to buy goods, or to promote services or some kind of social behaviour. The information offered may be selective, or may even tell half-truths.

Advertisements try to attract our attention, and to entertain us as well as persuading us. This is often done using the following language aspects:

- puns
- rhythmic phrasing
- verbal patterning
- imagery
- coined words (often as product names)
- attractive layout
- pictures.

We need to use inference when reading texts idealising a product. Here it is best described as understanding the difference between what is presented and what our general knowledge of the world tells us is true.

Consider the following advertisement, where the normal techniques used in advertising are used in reverse. The resulting humour proved to be very successful in promoting this club.

Join the pudding club.

No, they're not professional athletes. (How did you guess?) They're typical Edinburgh club members.

Their idea of exercise is getting up to change channels on TV rather than using the remote control. "Go for the burn" in our aerobics classes? The only time they feel the burn is when they have a barbecue. So why do they use our exercise machines and follow our fitness programmes? Well, you should have seen them *before* they joined.

From an advert for The Edinburgh Health Club.

Reading a variety of texts for implied meaning

Why does it make you laugh? It is partly that these ordinary-looking people are all members of a fitness club! The mismatch creates the humour; fitness clubs produce people with as perfect bodies as possible, we suppose from our general knowledge. How ever did you guess 'they're not professional athletes'? We are presented with a mismatch again. According to the text, they don't know much about fitness: they sit watching TV a lot and don't understand the meaning of 'go for the burn'. The final mismatch is in the last sentence. How can we credit that these people are following a fitness programme? The answer is 'Well, you should have seen them *before* they joined'!

Look at the following extract, which uses a jolly, bantering tone. Read it through and try to answer the questions that follow. The examiner's model answers are given below each question.

T H E   E D I N B U R G H   C L U B

All health clubs are chasing the 14 per cent of the population already in the market for a health club, that is, those who already participate in some form of exercise.

The phenomenon of the gym has grown through the 70s and 80s. It began as 'pumping iron', and evolved into aerobics. Consequently, the non-user's image of these clubs was that they were bursting at the seams with the kind of people who could easily be extras in *Baywatch*, and who would be competing with each other in front of full-length mirrors to present the best bodies.

The Edinburgh Club decided to target the 86 per cent of the population who were not using a health club and to identify behavioural characteristics within this group and go for the people with the greatest potential. To do this they had to establish why they were not using a club. Was it because they felt that getting fit was a waste of time and not for them, or were they inhibited by price or emotional barriers? It seemed that the fear factor of being looked down on in a health club by the beautiful people was the biggest turn-off. Price was an inhibitor, therefore The Edinburgh Club emphasised a reasonable price throughout the campaign. To reach the 86 per cent of people who would no more pull on a pink leotard than refuse that extra helping of custard with their apple pie, required an attempt to attract ordinary people who could get fit without feeling inadequate.

The Club disregarded received wisdom and aimed at a target audience that was not the sort you would expect to find in a health club at all. These would be older, more down-market people, often female, also those who had once been fit, trim and active, but in the last few years found that circumstances – children, pressure of work, ageing – had conspired to remove exercise from their lives. They wanted to be fit, but wouldn't be seen dead in a health club.

'OTHER FITNESS CLUBS'

The trouble with most fitness clubs is that they're full of fitness fanatics. It's no fun exercising next to guys who spend hours pumping iron, if you get knackered just pumping up a bike. Thankfully, the Edinburgh Club's more like Blackpool Beach than Muscle Beach. Our members are all ages, shapes and sizes. Most joined when they heard how good our teachers, equipment, leisure facilities and free classes are. (So good that some of our regulars are staff from rival clubs.) Why don't you phone for details or a tour? We can't guarantee you'll suddenly feel like Charles Atlas. But at least you won't feel like a right Charlie.

THE Edinburgh CLUB

Other fitness clubs. The Edinburgh Club.

The strategy was a great success. Here is a representative selection of comments from new club members:

"Mr Normal is welcome at The Edinburgh Club. I think the advertisements portray the club as it is now."

"The advertisements made The Edinburgh Club somewhat homely, which is a good feeling. They attract working mothers, older people."

"The advertisements are comical. They don't make it sound serious."

"My husband would not feel he was different in the sense that he looks like at least 90 per cent of the people here."

"It says the club is not draped in wall-to-wall Arnold Schwartzeneggers."

Now try to answer the questions. Compare your answers with the examiner's model answers below.

Question 1

What does the opening paragraph tell us about the general view of health clubs and people who usually attend them?

The opening paragraph tells us that the general view is that members have muscular and fit bodies, and would rival each other to keep in peak physical condition.

Question 2

What in your own words were the characteristics of the 86 per cent of the public that the club was trying to attract?

These people were weak-willed; they ate too much and were self-conscious about their physical condition. For some, changing life circumstances had made them lose the fitness they once may have had. Mostly they were women, not very well off, or older people.

Question 3

What would the 'received wisdom' that they disregarded have been?

It was that the club should target people who were already fit and who were keen to stay that way.

Question 4

Find an example from the members' comments where the meaning is indirect or implied.

'It says the club is not draped in wall-to-wall Arnold Schwartzeneggers.'

Compare the leaflet below. It is simple, but very persuasive, in a different style. Like the Edinburgh Club advertisements, though, it persuades through indirect means.

FITNESS WITH YOUR PERSONAL TRAINER

Are you **too busy at work to work at keeping fit**?

Are you **highly motivated**, a big achiever?

Do you want to **look good, as well as feel good**?

Do you want to **fit your role in life**?

Is it professionals that you are looking for?

Do you want to avoid the common herd in a large gym?

Do you want the **best equipment, the most skilled trainers, for superb results**?

Are you looking for **100 per cent attention for 100 per cent results**?

If you answered YES to any of these questions, you need **ACE PERSONAL TRAINING SERVICE.**

Come to **ACE** to meet the professionals with the knowledge to tailor-make a programme just for your own needs.

JOIN ACE TODAY

for

Attention   Commitment   Excellence.

(Rates: from $30 an hour)

Answer the questions and compare your answers with the sample student answers (in handwritten script) and the examiner's model answer below.

What is the purpose of the advertisement?

It is trying to talk people who have never seen the inside of a gym in their lives into having a personal trainer.

The purpose is to advertise the services of a personal trainer.

What type of client is this club hoping to attract?

It does not go into depth about training methods, so it is for people who do not know much about fitness. It is expensive and only for rich people.

It seeks to attract busy, probably business or professional people, who can afford to pay for individual attention, want to look good for work advancement but do not know much about fitness clubs.

Pick out three phrases which show this.

'$30 an hour'.

'Too busy at work to work at keeping fit', and almost any phrase in the first section. Also 'from $30 an hour', that is, you could end up paying a lot more than that!

How does the second half differ grammatically from the first?

There are a lot of questions and then answers.

The first half has all rhetorical questions. The second has forceful statements and some commands. All are directed at the targeted person – you.

What effect does this contrast have on the reader?

It paints a picture of people who want to please the customers.

The questions draw the reader's attention; the commands order you and also flatter you.

Give three examples of phrases which suggest quality.

Examples are 'most skilled trainers' and 'Excellence'.

'Most skilled trainers'; 'Excellence'; 'a big achiever'; 'the best equipment'; 'superb results'; '100 per cent attention for 100 per cent results'; 'commitment'.

What, in your view, would be likely to make you join the club, and what would dissuade you?

I wouldn't join because there are no details of what you get for all that money.

Though no specific information is given about the training, you are assured of great quality and it might suit very busy and status-conscious people very well; some people might be flattered to think that only high flyers would join the club.

What effect does the general layout and presentation have?

The key words are highlighted to grab the reader's attention, but the price is not – it's just put at the bottom.

The headings, use of capitals for emphasis, and the shaping of the text draw our attention. The price is not highlighted but, coming last, it would catch attention.

What is typical of advertisement style in the language?

It has got lots of words about what is good.

The punning echoes on 'work' and 'fit', the rhythmic effects of all the questions with the same grammatical structure, the patterned phrases (e.g. 'to look good as well as feel good'; '100 per cent attention for 100 per cent results'), and also the superlatives 'best' and 'most skilled'.

Now try one further question for yourself on the two texts.

Compare both texts and say which is more likely to persuade you to join a fitness club.

Your answer will have included quite a few of the points above, as well as your own personal preferences. You should have included somewhere, though, that in common they have an inference which is that they are exactly what you are looking for in a fitness club – even if it had not occurred to you before that you were looking for one at all!

Reading a variety of texts for implied meaning

Media

Articles in magazines and newspapers try to change our opinion by persuasion. They use some of the same techniques of presentation as advertisements, but rely more on selecting content in such a way that we will share the writer's opinion. Style is often fairly basic, with simple major or compound sentences. Vocabulary is also not too complex, but it is sometimes **loaded** (given a limited, biased or special meaning with which the reader is expected to agree). There will be aspects of style to entertain, much as in advertising.

From Air Malta In Flight magazine.

Read this article from an in-flight magazine. It is intended for relaxed reading.

Carnival 2000 – An Island's culture in colour

BY CHARLES COLEIRO

Fantasies spring to life when Carnival erupts in Valletta and neighbouring Floriana. Malta's own reign of mirth is an annual mid-winter spectacle which presents to the young-at-heart a carefree atmosphere of boisterous revelry with a crowd-pulling parade of grotesque floats, fancy costumes, bands and dancing in the streets.

The colourful days of Carnival are intertwined with frolic and fun, deeply rooted in a traditional past, which is likewise nourished by a mixture of spontaneous exuberance preceding what was known to be an austere and disciplined period associated with fasting and penance.

From the original Latin meaning and its Italian offspring in the coined phrase *carne vale*, it is easier to understand that Carnival days allowed for meals when meat dishes sparked lavish feasting for revellers who would abstain from meat during the 40 days of Lent that followed. It is therefore not without reason that the birth of Carnival rests in the cradle of a religious culture in countries with a predominant Catholic faith.

This time-honoured folk entertainment reached the Maltese Islands, proverbially known for their strong Christian inheritance, long before the arrival of the Knights of St John – the Knights of Malta. History records the year 1535, during the reign of Grand Master Pietro del Ponte, which saw the first organised event. It started with knights in armour being involved in a make-believe duel watched by an excited crowd.

This manifestation may also have prompted the later introduction of *Il-Parata*, a sword dance commemorating the Maltese victory over the Turks in the Great Siege of 1565.

But the first Carnival that really broke into general jollification was, according to historians, that of 1560 when a massed Christian armada was harbour-bound on the island before sailing for an assault on Tripoli. The Genoese Grand Admiral Andrea Doria sent his men ashore while Grand Master Jean de la Valette placed his stamp of approval on Carnival by sanctioning the wearing of masks in public.

Historic milestones on the path of the Maltese Carnival reveal that another Grand Master, Jean de Lascaris, instigated by the Jesuits, prohibited the wearing of masks by women in 1639 under penalty of whipping.

During the early days of British rule King Carnival nearly lost his throne. After the French blockade the Maltese population faced gloom and hardship, with outbreaks of plague and cholera leaving no eagerness for merrymaking. Neither were the British Heads of State, with their military background of hard discipline, very enthusiastic to play games. Nevertheless some show of Carnival continued and the English author George Percy Badger gave a good account, published in 1838, from his own personal experience.

The spirit of Carnival breathed once more in happier days and by 1910 its reign had already extended to non-urban districts outside Valletta and to the island of Gozo. The Three Cities in the Grand Harbour area had organised their own Carnival festivities even earlier. Many villages led the way in presenting the folklore features of the Maltese Carnival with bands, orchestras and dancing in the streets, forming what was known as *Il-Kumittiva*.

Another characteristic event which saw the light of day during the Knights' era and still survives in our age is *Il-Kukkanja*. This game, Maltese for "clique", was

probably imported from Sicily and introduced to the islanders by Grand Master Antoine Zondadari in 1721. *Il-Kukkanja* is a greasy-pole game giving males the right to take part in a struggle to seize food prizes – hams, sausages and poultry – hung on plain beams and camouflaged with tree branches.

Nearer our times, year after year the external activities are organised by the National Festivities Committee. The individuality of the Maltese Carnival has been retained, adding cash prizes for – among other attractions – companies in costume, floats, bands on parade and choreographed dancing. Children's participation, especially from schools and other institutions, has further contributed to a genuine expression of youthful glee. Carnival has also continued to extend its sovereignty in the villages. Particularly in Nadur, and Gozo, events take on a more liberal aspect with spontaneous humour and disguise.

These anecdotes recount, if somewhat briefly, the birth of the Merry Monarch and his uninterrupted command in present times. His domain certainly does not echo the sounds of samba one hears in Brazil's Rio Branco. This is Malta's own festival giving an insight of an identity synonymous with an island's anthropology and the way people go about traditional feasting.

Answer the questions, and compare your answers with the examiner's model answers below.

Question 1

What are the three major purposes of the article?

The three main purposes of the article are:
 (i)   to entertain passengers, to pass the time when flying
 (ii) to inform them about Malta's carnival
 (iii) to encourage people to visit the carnival, and Malta, too.

Question 2

For each of these purposes, pick out two groups of words that convey the point vividly.

 (i)   Any descriptive phrases of what the carnival is like.
 (ii) Any historical or background information.
 (iii) 'presents to the young-at-heart a carefree atmosphere of boisterous revelry'
       'a crowd-pulling parade ... dancing in the streets'
       'intertwined with frolic and fun'
       'cash prizes' and all the attractions listed.

Question 3

What is entirely absent from the article?

Anything negative or disadvantageous about the carnival.

Question 4

What is stressed as being distinctive about Malta's carnival?

It is religious, Catholic, related to the start of fasting. It has historical roots.

Question 5

What has been retained in this carnival over the years?

Its individuality has been retained.

Reading a variety of texts for implied meaning

What new things have been added in recent years?

Cash prizes, costume parades, floats, bands, dancing, children taking part and having fun. It has spread to the villages outside the capital. It is more liberal and fun nowadays.

Now read this article, from a national newspaper, reporting a special event, and try the questions on page 48. Compare your answers to the questions with another student's, in handwritten script. As the examiner's comments show, their answers are rather weak.

Who had the biggest bang of them all?

THE FIREWORKS

AROUND the globe from Sydney to New York, from Peking to Paris, the millennium arrived explosively, courtesy of gunpowder – invented more than 4,000 years ago.

But even before the last firework had been lit, a global debate had begun over who had provided the greatest pyrotechnic show on earth.

According to the BBC, London, Paris and Sydney were the top trio, with the UK most spectacular of all. An independent verdict came from the American station CNN, which declared London the winner.

The Paris fireworks were probably the most stylish, especially when coupled with more than 20,000 lightbulbs illuminating the Eiffel Tower.

London and Sydney, on the other hand, blasted their way in to Y2K with more than 30 tons of fireworks each. But Syd Howard, the man who designed both displays, didn't see either, spending Millennium Eve in bed at his Sydney home. He believes New Year's Eve is jinxed, after his father and grandfather both lost hands in firework accidents on the night, which is why he did not hang round to see his own work.

The biggest damp squib of the millennium had to be in Fairbanks, Alaska, where thick fog and temperatures of −40° C resulted in the city's firework show being cancelled for its 36,000 residents.

Which was better than anything on display in one global region where the country's new rulers, who came to power in a coup on Christmas Eve, banned fireworks for fear they would be mistaken for gunshots.

But, as befits the country which invented them at least 2,000 years before the arrival of the first millennium AD, there were spectacular displays throughout China.

From The Independent on Sunday.

Question 1

What is this article about?

It is about the fireworks set off for the millennium.

The candidate's sentence does not stress that these were the massive displays of fireworks in capital cities set off on the eve of the millennium as part of the international celebrations.

Question 2

Which places are said to have had the best displays?

Paris, London, Sydney.

The answer is correct, but it would have been better if expressed as a sentence.

Question 3

What does the title suggest about the fireworks?

It suggests that there was a competition for the best one.

The answer here is only partly right. The candidate has missed the inference in the word 'bang'; it is not just who made the most noise, had the greatest number or even created the best display, but it hints at dominance, rather than friendly rivalry.

Question 4

Trace the points throughout the article which support this suggestion.

It says that Paris, London and Sydney were 'the top trio' and the UK display was 'most spectacular of all'. It says the Paris fireworks 'were probably the most stylish'.

By missing the inference, the candidate also misses most of the answer to this question. The first paragraph, as is usually the case with newspaper articles, makes clear what the secondary meaning of 'bang' is, with the punning phrase 'arrived explosively, courtesy of gunpowder'. The literal meaning of this is that a vast quantity of gunpowder was used, but the associations are more with war than with entertaining fireworks. Further points to support this idea are 'even before the last firework had been lit, a global debate had begun'; 'blasted their way in to Y2K with more than 30 tons'; 'banned fireworks for fear they would be mistaken for gunshots.' There is irony here, though; the millennium began with friendly use of gunpowder. Let us hope that it continues that way.

Reading a variety of texts for implied meaning

Rhetorical texts

Rhetorical text is concerned with argument, another form of persuasion. You may not come across much of it written down, as it is most commonly used in public speeches. However, at school or college you may be asked to give a speech on a topic, arguing the case for or against. That is when rhetoric is extremely useful.

Because it aims to persuade, rhetoric involves a good deal of inference or indirect meaning. It may sound like a good idea to give people all the facts objectively all the time. However, if you do, you face certain disadvantages. Firstly, people may not have the will or patience to listen to your lengthy and detailed speech; secondly, they will certainly accept some of your points and reject others, so that you cannot be sure of their whole-hearted support.

Rhetoric has one main aim: to persuade listeners or readers to agree with you. To achieve this aim, you need to:

- select information that will cause people to agree with you (we will consider this in Chapter 4);
- choose a style that will cause people to agree with you (this will be dealt with in Chapter 5).

Here are some of the language strategies often used to create a rhetorical style.

Rhetorical questions

As their name suggests, these feature highly in rhetoric. The most successful way to use this device is as the triple **rhetorical question**. You ask your listeners or readers a question which they are expected to answer silently:

'Will the People's Party give you a better standard of living?'

While they are considering that, you follow immediately with a repetition of the question, in case some people have not heard and taken in what you said, and also to make it more emphatic:

'I ask, will the People's Party give you a better standard of living?'

Then you follow up with a really emphatic, challenging question of the same type:

'Will the People's Party give you a better standard of living? I ask, will the People's Party give you a better standard of living? Well, will they?'

Research has shown that many of the most successful public speakers in the world use the triple rhetorical question. (Note that three times is as much as the human mind will tolerate. Try asking the question four times and you will start your audience laughing; it is too emphatic then!)

Headline-punchline

When using the **headline-punchline** technique you make a statement, then repeat it again later in the speech:

> 'They say [a man] must lift himself by his own bootstraps ... It is all right to tell a man to lift himself by his own bootstraps, but it is a cruel jest to say to a bootless man that he ought to lift himself by his own bootstraps.'

Hearing the statement a second time, as an echo of the first, makes the audience pay particular attention.

Contrast

Here you make an antithetical statement (one with a **contrast**) in one sentence:

> 'This party is morally corrupt rather than well-intentioned.'

Balanced statement

Here you make two synonymous statements in one sentence:

> 'This party is morally corrupt and it is politically bankrupt.'

Ladder statement

A **ladder statement** builds up, step by step, to a conclusion. The steps are not necessarily logically linked, though:

> 'This party has wise leaders, good policies, real conviction in what it sets out to do, so it must be the one that will win the election.'

Conflation

Conflation is when two ideas, which look as if they are related but aren't really, are stated side by side:

> 'We will get a better environment and better living standards.'

Exaggeration

Here the case is overstated:

> 'Our party is the best this country has ever seen.'

Generalisation

In a **generalisation**, the broad statement puts the case, but it is so broad as to seem vague:

> 'Everything will get better for everyone.'

Persuader words

Persuader words are adverbs or adverbial phrases which are only put in to urge the listener or reader to agree:

'Surely you agree that our party will be very beneficial for this country.'

Let us take two examples of rhetoric, and you can see how far they fulfil their aim with careful choice of information and style.

There is no political content in the form of a manifesto: no policies, and no

Task 1

Read the text, an imaginary political handbill, looking out especially for what is <u>not</u> mentioned that you would expect to find.

REFUSE TO VOTE

Once again the carnival is upon us. The parties, all having ignored us since the last election, are busy promising us HEAVEN in order to give us HELL. And you vote People's Party to keep the Town Party out, Town Party to keep the Country Party out, and Country Party because no one can remember how bad the Country Party really was. Can *you* remember how bad the Country Party really was?

Take a *positive* step, and say NO to the negation of human individuality that is politics. THERE IS NO GOVERNMENT LIKE NO GOVERNMENT. If no one votes, no one gets in!

Together we will create the ANARCHY that alone will give all the people the chance to live their own lives in their own way. IT DOESN'T MATTER WHO YOU VOTE FOR – THE GOVERNMENT ALWAYS GETS IN!

CHOOSING MASTERS IS WRONG!

promises of better things to come in the future. The first omission is appropriate because anarchy means the opposite of rules and regulations imposed on us by other people. Why is anarchy a good thing, though? There is an **assertion** that 'Choosing masters is wrong' but this is completely unsupported by any reasons that might persuade us.

Task 2

Now read the text again. This time, look at how the writer uses a selection of language strategies to persuade us to agree with the point of view put forward.

Did you find some of the strategies listed earlier? Essentially, there is not much logical argument here. Instead, there are a lot of unsupported statements (known as assertions) and several of the devices of style mentioned earlier:

- rhetorical question: 'Can *you* remember how bad the Country Party really was?' Did you notice the persuader adverb 'really' slipped in there?
- generalisation: 'There is no government like no government.'
- effective contrasts: 'The parties ... are busy promising us HEAVEN in order to give us HELL'; 'Take a *positive* step and say NO to the negation of human individuality that is politics.'
- ladder statement: 'And you vote People's Party to keep the Town Party out, Town Party to keep the Country Party out, and Country Party because no one can remember how bad the Country Party really was.'
- conflation: 'Together we will create the ANARCHY that alone will give all the people the chance to live their own lives in their own way.'

Task 3

Finally, ask yourself 'Do I find this persuasive?'

If the answer is 'No' it is probably because you are aware of the rhetorical devices of style which are used, rather than the writer seeking to persuade through logical reasoning. If the answer is 'Yes' it is probably because you appreciate that these devices of style have been cleverly and entertainingly used, and the handbill has much distortion, but some truth. It is a fact that 'IT DOESN'T MATTER WHO YOU VOTE FOR – THE GOVERNMENT ALWAYS GETS IN!'

Here is a second piece of rhetorical writing, quite different in content but sharing some of the same strategies.

Task 1

Read the text thoughtfully, looking out for the hidden means of persuasion, then write a paragraph explaining what some of them are and whether they have made you sympathetic to the writer's viewpoint. Incidentally, this was written as an essay in the examination.

Hello Classmates!

Well, you're not really my 'mates' because you all hate me and it's probably my resentment of this that's brought me to the point of undermining your entire way of life. I'm going to talk to you about peer pressure in school and its main cause – insecurity with oneself. Throughout my life so far, I've lost more convictions than I will have gained if I live to be a hundred years old. Nowadays, I'll be debating with someone, only to ask myself 'Does he really think he's right? Is he just arguing with me because it's expected of him by his peers? Would he agree with me if I was one of his friends?'

See, I don't fit in anywhere. In my old school, when it was found out that the next year I would be coming to this school, I had to endure the agony of watching my friends drift into hostile territory, because now I was seen as a 'posh boy', and that was unacceptable to them.

So, I came here a refugee, because my old friends had a deep hatred for anything that wasn't them. I came to this school an outsider, with one friend out of nine hundred pupils. That friend was me. For me, school wasn't a positive learning experience, it was a place in which one masters one's fears. So I came in with guns blazing, and lost my chance of friendship. I was instantly different. Without knowing it, I'd let myself in for three years of misery. I remember living in a world where open eyes meant suicide or agony.

By having my own opinions, I had somehow threatened the very foundations of the peer group system, and was therefore made a scapegoat. Every society needs a scapegoat. The Romans had the Barbarians. The Barbarians had other Barbarians. This school had me. I was made an example of what would happen to you if you didn't conform. Then, in my fourth year at this school, I came to the conclusion that those who practise peer pressure do so because they believe they can't stand on their own two feet. THEY ARE INSECURE! And this is what baffles me, at the moment. Why can't people survive without a big group to help them along? I have managed, even with what seemed like the whole world turned against me. Why can't people just be individuals, and respect one another as individuals? Ask yourselves that. Ask yourselves WHO YOU REALLY ARE. We all can stand on our own two feet; it's just a matter of getting up.

Thank you.

This has fewer of the strategies already discussed. However, there are several that stand out. You will have noticed the triple rhetorical question: 'Does he really think he's right? Is he just arguing with me because it's expected of him by his peers? Would he agree with me if I was one of his friends?' and again, later, two separate rhetorical questions: 'Why can't people survive without a big group to help them along?' then 'Why can't people just be individuals, and respect one another as individuals?' There are some striking contrasts: 'For me, school wasn't a positive learning experience; it was a place in which one masters one's fears'; 'I came in with guns blazing, and lost my chance of friendship.' There is a ladder sentence: 'Every society needs a scapegoat. The Romans had the Barbarians. The Barbarians had other barbarians. This school had me.' Finally, there is a good headline-punchline. Relatively early on, the candidate introduces the idea of independence of thought and speech with the sentence 'they can't stand on their own two feet'. At the very end he returns to this idea, restating it slightly to make a memorable ending, which carries conviction: 'We can all stand on our own two feet; it's just a matter of getting up.'

Reading literary texts

More than any other kind of writing you are likely to meet, literary text frequently relies heavily on inference to convey meaning.

Read the following extract taken from a literary biography.

WHERE ARE THE CHILDREN?

Both house and garden are living still, I know; but what of that, if the magic has deserted them?

....

It would happen sometimes long ago, when this house and garden harboured a family, that a book lying open on the flagstones of the terrace or on the grass, a skipping-rope twisted like a snake across the path, or perhaps a miniature garden, pebble-edged and planted with decapitated flowers, revealed both the presence of children and their varying ages. But such evidence was hardly ever accompanied by childish shouts or laughter, and my home, though warm and full, bore an odd resemblance to those houses which, once the holidays have come to an end, are suddenly emptied of joy. The silence, the muted breeze of the enclosed garden, the pages of the book stirred only by invisible fingers, all seemed to be asking, "Where are the children?"

It was then, from beneath the ancient iron trellis sagging to the left under the wisteria, that my mother would make her appearance, small and plump. She would scan the thick green clumps, and raising her head, fling her call into the air: "Children! Where are the children?"

Where indeed? Nowhere. My mother's cry would ring through the garden, striking the great wall of the barn and returning to her as a faint exhausted echo. "Where ...? Children ...?"

Nowhere. My mother would throw back her head and gaze heavenwards, as though waiting for a flock of winged children to alight from the skies. After a moment she would repeat her call; then, grown tired of questioning the heavens, she would crack a dry poppy-head with her finger-nail, rub the greenfly from a rose

---

Reading a variety of texts for implied meaning

shoot, fill her pockets with unripe walnuts, and return to the house shaking her head over the vanished children.

And all the while, from among the leaves of the walnut-tree above her, gleamed the pale, pointed face of a child who lay stretched like a tom-cat along a big branch, and never uttered a word. A less short-sighted mother might well have suspected that the spasmodic greetings exchanged by the twin tops of the two firs were due to some influence other than that of the sudden October squalls, and in the square dormer window, would she not have perceived, if she had screwed up her eyes, two pale patches among the hay – the face of a young boy and the pages of his book?

But she had given up looking for us, had despaired of trying to reach us. Our uncanny turbulence was never accompanied by any sound. I do not believe there can ever have been children so active and so mute. Looking back at what we were, I am amazed. No one had imposed upon us either our cheerful silence or our limited sociability. My older brother, engrossed in constructing some kind of apparatus out of linen, strands of wire and glass tubes, never prevented the younger, aged fourteen, from taking apart a watch. He did not even interfere with his junior's incomprehensible passion for decorating the garden with little tombstones cut out of cardboard, and each inscribed with name, epitaph and genealogy of the imaginary person.

My sister with the long hair might read forever with never a pause; the two boys would brush past her as though they did not see the young girl sitting abstracted and entranced, and never bother her. When I was small, I was at liberty to keep up as best I could with my long-legged brothers as they ranged the woods.

"Where are the children?" She would suddenly appear, the over-solicitous mother, breathless, pursuing her constant quest, head lifted and scenting the breeze. Sometimes her white linen sleeves bore witness that she had come from kneading dough for cakes or making the pudding that had a velvety hot sauce of rum and jam. If she had been washing the Havanese bitch, she would be enveloped in a long blue apron, and sometimes she would be waving a banner of rustling yellow paper, the paper used round the butcher's meat, which meant that she hoped to reassemble, at the same time as her elusive children, her carnivorous family of vagabond cats.

To her traditional cry she would add, in the same anxious and appealing key, a reminder of the time of day. "Four o'clock, and they haven't come in to tea! Where are the children?... Half-past six! Will they come home to dinner? Where are the children?"

Our only sin, our single misdeed, was silence, and a kind of miraculous vanishing. For perfectly innocent reasons, for the sake of a liberty that no one denied us, we clambered over the railings, leaving behind our shoes, and returned by way of an unnecessary ladder or a neighbour's low wall.

"Tomorrow I shall keep you locked up! All of you, do you hear, every single one of you!"

Tomorrow! Next day the eldest, slipping on the slated roof where he was fitting a tank, broke his collar-bone and remained at the foot of the wall waiting, silent and half unconscious, until someone came to pick him up. The next day an eighteen-rung ladder crashed on the forehead of the younger son, who never uttered a cry, but brought home a lump like a purple egg between his eyes.

"Where are the children?"

From My Mother's House *by Colette.*

When reading a literary text like this, you will find that you cannot just skim it and get the sense. You have to slow down, because it is slow-paced writing.

At first reading, this text doesn't seem to have much content. It is about a group of children from the same family, playing in and around their garden and not responding to their mother's calls to come. It seems a simple and common experience.

Try to answer the two questions below, which seem to be equally simple. You may be surprised to find that it is difficult to answer these, even after intensive reading of the text, in a way that really seems to get to the bottom of the matter. Consider the answers shown in handwritten script and the comments below.

Question 1

Why is the mother calling?

She is calling because she wants her children to come in to tea or dinner.

This is not wrong, but it seems inadequate. It can't be that important to her because she soon becomes distracted, doing something else in the garden, or else she just returns to the house. However, she comes out regularly throughout the day, threatens her children with forcing them to stay in the house when they are doing no harm. You begin to sense that the real answer is more subtle. Using your skill of inference, you decide that it is just because she is a mother, always anxious about her children, hoping they are coming to no harm. They are always on her mind.

Question 2

Why don't the children answer?

The children are busy reading, wandering in the woods or doing things that interest them.

This answer isn't wrong either but, again, it does not seem to be enough. The children are often in the garden, watching their mother calling. We are told they keep a 'cheerful silence' so they are not afraid to answer her. You reflect, having been a child yourself, and realise that the answer is there in the text after all: 'vanishing ... for perfectly innocent reasons, for the sake of a liberty that no one denied us ...' It is because they are children, with their own interests but also their own individuality, their private lives; we might say now 'having their own agenda'.

In the examination you will usually find two texts on the same theme. Look back at the earlier passage entitled *Shy prodigy 'stretching her wings'* on page 35 and try to answer Question 3 about both texts.

Question 3

What do both passages have in common?

Both passages are about children, or young people, who disappear, and about anxious adults who worry about this.

This is an answer based on explicit reading of the text. I expect that your answer is fuller than this. Both passages are about children or young people who disappear, and about anxious adults who worry about this. When we put them together, we see that they are also about the need for young people to claim their liberty. They are aware of their parents' wishes for them and may love their parents, but every child is his/her own person and, sooner or later, children will let the parents know this. It is as natural as the bird leaving the nest. In the first passage this idea is suggested by the title; the second also has a direct reference to children who 'take flight'. The mother looks upward, 'as though waiting for a flock of winged children to alight from the skies.'

Did you get the final answers suggested above? If you did, you have been doing some productive reflective reading.

Sample exam questions and answers

This passage is from a short story about a very fit boy who is training to run a long distance race. Read it through slowly, reflecting as you do so.

So as soon as I tell myself I'm the first man ever to be dropped into the world, and as soon as I take that first flying leap out into the frosty grass of an early morning, when even birds haven't the heart to whistle, I get to thinking, and that's what I like. I run my rounds in a dream, turning at land or footpath corners without knowing I'm turning, leaping brooks without knowing they're there, and shouting "Good morning!" to the world. It's a treat, being a long-distance runner, out in the world by yourself with not a soul to make you bad-tempered or tell you what to do. Sometimes I think that I've never been so free as during that couple of hours when I'm trotting up the path out of the gates and turning by that oak tree at the lane end.

Everything's dead but good, because it's dead before coming alive, not dead after being alive. That's how I look at it. Mind you, I often feel frozen stiff at first. I can't feel my hands or feet or flesh at all, as if I'm a ghost who wouldn't know that the earth was under him if he didn't see it now and again through the mist. But even though some people would call this frost-pain suffering, I don't, because I know that in half an hour I'm going to be warm, that by the time I get to the main road and am turning onto the wheatfield footpath I'm going to feel as hot as a stove.

It's a good life, I'm saying to myself. Trot-trot-trot, puff-puff-puff. Slap-slap-slap go my feet on the hard soil. Swish-swish-swish as my arms and side catch the bare branches of a bush. Trot-trot-trot, over the stream and into the wood where it's dark and frosty. Twigs are stinging my legs. I see my smoky breath going out into the air as if I had ten cigars stuck in my mouth.

By the time I'm half way through my morning course, when after a frost-bitten dawn I can see a bit of sunlight hanging from the bare twigs of beech and sycamore, and when I've measured my half way mark by the shortcut scrimmage, I make my way down the steep bush-covered bank and into the sunken lane, when still there's not a soul in sight and not a sound, except the neighing of a foal in a cottage stable that I can't see, I get to thinking the deepest thoughts of all. To go down the bank is a risk, it's the only risk I take on the run and it's excitement I feel as I'm flying flat out like one of the pterodactyls from the 'Lost World', scratching myself to bits and almost letting myself go, but not quite. It's the most wonderful minute because there's no one thought or word or picture of anything in my head while I'm going down the bank. I'm empty, as empty as I was before I was born.

When I've passed this half way mark I often think that every run I do is a life – a little life, as full of misery and happiness and things happening around you as you can ever get – and I remember that after quite a few of these runs I thought that it didn't need much understanding to tell how a life was going to end, once it had got well started.

From The Loneliness of the Long Distance Runner *by Alan Sillitoe.*

Now answer these questions. Look at the three sets of answers given by three different students in the examination. Decide which you would grade highest.

Question 1

Why does the runner think he is 'the first man ever to be dropped into the world?' **(5 marks)**

Student 1

The runner thinks he is the first man ever to be dropped into the world because he takes his first flying leap out into the frosty grass of an early morning when even the birds haven't the heart to whistle.

Student 2

He thinks that he is the first man to be dropped into the world because at that time, early in the morning, it is so silent and calm with no one about and not even the birds had started to sing. Every animal seems 'dead' asleep. He is the first to touch the frost with his feet and he is all alone.

Student 3

He thinks this as it is still dark when he begins running. There is frost on the grass and no one is around.

Question 2

Give three different examples of the boy's mood as he runs. **(3 marks)**

Student 1

The boy's mood is that in half an hour he is going to be warm, he is going to be as hot as a stove and he sees his breath going out into the air.

Student 2

The boy's mood is day-dreaming: 'I run my rounds in a dream.' It is cheerful: 'with not a soul to make you bad-tempered'. He tastes freedom: 'I've never been so free.'

Student 3

The boy's mood is that he is happy, excited and in a deep-thinking mood.

Explain in your own words what the writer means by the following: 'I often think that every run I do is a life ... well started.' **(4 marks)**

Student 1

It means that if he runs well he is living well.

Student 2

It means that you can be given a good start in life the same as you can get off to a good start running.

Student 3

It is that if your life starts off well you have a chance to do well and be happy later on, like starting a race well and being pleased because you are ahead.

Give in a single word or short phrase the meaning of each of the following as used in the passage:
'I'm empty';
'I'm flying flat out';
'it's dead before coming alive'. **(3 marks)**

Student 1

'I'm hungry'; 'I'm running so fast I'm tired'; 'It hasn't come alive yet.'

Student 2

'I'm not thinking of anything'; 'I'm running as fast as I can'; 'Spring hasn't come yet'.

Student 3

He wants something to eat. He is going really fast. Everything is still dead.

I hope that you gave Student 2 the best mark, as all the answers are right. Student 3 gave the best answer of all to Question 3, though, a difficult question that needs reflective reading to understand the inference.

In an exam, this text might be paired with the texts *The Edinburgh Club* (see page 39) and *Fitness with your personal trainer* (see page 42) from earlier in the chapter. The subject matter is similar, though the tone of this text is more serious than that of the Edinburgh Club article.

Reading a variety of texts for implied meaning

Inference in your own writing

Finally, remember that as you read you learn ways of writing with greater skill and maturity. You can use inference in your own compositions. Here are three essays written by students on the same topic – dancing.

Read each in turn, and write down a sentence or two about the writer's approach. Ask yourself the following questions:

- Is there a good deal of action in the piece?
- Is the dancing described in detail?
- Does every paragraph take you a little further in understanding this dancing?

As you try to answer the third question, a fourth may come into your mind:

- Is the writer telling you about something else besides dancing?

DANCE REHEARSAL

As the dance instructor called them to order, the dancers took their places at the bar.

"Firstly, we shall begin with warm-up exercises with the placing of arms, and matching footwork in 1st, 2nd, 3rd, 4th and 5th positions, involving half and full turns, along with stretches. Secondly, I would like all dancers to position themselves in their proper places centre floor to begin rehearsal for our current production of Romeo and Juliet. Quiet, dancers," called the instructor. "Now centre floor, with principal dancers leading." Once the dancers had taken up their positions, the instructor motioned the pianist to begin. As the music started, the instructor counted with the music: "One and two and three and four and ..."

Suddenly he shouted "No! No! No! It's all wrong! You must feel the music, live the music, be the music and, above all, dance the music as if it were your very last breath of life." With this in mind, the dancers gracefully moved across the dance floor with much magnitude of splendour. Upon their completion of the rehearsal piece, the instructor beamed and cheered: "Bravo! Well done!"

This piece is carefully explicit. We are invited to see and hear exactly what takes place during the dance session. First the instructor calls the dancers together and they all do warm-up exercises. Next, they take their places on the floor to begin the actual rehearsal, obeying the instructor's shouted instructions as the music plays. This is interrupted by the instructor's sudden shout, which seems to inspire the dancers to do their best, moving, as this fine phrase tells us, with 'much magnitude of splendour.'

Now read the second piece on page 62, asking yourself the same questions.

GOTTA DANCE! GOTTA DANCE! GOTTA DANCE!

For sixteen years of my life, five days a week, I would walk up steps covered with a worn brown carpet and push open an old wooden door. Inside were little children running around, middle-school students lying on the floor finishing homework, loud music, and the booming voice of the dance instructor counting to the beat of the music.

Although chaotic and noisy, the dance studio was a place of warmth, a place of release, and was a place that became my second home. I would always peek around the corner after closing the door and watch the pupils struggle to keep up with the relentless beat. I would then frantically change my shoes, tie my long hair back into a careless bun, and run to join them on the dance floor. Flashing a smile at my friends and the instructor, I would find my way to a spot in the front of the room. I always found time to glance into the mirror and adjust my hair and attire, just as the next routine started. It was always the same routine, but it was a preparation before I could release the pressures of home, school and set my spirit free.

John, a middle-aged man with a bald head and a round stomach, from the large amount of coffee, doughnuts and cigarettes he consumed, would instruct the class to quieten down. It was a loud yell that sounded as if he was irritated by our behaviour, but he would always proceed to tell us a series of jokes and then tell us the goals for the class during the hour. We always had a good laugh, which was liberating to the soul and helped to release anxiety from our school day.

Our goals for the hour were always challenging, and I would often become frustrated with myself because I do not have a natural talent for dance, and had to work very hard to reach my level of success. However, overcoming the difficult steps was well worth the hard work because it would set my spirit free and the motion became easier and more fluid, allowing better self-expression through my own style of dance.

Through the art of dance I can reveal myself, the world inside me, and find myself psychologically and emotionally. It sets me free, helps release my stress, and helps me to understand myself better. I often have a difficult time expressing myself with words on paper and verbally with others; dance allows me to express myself physically. As a performer, I often let my 'actions speak louder than words' when communicating with both strangers and loved ones. Although I can be shy and reserved at times, dance allows me to express my emotions freely, confront my problems, find myself, and let my body rhythm and movement convey my feelings towards others.

Dance is always my means of releasing tension. Whether I slap my feet on the floor to tap rhythms or twist and contort my body to lyrical ballet dance routines, I release the worldly pressures from my body. The motion, the inspiration of others, the passion of the art of dance, and the pure enjoyment of dancing sets my spirit free. To connect with my spirit, remember my spirit, express my spirit and free my spirit ... in the words of that great American dancer Gene Kelly, "I gotta dance! Gotta dance! Gotta dance!"

Reading a variety of texts for implied meaning

This piece begins in a similar way. We are taken into a dance hall, accompanying the narrator. The young dancers come together, taking their places on the floor, just as in the first piece. We find out much less about the dancing and soon it seems to be over, but the writing continues. Now, the writer is telling us about one of the dancers – herself. We are invited to identify with her responses. We find many statements which show her feeling of relaxation and liberation, for example, 'I could release the pressures of home, school and set my spirit free.' The session is 'liberating to the soul and helped to release anxiety'; 'it sets me free, helps release my stress.' Another idea begins to come in – that of self-expression: 'the motion became easier, allowing better self-expression'; the dance 'helps me to understand myself better'; '[I] let my body rhythm and movement convey my feelings towards others.' This running line of comment on self-expression and release of tension seems almost like a part of the music, and it grows to a point of crescendo, just as music does – 'To connect with my spirit, remember my spirit, express my spirit and free my spirit ... in the words of that great American dancer gene Kelly, "I gotta dance! Gotta dance! Gotta dance!"'

Don't you agree that there is comparatively little explicit comment about dancing here, but a great deal about the effect of dancing on an individual? You understand the effect by adding together all the references listed, and they make up the real meaning of the piece.

Now read the third piece. Again, ask yourself the four questions.

THE WAY I USED TO

I used to dance. The dance itself was not an ordinary dance, it was a lot more than that. The first steps I learned at the age of six, but the real meaning of the dance I realised much later, in a country far away.

Every national dance represents one particular region. This one combined various cultures. Music, costumes and steps were highly influenced by different religions and great variations of style have been developed: Circle, Chain, and Couple were the most typical.

Circle used to promote a feeling of unity among the dancers, symbolically among nations. Chain dances usually had a leader. They involved serpentine or spiral formation, as well as straight-lined patterns. The dancers used to be lined up side by side, or they used to follow one another. However, if they touched, the contact was made in various ways: holding hands, linking arms, even grasping one another's belt if the rhythm became really fast.

Couple was the most romantic formation of all: man's arm around the girl's waist. It happened more than once that the dancing couple ended up married in real life.

Men's and women's movements were usually different. Men used to step vigorously and execute spectacular leaps. Women's styles were generally less energetic, calling for graceful movements with smaller steps and fewer jumps and kicks.

But the real beauty was found in their costumes. Wearing them, it felt like carrying years and years of people's history on your shoulders. The costumes were authentically made out of natural fabric such as cotton, linen, wool and silk, hand-sewn and embroidered in bright colours. The dancers used to wear everything from turbans and Turkish pantaloons from regions in the south of the country to heavy, fur capes and hats from the mountainous regions. At some point they would allow you to see nothing but a spinning wheel of full skirts and handkerchiefs. Men in some dances used to wear small bells on their high-topped black boots. As they would prance and stamp their feet, the differently pitched bells sounded like an orchestra of sleigh bells.

To emphasize the rhythm and accent when we danced, we used to clap or click our fingers. Very often, to punctuate our movements, we would produce vocal sounds such as yells, yips and yodels. At that moment the dance would reach its climax and the feeling among us, as we danced, was simply indescribable. As I said before, it was a lot more than just a dance. It was something that you are born with: music in your heart, rhythm in your veins was coming to the surface every time we were on stage.

The country from where I come has fallen apart. The unity is broken. The music has stopped. I live far away now. I will never dance again the way I used to.

This seems to do much the same as the first and the second pieces. There is a great deal of exact description of particular dances. In fact, you would probably recognise Circle, Chain, and Couple if you saw people dancing them, because the writer has given you a precise account. This careful description of the series of dances concerns the dancers, too, but chiefly concentrates on how they move and what they wear. This dance also moves to a climax, at which point we are told of the feeling which was 'simply indescribable' (i.e. you can't write down explicitly what that feeling was like). The feeling, like the rhythm of the music, is 'inborn' – national.

Then the writer moves one step further. The final short paragraph comes as rather a shock. The unity of the dance is broken, the nation whose rhythm is in the blood of these dancers has 'fallen apart', the music is over. The dancers are scattered. Reading the final sentence – 'I will never dance again the way I used to' – we see that it carries a complex message: not just no more national dances, but no more living in your own country, no more of the feeling of release and happiness among your family and friends there, no more celebrating the love of your country through your own culture at home. This is all there, but you, as reader, add together the preceding ideas and can appreciate the full force of the meaning in the phrase of the title, because you can measure in your own mind and heart what such a loss would be to you.

We hope that you feel confident now that you can respond well to implied meaning when reading, or when writing. The next chapter moves on to look at responding to more texts with a common theme.

3

From reading to writing

In the examination, you will be asked questions on a range of texts which are linked or themed in content. For this chapter we have chosen a topic which has fascinated individuals and researchers for many years – sleep and dreams.

You may have your own experiences and theories about this topic, but you must be careful not to be influenced by your own ideas unless a question asks you to give a personal response.

Section A: Comprehension

In Section A of the exam paper, you have to answer directed questions about the content, language and layout of the related texts.

You are going to look at a variety of texts on the topic, all from different sources. After reading the texts and making notes on them, you will be asked to compare two of the texts, using your notes.

Read the following extract from a magazine advertisement.

Text A

ADVERTISEMENT

Pillow Talk.

We're all much happier for it. It's guaranteed to make even Monday morning feel better. What is it?

Sleep, that's what. Nothing sets you up for a good day like a good night's sleep. Here we take a look at what steps you can take to make sure you get one.

Sleep is good for us in so many ways; repairing and refreshing the mind and body. But not sleeping is a common problem, with over one in three people suffering at some stage. Because it's so common you could think of it in the same terms as, for example, a headache – an ordinary, treatable condition.

There are a number of things you can do to help get a good night's sleep, like making sure your bedroom is dark and quiet, that your bed is comfortable and not too hot or cold, and avoiding caffeine, cigarettes and even exercise close to bedtime. If you're lying awake worrying about stuff you may find it helps to write things down.

But if you've tried all that and you still can't sleep, you could try taking Nytol before you go to bed. Just think of it as a bridge back to a normal sleeping pattern.

Nytol and Nytol One-A-Night contain diphenhydramine, a tried and trusted antihistamine – take it twenty minutes before going to bed and it'll gently help you fall asleep. And because it's only a sleep aid, not a tranquiliser, it'll help you wake up feeling bright and refreshed. What's more, tests show not only that it works but when used according to the instructions, there's no evidence to suggest you'll grow to rely on it. Nytol is also like a headache tablet in that you use it as and when you need to, you don't need a prescription and there's no course to take.

Meanwhile, if you prefer, there's Nytol Herbal*, a traditional remedy to promote calmness and natural sleep. Just two tablets at bedtime will help you gently drift off.

Nytol is used by millions all over the world and you can trust it just as they do. So, if you're tired of not sleeping, ask your pharmacist for Nytol. Good mornings follow a good Nytol.

*Nytol Night Time Herbal Sleep Aid. Always read the label/leaflet. D04170

Adapted from Red *magazine.*

Task 1

Think about what makes this a good advertisement. How is the reader drawn into reading the advertisement? How is it effective in achieving its aims of:
a) making the reader aware of the product;
b) making the reader buy the product?

You are not being asked for a judgement about the worth of the text, but to explain how effects are achieved using both layout and content, and maybe to show that you have the skill to use such effects in your own writing (this will come later in the chapter).

Visual impact

First, let's consider the visual impact of the advertisement. At first glance, it looks like an article rather than an advertisement. After all, it appeared in a women's magazine which deals with topics such as relationships, and the image of a smiling woman and the headline 'Pillow Talk' might suggest a discussion on what people talk about in bed.

In fact, when first reading it, one might be unsure until reaching the end of the first main column of text that it was an advertisement. Intentional? Yes! Clever? This will depend on your viewpoint. It certainly catches the reader's attention.

Task 2

How is the layout of the text arranged? Is it spaced out or crowded?
Do the typefaces and sizes vary? If so, how and what is the effect?

You can see, whatever the language in which the text is written, that there is plenty of white space. What is the effect of this space? Can space be used to set a mood? A crowded page might convey stress and pressure, so maybe a more restful feeling is communicated by white space.

The typefaces are two main styles, one for the headline and side introduction, one for the main body of the text. They each have some variety of size or density (emboldening) to fit the layout and position of the text.

The two main columns have paragraphs of varied length. What is the purpose of this? Look at the fourth paragraph, which wraps around the columns. This is much longer than any of the others. Why? What is the reason for placing it in the middle of the text? Would you have read the piece if that paragraph had been at the beginning? The answers to these questions may be clearer once you have considered the content and style of the text.

Task 3

What other features might you comment on about the layout?

Did you notice the blocked and centred heading ADVERTISEMENT at the top of the page? Not very eye-catching, maybe, but it is a legal requirement to distinguish advertising from other material. What about the small print at the foot of the page? Did you notice it on your first look at the text? The use of the asterisk allows the writer to explain or develop an idea without interrupting the reader's flow, but it might seem like an afterthought, a postscript. On the other hand, it is followed by the 'health warning' that has to appear on any medication, so the footnote serves a dual purpose.

It is important to examine the text as a whole, not only the main sections, as there could be important clues about its function or purpose which you could miss.

Style and content

Now we have looked at the appearance of the text, let's look more closely at the style and content.

Task 4

What words could you use to describe the image the advertiser is trying to convey to readers? Which of the following would fit?

relaxed   happy   refreshed   positive   sexy   tired   sluggish

You may be surprised at some of the adjectives above, but when we examine the text, not all the images are positive. After all, an advertisement for a sleep remedy has to appeal to those who have difficulty sleeping, not those who sleep easily.

Task 5

What do you notice about the style of the title and the introduction?

You could comment on the title and the side column introduction first – it is logical, and probably the order in which most readers approach such a text. As indicated in the previous section, the title 'Pillow Talk' is deliberately ambiguous, posing such questions to the reader as 'What is this about?' and 'Am I going to find it interesting?' The side section continues this teasing approach, with assertive statements and a question – you have to read on to discover the topic.

Task 6

What is the effect of the first main paragraph, in bold type?

The first main paragraph assumes that you have read the introduction. It would seem rather odd if you hadn't – 'Sleep, that's what' is an incomplete or **minor sentence**, quite common in advertising and in response to a question. This is followed by another bold assertion, with the positive adjective 'good' repeated. The final sentence in this paragraph uses 'here' to focus on what follows and 'we' to suggest a joint approach – the writer and the reader together.

Now we have looked at some elements of the text, try to write five sets of short notes to answer these questions. Look only at the second paragraph of the text. Compare your answers with the students' ideas in handwritten script.

Question 1
───

What kind of readers is this aimed at?

general public

Question 2
───

What is the evidence for your answer to Question 1?

'a common problem', 'over one in three people'

Did you try to answer Questions 1 and 2 together? Look carefully at how questions are phrased, or you might find yourself duplicating material between questions.

Question 3
───

Identify four key words or phrases that set two contrasting tones within the paragraph.

'good for us', 'repairing and refreshing'
contrast with 'suffering', 'treatable condition'

What is the effect of the order of the content?

The positive aspects of sleep, followed by the shared problem of sleeplessness and a possible solution promotes the benefits of sleep and suggests a way to achieve it.

How does the writer establish a sort of relationship with the reader? Give at least three examples of how language is used to do this.

- *The use of personal pronouns ('Sleep is good for us'; 'you could think of it') rather than the more distant 'one', or 'they'.*
- *Reassuring semi-medical tone; alliteration (repetition of the same initial sound, as in 'repairing and refreshing'); and gentle sounds.*
- *Showing the reader is not alone or unusual ('common problem').*
- *Showing there's nothing to panic about and a solution is available ('ordinary, treatable condition').*

Now use the following questions to help you analyse the remainder of the text. Remember, only make notes at this stage.

Your turn

1 Is the tone formal or informal? Give at least three examples to support your answer.
2 Where does the tone change from reassuring to persuasive? Give a line reference or a quotation here.
3 What is the difference between the fourth paragraph and the rest of the text? You may wish to look back to the section on layout when you answer this question.
4 What are the different effects of 'could' ('you could try'), 'will' ('will help you') and 'can' ('you can trust it')?
5 What is the effect of the last sentence?

Now go through the whole text and note any expressions or ideas which you might use in a more detailed analysis of the style and content of this advertisement. Keep your notes safely for a task later in this chapter.

The next extract consists of the introduction and some short extracts from a website on sleep. Read the piece twice, first to get a general idea of tone and structure, then more carefully to understand the content.

Text B

What is sleep...
and why do we do it?

We spend about eight hours a day, 56 hours a week, 224 hours a month and 2,688 hours a year doing it ... that's right ... SLEEPING. One third of our lives we are apparently doing nothing. But is sleep really doing nothing? It looks like it ... a person's eyes are closed; muscles are relaxed; breathing is regular; there is no response to sound or light. However, if you take a look at what is happening inside the brain, you will find quite a different situation – the brain is very active.

Scientists can record brain activity (or waves) by attaching electrodes to the scalp and then connecting these electrodes to a machine.

Stages of sleep
Sleep follows a regular cycle each night – the brain pattern changes in a predictable way several times during a single period of sleep. There are two basic forms of sleep: slow wave sleep (SWS) and <u>rapid eye movement (REM) sleep</u>. Infants spend about 50% of their sleep time in SWS and 50% in REM sleep. Adults spend about 20% of their sleep time in REM and 80% in SWS sleep. Elderly people spend less than 15% of their sleep time in REM sleep.

Did you know?
Did you ever think about how much you sleep and dream? The 'average' human sleeps about eight hours every day. That's one third of your life! In other words, you sleep for about 122 days every year. A 75-year-old person would have spent a total of about 25 years asleep. There is a wide range in the amount of <u>time different animals spend sleeping</u>.

As for dreaming ... we enter REM sleep about five times in an average eight-hour period of sleep. If we assume that we dream during each of these REM periods, then in one year, we will have had 1,825 dreams! Of course we don't remember all of these dreams. A 75-year-old person would have had about 136,875 dreams!

Why sleep?

Why sleep at all? It seems like a big waste of time. Think of all you could be doing if you did not sleep. Nevertheless, sleep appears to be necessary. There is a continuing debate going on as to why we sleep. Why do most animals sleep? How much sleep is required?

Most 'higher' animals <u>appear to sleep</u> during some portion of the day and/or night – they are quiet; they rest; they do not move. Scientists have recorded sleep-like brain patterns in birds, reptiles and mammals.

No one knows for sure why we sleep, but here are two basic theories:
- sleep has a **restorative function**;
- sleep has an **adaptive function**.

Sleep as a restorative process

This theory of sleep suggests that sleep helps the body recover from all the work it did while an animal was awake. Experiments have shown that the more physical exercise an animal does, the more SWS an animal will have. Also, if people are deprived of SWS sleep by waking them up during it, then they complain of being physically tired. If people are deprived of REM sleep by waking them up during REM periods, they can get anxious and irritable. If animals are deprived of REM for several days and then allowed undisturbed sleep, they will go into 'REM rebound' – this is when REM periods of sleep will happen more often and for a longer time than normal.

Sleep, especially REM sleep, has also been thought to be important for memory and learning. Perhaps sleep in some way helps in the formation of memories.

Sleep as an adaptive process

Sleep may have developed because of the need of animals to protect themselves. For example, in some animals, the search for food and water is easier during the day when the sun is out. When it is dark, it is best for these animals to save energy, avoid getting eaten, and avoid falling off a cliff that they cannot see. It is interesting to note <u>which animals sleep the most and which sleep the least</u>. In general, animals that serve as food for other animals sleep the least!

Now make notes on these questions on visual impact, style and content, which are similar to those on the previous advertisement. Some advice is given below each question.

Visual impact

Question 1

What did you notice first about this text?

You could comment on blocks of material, type sizes, cartoons or illustrations, underlining, humour, etc.

Question 2

Which of these devices did you find most effective, and why?

Now you are beginning to use observation and analysis to explain a personal visual response to a text.

Style and content

Question 3

What kind of readers are these pages aimed at?

These web pages came from a site called 'Neuroscience for Kids – Sleep' (http: faculty.washington.edu/chudler/sleep.html). (It would have been too easy to tell you that at the beginning!) Would you like to change any of your answers in the light of this new information? This may show you how close attention to a text or even a heading may reinforce or alter a first impression, as with the advertisement we first looked at in this chapter.

Question 4

What is your evidence for your answer to Question 3?

There are lots of facts in the text, but they are presented quite simply. The style is also quite light and friendly, and the cartoon pictures are fun.

Question 5

Identify four words or phrases that set the tone of the extract.

The style is quite chatty, with phrases like 'that's right ... SLEEPING' and 'as for dreaming', but it's educational too, with lots of questions. Phrases like 'Did you know' are both chatty and educational in style.

Question 6

Look at the section headings. What do these headings tell you about the purpose of these pages?

Did you notice that lots of the section headings are in the form of questions? This helps set an educational tone.

Question 7

Why does the writer use a question and answer pattern? For example 'But is sleep really doing nothing? It looks like it ... the brain is very active.'

Did you comment on the teaching-type style of communication? This may be an attempt to engage the reader in some thoughts of their own before giving the answers, as a teacher may do.

Question 8

Identify at least four different types of punctuation, apart from commas and full stops. What is the effect of each of these?

The varied punctuation, such as leader dots and exclamation marks, contributes to this conversational tone. Conventions of a website are also used, for example indicating links by using bold type or underlining.

Question 9

What do you notice about the language used in this text?

Did you notice how much information was repeated, particularly key terms? This again may be an attempt to reinforce ideas and concepts, like stressing them in speech, to make them stay in the viewer's mind. After all, a web page needs to attract attention, as viewers may choose just to skim it for interest or information, to ignore or close it.

Once again, keep your notes for use later in the chapter.

Now we have two more extracts on sleep. Each is taken from a quality daily British newspaper, but they are very different in appearance and style from both the two previous texts and each other.

Read this extract, which came from the news analysis pages of a newspaper.

Text C

Body suffers symptoms of age with too little sleep

Sarah Boseley
Health Correspondent

Sacrificing sleep to longer working hours and nights on the town could bring about changes in the body similar to ageing, according to new medical research.

A study of the effects on the body of the sort of sleep-debt that is increasingly common at the end of the 20th century has had startling results. Although the study was small – 11 young men aged between 18 and 27 took part – it found 'striking alterations' in the way their bodies functioned, according to a report in this week's *Lancet* medical journal.

The Chicago-based scientists found that successive nights of four hours' sleep took its toll on the metabolism and endocrine (hormonal) functioning of the body. These alterations 'mimic some of the hallmarks of ageing.' The scientists suggest that chronic sleep loss could increase the severity of age-related diseases such as diabetes and high blood pressure.

They also suggest that young, healthy adults may need more than the standard night's sleep. Their volunteers biologically performed better when they had slept for more than eight hours.

From The Guardian.

Make notes on the following questions. Some thoughts on these questions are given below each question.

Question 1

What is the target audience for this article?

The article itself is a summary of a piece of research which appeared in a professional magazine for doctors. Any doctors who noticed it could go to the magazine or website for more detailed information. So maybe the target audience is readers who are worried about their health or their lack of sleep or feel guilty about not getting enough sleep. Maybe here is the evidence they need to prove that too little sleep is bad for you!

Question 2

How are quotations and brackets used in this text?

Look at how quotation marks are used where some of the ideas can be best reported in the original words from the text. Brackets are used to explain or gloss a technical term – a more knowledgeable reader would not need to read the explanation.

Question 3

Is the first paragraph an adequate summary of the text?

The use of a summary in the first paragraph is a usual newspaper device in news or comment articles. It helps the busy reader skim the paper for items they would want to read in depth and also is a journalistic convention, as items tend to be shortened from the end to fit the space available, so the most important ideas need to come early on.

Question 4

The article continues by giving more details about the study and its findings. What sort of readers might want to read the whole article?

The answer to the final question is really in the ideas above – those who have time, have more than a passing interest in health issues and who are not put off by the scientific references.

Now read the last piece on dreams. It is from an article that appeared in the same newspaper as the previous one, in the magazine section on work issues rather than the news analysis pages.

Text D

In the 80s sleep was for slackers. Now it's the new status symbol. Angelique Chrisafis finds out why everyone who's anyone is getting the full eight hours.

Dream on

Recently the Wall Street Journal called sleep the new status symbol. At a time when most people complain that they stay at work too late, it's now a sign of class to refuse to sacrifice your normal brain function to the 24-hour industrial beast. Sleep snobs are dismissing the late-nighters as daft.

"The four-hours-a-night fad was hype, lies and absolute nonsense," says Ruth Lea from the Institute of Directors. "Most directors average eight hours. They get in at 9.30 am, work very hard and go home. Lately I have found that directors aren't complaining about sleep. They are sensible, normal people who try to get as much as they need."

But there is a horrible smugness about the new refreshed executive. A US anthropologist says that showing off about your eight hours is classic one-upmanship. "There is an implication in the 'sleep-a-lot' boast that you are so well organised and such a neat delegator that the world can persist adequately even while you are comatose. This is a tribute to how splendid you are when you are not comatose."

The eight-hours-a-night brag by directors would be brilliant if it were accompanied by a nicer workplace which everyone left at 5 pm. But it is not. If sleep is a status symbol, a class system is emerging in which the slumber-rich snuggle down at the expense of their exhausted staff.

A specialist in shift-work fatigue says that there is evidence to suggest that British workers are sleeping less than ever. Junior doctors still regularly sleep four-hour nights. One headteacher admits to working until 3 am and sleeping bolt upright in an armchair to ensure he wakes at seven. In stress-management workshops it has been found that the average British office worker goes to bed at 11 and wakes at 3.30 am worrying about work.

From The Guardian.

From reading to writing

Your turn

Write notes on the following questions.

1 Who might be attracted to this article?
2 What sort of people claim to be sleeping eight hours or more?
3 What types of people are not sleeping as much as this?
4 Look at the following sentences from Paragraph 2:
'The four-hours-a-night fad was hype, lies and absolute nonsense'
'They are sensible, normal people...'
First of all check your understanding of all the words used here, some of which might be described as 'slang'. Even if you are unsure of the exact meanings, can you comment on the contrast in tone between the two sentences? How could you now describe the attitude of the writer, and therefore what she wants her readers to think?

Comparing texts

You have now looked at four different pieces on the same theme. You have tried to answer a range of questions on each piece, on layout, style and content. You could be asked similar questions in the examination, on one or more pieces. There will usually be two texts on the same theme, not necessarily factual or media pieces. Questions will normally focus on aspects of language use and meaning, but understanding how layout works will help you to compare and contrast texts.

Now, using your close reading and your notes, plus the ideas in this chapter, answer the following question in not more than 200 words. Compare your answer with the sample answer and examiner's comments below.

Question

Choose two of the texts: A or B and C or D. Write a comparison, using the following points as guidelines. Use brief quotations to support your ideas.
- **How do the pieces differ in target audience?**
- **How do they differ in purpose?**
- **Are there any similarities between the pieces you have chosen?**
- **Identify any stylistic devices that you feel have been well used by the writers and explain the purpose and effect of these devices.**

Sample answer: comparison of Texts B and C

The target audience for the website is young people interested in science, especially the workings of the brain, and in sleep or dreams; the newspaper article is aimed at adults with an interest in health issues, particularly a possible link between sleep deprivation and ageing.

The purpose of the website is to inform, entertain and stimulate readers to follow up cross-references. The article aims to summarise a report on medical research for lay (non-specialist) readers, informing them of the main findings and indicating the original source for those who want more detail.

Similarities – each takes sleep as the main topic, with references to eight hours a night as 'standard' or 'average'. They each use glossing to explain technical terms or expand ideas, with brackets and dashes. They each consider the benefits of sleep, particularly the final sentence of the article and the detail on the restorative function in the web pages.

Stylistic devices – the web page uses a chatty style, with questions and answers, headings, varied punctuation, repetition of content and structures, figures and numbered points, which are slightly altered in the sub-headings, to reinforce without boring the reader. Abbreviations are also used to speed up the reading. The overall impact is attractive, with illustrations and cartoons to set the tone of entertainment, but sufficient technical detail to satisfy a more demanding reader. The interactive style is appropriate, although at times it may seem patronising.

The newspaper article uses alliteration in the headline and the opening sentence. The first paragraph is a bold statement followed by the source of the information. The findings are summarised in the introductory paragraph. Each subsequent paragraph uses a similar pattern of stating a key point and then building up details, so a reader could scan the article for the main points. The writer uses emotive language to attract attention - such as 'sacrificing' as the first word, 'sleep-debt', 'startling', 'striking'. Quotations also draw attention to key points. The writer does not assert facts, using words such as 'could' and 'suggest' to avoid accusations of scaremongering.

This is a detailed response, longer than the 200 words required but following the suggested structure. Brief quotations are used appropriately to support points about Text C, but not Text B. There are some personal judgements, which were not asked for, but are understandable. The writer could have summarised the comparisons in a chart, but as the texts are so different in style, paragraphs allow more freedom to develop ideas.

We hope this example helps you to analyse and compare texts and to gain some ideas of appropriate styles to use in your own writing. Now you could write a similar comparison of Texts A and D.

Section B: Summary and directed writing

In Section B of the exam paper you will be asked to complete a task that requires you to select and summarise information from one or more of the texts and to re-present it for a new purpose and audience.

Task 1

> You work for a newspaper. The editor has asked you to write a shorter version of Text D for the news analysis page. You have a limit of 150 words for the article, including your headline.

Compare your answer with this model answer and comments below.

SLEEP – THE NEW STATUS SYMBOL – but for whom?

By our business correspondent

A change in attitudes to working hours is being led by company directors, according to a spokesperson from the Institute of Directors.

They are boasting that they are so well organised during their working day that they no longer need to work excessive hours and can afford to sleep for at least eight hours a night. Their companies, in effect, can function without their continual presence.

Although this may be true, other findings suggest that not all workers benefit from their bosses' change in working and sleeping habits. Employees are working long hours to support this new attitude from above. Junior doctors, head teachers and the average British office worker are managing on only four hours' sleep a night – but maybe 'managing' is the wrong word for this enforced sleep deprivation.

We await a response from the unions that represent these employees.

This article is just within the word limit and largely follows the structure and style of Text D. The writer has used a quotation, with alliteration and a question in the headline, to attract attention and suggest controversy. Some of the paragraphs follow the structure of Text D, with a key sentence and then expansion or detail. There is, however, more variety in paragraph style and length.

The content is appropriate for the change of purpose and position in the newspaper. Some words echo the original article, but the organisation and tone are altered. Apart from the headline, there are no quotations, which would lengthen the piece and slow down the reader. The article ends with a challenge to the unions to respond – the writer's own slant on the task.

This is a good response in terms of content, style and accuracy, built on the analytical skills practised in this chapter.

Task 2

Write a letter to your boss, asking him to consider giving you the same working hours as he enjoys. Use ideas from Texts C and D.

Here is one sample answer.

27 Allan Lane
Hounsleigh
Edinburgh
ED3 7JQ
27 December

Dear Sir,

I am unable to attend work today as my car has broken down and there is no public transport as the rest of the country is on holiday.

I was unable to contact you to let you know as you are in the Scilly Isles.

I must admit that I was reluctant to go to the office today anyhow, as I feel bad that you had asked me to work to cover for absent staff who are still relaxing with their families.

I do not think that it will have made much difference, as there would not have been much work to do anyhow.

Yours faithfully,

Chris Brown

Office Junior

Do you think Chris Brown would still have a job in the New Year?
This letter reads as if the writer had not studied any of the texts in this chapter. It is also rather casually expressed, with some repetition of phrases and structures, such as starting every sentence with 'I', and does not really answer the task set. The tone is rather offhand, almost rude.

Look at the next attempt.

31 Crystal Mansions
LONDON
EC1 3LT
30 December

Dear Mr Robinson,

I hope you are enjoying the break with your family. I have been able to relax and catch up on some reading.

I came across some interesting articles on the effects of shortage of sleep on the workforce. Apparently research has discovered that lack of sleep can lead to premature ageing and associated diseases. Young adults function much better when they have had at least eight hours' sleep.

The new trend, followed by many leading industrialists, is to aim at eight hours' sleep a night, with regular and limited working hours. I am sure you will agree with this, as I understand you try to follow this pattern yourself.

I have enclosed copies of the articles for you to study. I think you will find some of the conclusions could be applicable to our firm's working practices.

I'd like to request that you put the topic of working hours for all staff on the agenda for the next resources management meeting, with a proposal to set up a sub-committee to look at the research in more detail – I have addresses of websites. The whole company could benefit from healthier working practices if changes in working patterns for all staff were implemented.

Information is available in a variety of different formats which could also be used on posters throughout the offices if you decide to tackle the problem.

I look forward to receiving your response to my suggestion.

Yours sincerely,

Jan Edmonsen

Staff representative on Management Committee

What sort of response do you think this one will receive?

Not only is it more polite and formal, but it has both personal touches and a strong conclusion which expects a reply. It uses varied sentence openings and constructions, with active and passive moods. It also addresses the task, in that it refers to the topics and varied material of the texts and relates them to the situation outlined, with creative and realistic touches. The writer shows a clear understanding and focuses on appropriate details. This is a much better answer than the first letter, in content, use of ideas and style.

Your turn

Write what you would say to a friend who is worried about sleep and dreams, using information from Texts A and B. Your aim is to reassure your friend about sleep patterns and to suggest they should seek professional advice if the problem persists.

Remember to avoid an over-chatty style, both because the subject matter is quite serious and you need to remember the examiner as your 'other' audience.

Section C: Essay

The tasks you will be asked to tackle in Section C of the exam paper are also thematically linked to the pieces you have read and studied for the other sections. You could be asked to produce any one of a range of types of writing. Here are some questions you might be asked in this section on the theme of sleep and dreams:

- Write a dramatic story about what happens when someone falls asleep on the job.
- My worst nightmare.
- Write a speech to a conference on 'A healthy workforce is a productive workforce.'

Task

Try answering one or more of these questions in timed conditions (that is, in under an hour for planning, writing and checking). Exchange your piece with a fellow student who has also studied this chapter. It will be interesting to compare your ideas and treatment.

Here is an answer to the third question given above.

> *A HEALTHY WORKFORCE IS A PRODUCTIVE WORKFORCE*
> *Good morning, fellow delegates.*
> *We have heard some very interesting contributions from management and unions so far in this conference. They have given their viewpoints on what should be done to increase productivity (and pay) through a greater awareness of risk factors. A shared responsibility for Health and Safety is a legal requirement for each of us.*

My theme, however, is rather different, so I suggest you put away your clipboards and just listen.

Today, we are at a luxurious conference centre, set in lovely grounds, with a pool, a health spa, a golf course and three restaurants. How many of us are familiar with such facilities in our daily lives? Most of my colleagues would smile wryly if I showed them the glossy brochure from reception, not necessarily because they couldn't afford the extravagance occasionally. Why would the idea of using a gym or a pool or playing golf, even enjoying a pleasant meal, amuse them, do you think?

The answer, delegates, is that their lives are too constrained to be able to relax. It is time which dictates the rhythm of their days and weeks: as they race to be at their desks; as they catch the 6.30 train with laptops and briefcases; as they grab a caffeine-laden expresso at Waterloo Station; as they munch a sandwich at their desks for their version of a working lunch; as they guiltily jerk awake on the 5.50 return train (4.50 if they're lucky on Fridays).

Even their weekends, supposedly for families, cutting the grass, relaxation, football or cricket, are affected by the time pressure – the nagging thought of deadlines, the unfinished report, the presentation to be polished, the sale to be clinched.

And where is this leading the ambitious middle manager? Not to a seat on the board or even early retirement to enjoy the fruits of their labours. The likelihood is that most of my colleagues, maybe myself, will fall prey to a stress-induced illness which, even if not fatal, will mean lengthy absences from that desk. This increases pressure on the rest of the workforce, who in turn will fall ill. What happens to productivity then?

What is the solution to this doom-ridden scenario?

The answer is not in medical experts or in the ideas of previous speakers. It is in our own hands, and it is up to all of us to make it happen. We have to change the pace and length of our working lives. Instead of competing to be first at our desks each day and yawning away the last hour of the early evening, to be seen carrying files home, let's have a quiet revolution.

"What is this revolution?" I hear you ask.

Let's change our working practices: instead of stretching the boundaries of work, let's limit them, ring-fence them, maximise their effectiveness. Let's ban work outside core-time, in the office, on the train, at home. Let's reduce the length of the working day, with a compulsory lunch break. Holidays will be obligatory – instead of extra pay for working during holidays, we'd impose a fine on anyone who overworked.

I promise you that research has shown that a workforce which feels valued and is able to relax is both healthier and more productive – the keynotes of this conference. The financial implications I leave to the accountants.

Who fancies a swim before lunch?

Did you recognise some of the rhetorical features which make this read like a speech rather than an essay? Note the direct address, reinforced at several places in the text, and the first and second person pronouns: 'I', 'we', 'us' and 'you'. The opening acknowledges other contributions, although they are discounted later on, and sets a context. The use of 'however' and the suggestion that they just sit back and listen should wake up the delegates and may intrigue them. Direct, if rhetorical, questions should also keep the listeners on their toes.

The concrete examples of the typical working day and the missed opportunities at weekends should also strike home to most of the audience. The change of mood with the reference to 'stress-induced illnesses' would probably remind them of past colleagues and their own doctors' warnings about their lifestyles.

The paragraph on change of working practices includes two lists of three – did you notice them? These give the speaker a chance to build to a crescendo and the audience will be waiting for the third example in each case. There is also a repetition of the structure 'let's', which, as well as hammering home the points, emphasises the shared responsibility. 'Holidays will be obligatory' is much stronger than the more tentative modal verb 'would', and should also make the audience sit up and take notice.

'I promise you' uses a personal approach. The title of the conference is echoed in the conclusion, and the final line is likely to produce a laugh and warm applause.

This answer does not use any of the texts directly, but picks up on the idea of long hours and competition. There could have been more direct references to sleep, but work in Section C, unlike in Sections A and B, does not have to take ideas from the texts; it can develop the theme in a variety of ways. We hope this example has shown you how to use your original ideas and approaches, while writing relevantly. If you enjoy writing, your audience should enjoy reading.

The following chapter gives you further advice on how to select and present ideas from the texts in the exam.

4 Presenting information from your reading

In this chapter you will practise:

- selecting the main facts and related ideas from texts
- understanding supporting detail in texts
- presenting information in your own words

One of the tasks you will be given in the examination is to read some text, for example from a leaflet, a handbill, or a non-fiction book, which gives information to the public. You will be asked to pick out the main ideas and some of the other parts of the argument, organise them and write them out again for a reader who has not seen the original text.

On first consideration, this seems a straightforward thing to do, but there are pitfalls along the way. When you know what they are, and have learned some techniques to help you avoid them, you will find that this part of the examination is something that you can practise and learn to do well.

Identifying the main and related ideas

You often hear people say 'That's a fact' as though it were easy to be sure about it. Most texts, if they contain several paragraphs of even basic information, can be more complex than they seem to be at a quick reading. Let us sort out what such a text would contain.

The main idea

This is what the piece of writing is about. It may be clearly set out, often as a heading. It may emerge gradually from a number of minor points.

Related ideas

Usually, there is a **key idea**, which may be stated in a few words, and a set of **related ideas**. It is like the framework of a building: the main ideas are the main timbers or girders, but there will also be related ideas, like smaller supporting timbers or girders, which form the structure. When presenting information from a text, your task will be to find the main idea and related ideas, decide how they fit together and discard the rest.

Some people find it helpful to draw a simple diagram to show this structure.

MAIN IDEA

Restatement of main idea in conclusion

First related idea ➡ Second related idea ➡ Third related idea

Examiners often find these diagrams in pencil before a candidate's answer. When they see them they know two things: the candidate has slowed down after maybe a quick read through the text, and can make confident judgements about the relevance of what is read. The diagram shows that they have selected some material and usually left out the non-essential details. They may return to these details later, and find that there is room to include some of them – but more of that later.

Look at this leaflet, produced for tourists to London, telling them something about Tower Bridge.

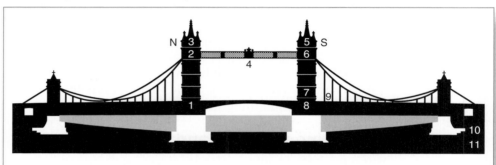

North Tower

① **Ground level**
Ticket office and entrances to lift and stairs.

② **Level 3**
Exhibition STRUCTURAL TRIUMPH explains the structural and hydraulic engineering of Tower Bridge. Video film, design drawings and photographs show how the bridge works.

③ **Level 4**
Information and sales counter where you can buy the colour souvenir brochures, postcards and special postal covers.

Walkways

④
The two glass enclosed walkways afford panoramic views across London. Captioned photographic panels are provided to help you identify the many famous landmarks. Photographers will find special sliding windows are available for them to record unobstructed views. Further exhibitions, public lavatories and the exit are in the South Tower. There is no exit from the North Tower except in an emergency.

South Tower

⑤ **Level 4**
Exhibition THE CITY'S BRIDGES traces the history of the City's bridges from Roman times.

⑥ **Level 3**
Exhibition THE WONDER BRIDGE illustrates, with a large model, photographs and a collection of mementos, how the bridge was built, its opening in 1894 and subsequent historic events.

⑦ **Level 1**
Public lavatories, reached by stairs only.

⑧ **Ground level**
Beside the lift exit one of the original control cabins can be viewed.

Museum

⑨
From the South Tower exit walk along to the steps leading down to the Museum entrance beneath the road arch.

⑩
The Museum contains the original boilers, steam and hydraulic engines and accumulators which powered the bridge prior to electrification. Animated diagrams, a video film, a model and reconstructed mechanisms explain the complete workings of the bridge.

⑪
The Museum shop stocks publications, gifts, postcards and postal covers.

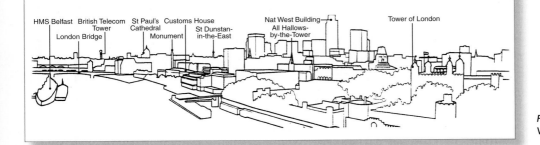

Welcome to Tower Bridge

How to use the lift service:
North Tower
The lift goes directly from ground level to the top of the tower but does not serve intermediate levels. The climb is worth the effort in order to see the restored original interiors. There are seats on the way.

South Tower
This lift is also express from top to ground floor level. The walk down the stairs is easy. There are seats at Level 2 and public lavatories at Level 1.

Wheelchairs
There is easy access to the tops of the towers and the walkways. Help is available from attendant staff. There is a lavatory for the disabled in the Museum.

Some of the buildings to be seen from the high level walkways.

HMS Belfast | British Telecom Tower | St Paul's Cathedral | Customs House | St Dunstan-in-the-East | Nat West Building All Hallows-by-the-Tower | Tower of London
London Bridge | Monument

From a leaflet entitled Welcome to Tower Bridge.

Task 1

> Now put yourself in the shoes of a visitor who has decided to visit the famous bridge and comes across this leaflet the day before. Glance at it quickly for a second or two, to take in the main contents and how they are set out.

You will spot an outline of the bridge, some headings in bold and probably a set of numbers on the outline, which look a bit complicated. This reading activity you now know as skimming. Most of us can decide if a text is helpful to us or not in this very short space of time.

Task 2

> Next, look again, making sure that you have taken in all the small blocks of text, without settling down to find out exactly what is written.

Now you become aware that the information is set out in four columns: about the North Tower, the South Tower, the walkways and the museum. The top two thirds of the page gives information mainly about what you can see at the bridge and in its towers. The lower third of the page tells you about how you can move around when you are there. This reading activity is called **scanning**: it allows the reader to get a general idea of the range of material and how different parts of the information are distributed. In life, most tourists would not do more than this, would they? They would not sit down and study it intensively. Writers of information leaflets have to bear this in mind when they plan a leaflet. There will be opportunities for you to practise writing like this elsewhere (see Chapter 5).

Task 3

Now, write down the main idea and the related ideas.

It should look something like this:

INFORMATION FOR VISITORS TO TOWER BRIDGE
Main idea: the two towers and the top and lower bridge
Related ideas: the different levels
*   services for the public*
*   things on view*

The related points may be put in a different order.

In practice, if you were really visiting the bridge, you would probably look again at the public services information, trying to decide the best point to start from and how to move around.

Task 4

Now, read the bottom third of the leaflet more carefully, so that you can remember and then write down the information.

This type of reading is called **search reading**, that is, you know now where to find this information because of your earlier skimming and scanning; now you want to read it really carefully to retain the information.

Task 5

You would then want to sort out how the different towers and levels were related and what would be worth seeing where. Imagine that as a visitor, you have decided to make a note of this essential information for others coming with you who do not have the leaflet. Write it down in outline.

Here is the set of points you could have made:

Enter at ground level in the North Tower (1) to buy a ticket. Walk up the stairs to see the exhibit 'Structural Triumph' (2). Next, walk across the upper bridge (4) and look out at the sights of London. Then, reach the South Tower but miss out the exhibition 'The City's Bridges' (5). Walk down one flight of stairs to the exhibition 'The Wonder Bridge' (6). Exit at the ground level in the South Tower (8). Walk along to the Museum to look at the boilers and engines there (10). Watch the film, if time allows. Visit the shop briefly to buy postcards (11). Go out through the Museum back to the bridge on the south side of the river.

Task 6

Now, suppose you were a disabled visitor. The essential information would be rather different, wouldn't it? This is the kind of task you will find in the examination. Try writing a second version of the most important points, bearing these different needs in mind.

Here is a possible answer:

Enter at ground level in the North Tower (1) to buy a ticket. Take a lift to the top of the Tower (3) where you will find postcards. Return in the lift to the ground level (1). Cross the bridge to the South Tower. Have a look at one of the old control cabins (8), then take the lift again, this time to the top of the South Tower (5) to see the exhibition 'The City's Bridges'. Return by the lift to the ground level and exit (8).

Task 7

Not only would this be a very different experience but this visitor would find the leaflet puzzling in one or two places. See if you can find the problems in the text.

The problems are as follows:

- Both lifts go straight from bottom to top and down again (see 'directly', 'express'), yet we read 'there is easy access to ... the walkways.' How can this be if the lifts do not stop at the higher level? Maybe there is a ramp, but it does not say so.
- There are steps going down to the Museum but we read 'There is a lavatory for the disabled in the Museum.' How, if a visitor were in a wheelchair, would he or she reach the Museum? The leaflet does not tell us.

These two examples show the pitfalls of designing and writing such a leaflet. Sometimes, something vital is left out. A disabled visitor might be very concerned before setting out because of these omissions. So, to return to an earlier idea: even a one-page information leaflet may make us pause before we say "That's a fact"!

Understanding supporting details

Given that there are four special exhibition areas (including the Museum) at Tower Bridge, and time may be limited, a visitor may have to choose between them.

Task

Look at the leaflet. Imagine you are visiting London and making a quick visit to the bridge. Choose either 'Structural Triumph' (paragraph 2) or 'The Wonder Bridge' (paragraph 6) and note down a list of details that interest you, justifying your choice.

If you are interested in engineering, you may decide to visit 'Structural Triumph' (2) for the following reasons:

- This exhibition explains how the bridge works. It is almost unique in its workings because the top walkway divides so that each half can be raised and lowered.
- It has lots of detail about the structural and hydraulic* engineering of the bridge.
- There are a range of different audio-visual displays (video, design drawings and photographs).

If you are interested in history, you might prefer to visit 'The Wonder Bridge' (6) for the following reasons:

- This exhibition tells us about how the bridge was built and when it opened.
- It also tells us about Tower Bridge over the years (the phrase 'historic events' tells us this).
- There are lots of photographs and mementos (things which remind us of the past).

In terms of the range of information in the leaflet, this information is minor detail, though in reality the exhibitions maybe the high point of your visit. The purpose of the leaflet is to encourage you to look at them but the focus is on the bridge itself and how going to it would affect every visitor.

Did you know the word 'hydraulic'? It is the one word which gives a clue to what happens when the two halves of the top walkway can be raised or lowered.

If you were to visit Tower Bridge, you would find some additional information not printed in the leaflet here. The video shows dramatic footage of vehicles leaping the gap between the two halves of the bridge when they misjudged the situation and set off to cross just as the bridge was opening. (This cannot happen now, as access is closed before the hydraulic power starts operating.) You might also hear a joke about the business tycoon who bought the old London Bridge – a stone structure, a little further along the river – took it down stone by stone and reassembled it near his works overseas. When it was finished he telephoned to complain: "I can't get it to go up and down!"

Presenting information in your own words

When visitors jot down the main points of interest, I wonder if they would copy them straight from the leaflet or put them down partly in the words found there and partly in their own? Information in a leaflet is ink on paper; it is only 'live' when it has been read and registered mentally. In the examination you will be asked to make your reading 'live' by selecting parts of a text and expressing them chiefly in your own words.

This does not mean that you may not use any word in the passage. For example, if you wrote 'See the movement of fluids through pipes as a means of giving power to the levels that raise the top section of Tower Bridge' instead of using the word 'hydraulic', that would be absurdly wordy. The instructions on the paper say that you may use words or phrases which cannot easily be conveyed in other words, so here you would be right to use the word 'hydraulic'.

What should you do, though, if the word or phrase is the key idea of the passage? How can you show that you understand it? I recall an example of a student who wrote an account of something he had read about deforestation, using the word 'desertification', which cropped up very regularly in the passage. As I continued reading I had a moment's doubt about whether he had understood the word or was just copying blindly, because he wrote 'This is an article about man-made desserts', that is, sweets prepared by a chef to be eaten after dinner! It was just a spelling error, of course.

Task

Look at points (10) and (11) in the text on page 88, which gives a short account of the Museum. Try to write this information yourself in a short paragraph using your own words.

Sometimes students copy every word of their answer directly from the text, even when the examination paper asks them to use their own words as far as possible. This is known as **verbatim copying**, and will get no marks for style. That is fair, because the words are the author's and not those of the candidate.

Also, though the selection of the words copied may show broad understanding of what the text is all about, it is usually a very hit-or-miss affair. Avoid verbatim copying unless you are actually asked to quote from the text.

Here is one possible version:

> The Museum exhibits include the first boilers and engines: these were not electric, but driven by steam, probably from coal furnaces. These engines raised and lowered the top walkway on the bridge. There are cartoon-style pictures, a video and a model, built to show the working of the bridge. When you have finished looking, you can buy presents, books and other reading material, postcards and stamped envelopes.

You may find that it takes more words to explain some of the ideas you find than are used in the original text. The writing then becomes 'wordy' or expansive. Sometimes you will find that a question of this kind has a word limit as in 'Write instructions for a visitor to Tower Bridge using not more than 120 words.' You are not expected to count every word! The limit is a guide to help you to keep to the point.

A simple way of being concise is to draw a grid in pencil, with ten spaces across and twelve lines down, and then to write in the grid.

When	you	visit	Tower	Bridge	you	should	first	buy	a
ticket	at	the	ground	level	office	in	the	North	Tower
and	walk	up	the	stairs	to	see	Structural	Triumph,	an
exhibition	which	explains	the	working	of	the	bridge.	Next,	you
may	decide	to	go	along	the	top	walk-	way,	seeing
how	many	London	sights	you	recognise	or	taking	photo-graphs	through
the	window	that	slides	back	to	give	a	clear	view.
After	taking	the	lift	straight	down	to	the	bottom	of
the	South	Tower,	you	will	leave,	passing	one	of	the
early	control	cabins	on	your	way	up	the	steps	which
lead	to	the	Museum.	Look	around	and	watch	the	film
before	buying	postcards	and	making	your	way	out	again.	

This method can be helpful at the very start if you find it really difficult to write briefly. You should think of it only as **first draft** work, though, and write your answer out freely as soon as you can do so.

This seems to meet the need to explain information you have read accurately, in your own words and concisely, but who are you writing for? Your writing is for the examiner, of course. In life, you do not write things as an exercise but usually for a practical purpose. For the new syllabus you are asked to do the same. Your first draft will need to be adapted when you consider who are your likely readers. In this case they are tourists. You will need to bear that in mind. (Chapter 5 deals in more detail with writing for a particular audience.)

Sample exam questions and answers

Try these questions, which are exactly of the kind you will find in the examination, for yourself. Sample answers and examiner's comments are given below each question.

Question 1

> Read the text on page 96, taken from a leaflet on the Tower of London, giving information to help tourists.
>
>   (i) Read the text and list FIVE things that are typical of the Tower that visitors will see. (5 marks)
> (ii) Pick out FIVE adjectival words or phrases which describe the Tower of London in a way that would attract visitors. (5 marks)
> (iii) Suppose that you are writing a textbook for school children. Write a paragraph or two for the book, giving just the historical facts about the Tower of London in about 150 words. (10 marks)

> *(i) The Great Tower or White Tower / boundary walls / moat / ravens / Crown Jewels.*
> (5 marks)

This is an orderly answer. This answer is correct. Alternative points are Wharf / Yeoman warders / their lodgings / Wakefield Tower.

> *(ii) Famous / historical / talked-about / unchanged / frightening.* (5 marks)

This is mostly correct. The one doubtful word is 'frightening', but then some people enjoy being frightened, so that would be accepted. Other possible words and phrases are 'well preserved', 'awe-inspiring', 'important' and 'essential'.

> *(iii) The Tower of London, or the Great White Tower, as it has also been called, was built by William I in the eleventh century in England, after he had killed King Harold II and conquered the country. It is situated on the north bank of the Thames in London. About a hundred years later, two huge walls were built and surrounded by a huge ditch or 'moat' to defend the tower.*

There are ravens nesting there and a prophecy once foretold in the times of Charles II that if they ever left, the English monarchy would fall. There is still a monarchy in England and its Crown Jewels are kept in the Tower, where they were put in the fourteenth century for safe-keeping, when not being used by the Queen. (9 marks)

This is a good answer in two paragraphs and 131 words, well within the limit. It covers all the historical points mentioned and wisely cuts out extra details, such as the dates of the reign of William the Conqueror, and the attitudes of the Anglo-Saxons to their new ruler.

WHAT TO SEE

The Tower of London is by far one of the most famous and well preserved historical buildings in the world. From its earliest structural beginnings by its founder William I of England, better known as William the Conqueror (1066–87), the Great Tower or White Tower as it later came to be called was fast becoming the most talked-about building in England. The White Tower was also the most awe-inspiring and frightening structure to the Anglo-Saxon people, who were trying to get used to the rule of their new Norman king, the destroyer of their own ruler, Harold II, at the Battle of Hastings in 1066. Within three months of his victory William the Conqueror had begun to build a castle on the north bank of the River Thames in London.

The Crown Jewels

The Tower of London has been home to the world famous British Crown Jewels since the beginning of the fourteenth century. Still used by the Queen and her family today, the Crown Jewels are an essential part of your visit. (See also The Wall Walk – the related Crowns and Diamonds exhibition.)

The Ravens

Legend has it that Charles II was told that if the Ravens left the Tower, the monarchy would fall; so he ensured that a limited number would be kept here permanently. The Ravens are cared for by one of the Yeoman Warders, with the title of Ravenmaster. Their lodgings, next to the Wakefield Tower, can be visited.

The development of the Tower

The Tower of London was begun in the reign of William the Conqueror (1066–87) and remained unchanged for over a century. Then, between 1190 and 1285, the White Tower was encircled by two towering curtain walls and a great moat. The only important enlargement of the Tower after that time was the building of the Wharf in the fourteenth century. Today the medieval defences remain relatively unchanged.

From the Tower of London orientation leaflet.

Printed below is a handbill advertising a *Son et Lumière** show at the Red Fort in Old Delhi, India.

  (i) Read the handbill and find four contrasts made in the text. (8 marks)

 (ii) Pick out six words or phrases which convey the noise and action of the *Son et Lumière* show. (6 marks)

(iii) Imagine that you have seen the show and are writing to a friend about your trip to Delhi. Write two paragraphs about your experience of the show, using ideas from the handbill. Do not exceed 150 words. (16 marks)

This is held in the evening and images are projected onto the walls of the Fort, while the audience listens to a recorded commentary about the history of the Red Fort, as well as plenty of sound effects.

Red Fort Spectacular
The story of the historic Red Fort
comes alive in sound and music

The picture show starts on the city side of the towering red sandstone walls where Shah Jahan began construction in 1638. The fort was finished by 1648, with lower walls on the river side, which was easier to defend.

The gardens, which by day are quiet and peaceful, are alive with a riot of colour and noise at night. Amid the crackling fire and exploding fireworks the story is played out.

From the clarion call at the start to the beautiful sound of the musicians playing sitar music, and the beat of the drums at the end of the show, you will find every moment grips.

- Watch amidst the blaze of lights the darkened walls of the Fort.
- Listen to the gallop of horses' hooves as the ambush closes in.
- Hear about the capture and imprisonment of Jahan in Agra Fort.
- See how Aurangzeb was the first and last ruler here.
- Watch the emperor's elephant, magnificently decorated with jewels and gold.

Be part of the thrill!

(i) The walls of the Fort are low on the river and high on the city side.
Building started in 1638 and ended ten years later.
Aurangzeb was the first and last ruler here.
The fort is calm in the daytime and noisy at night. (5 marks)

Overall, this is a passable answer, as indicated by the marks allocated, but there are some problems.

Some of these pairs aren't really good choices. 1638 and 1648 are two different dates but they belong to the same building period, so this part of the answer is wrong.

'First' and 'last' are also contrasts, but here they indicate the start and finish of the same reign. This is not the best choice, but some credit would be given.

The candidate could also have chosen 'darkened walls of the Fort' / 'blaze of lights surrounding them' – this is a more obvious contrast.

(ii) 'musicians playing sitar music'; 'riot of colour and noise'; 'crackling fire'; 'exploding fireworks'; 'gallop of horses' hooves' (5 marks)

All these are good choices, but there is one missing: 'beat of the drums'.

(iii) It was very quiet as the show was about to begin even though there were a couple of hundred people watching. It opened with a lazer beam of light and a call played on an instrument like a trumpet. The emperor appeared, looking very grand, riding on the back of an elephant. Soon everything went mad. Shah Jahan was captured in a noisy battle and taken by his son to be put in prison in Agra fort. I felt really sad for him. There was a lot of fire and it was hard to see what was going on sometimes but you could hear the noise of the horses and the sound of fireworks, shooting up into the sky. At the end a group of musicians with Indian instruments played, while the crowd slowly broke up. I was so interested in it all that I wasn't aware of anything else, but next day I woke up and found I had been bitten by mosquitoes! (11 marks)

The paragraph includes quite a lot of relevant information which is also correct. The reader gets a sense of the atmosphere of the show. Bearing in mind that it is part of a personal letter, space is given to the feelings of the writer, and a personal mishap. The style is relaxed but not too casual. Sensibly, the candidate remembers that as well as writing part of a personal letter, he or she is also writing an examination answer.

One problem here is length. This answer exceeds the word limit but only to a very slight extent, so that would not lose many marks. Two paragraphs were asked for and the candidate has written only one.

Compare your answers with those above and you will get some idea of how well you can manage this type of question now.

Read the extract printed below from a history of Indian art and look again at the Red Fort Spectacular handbill. Imagine that you are a guide, taking visitors around the Red Fort and the palace. In not more than 200 words, your own as far as possible, write your introductory speech. The speech should include material from both extracts and cover the following:

- Some brief welcoming remarks.
- Information about the Mogul emperors associated with these sites.
- Information about the flourishing arts of painting and decoration in Mogul times.

THE GLORY OF THE MOGULS

Once Akbar began his reign, the arts in India blossomed under his enlightened patronage.

The outpouring of artistic production was governed by highly sophisticated standards, and the next emperor, Jahangir, was proud of his expertise in judging the quality of the work. "If there be a picture containing many portraits and each face be the work of a different artist, I can discover which face is the work of each of them", he claimed.

The superb portrait of Jahangir's son, *Shah Jahan as a Prince* isolates the orange-robed figure on a flower-spattered, deep green ground. Festooned with precious stones, he holds a gold turban decoration set with particularly sumptuous emeralds and diamonds. The richness of the jewel-encrusted court is astounding; under Shah Jahan the image of the golden age took hold. The ruler responsible for the Taj Mahal, he favoured the theme of a flowering plant – whether decorating wall-hangings, beakers, tiles or bowls. The outcome evoked a heavenly garden, and an inscription in the palace at Delhi resoundingly declares: "If there be Paradise on the face of the earth, it is this, it is this, it is this."

But the Mogul Eden could not last forever. Shah Jahan's reign ended in appalling butchery, and under his successors the court art gradually lost its vitality.

Here is a sample answer; compare it with the mark scheme given below.

Now we are standing in the famous Red Fort, built by Shah Jahan in 1638 and finished ten years later. Here he was captured and imprisoned by his own son, Aurangzeb, who ruled instead of him. His reign brought to an end the glorious rule of the Moguls and their wonderful tradition of art.

Originally, under the patronage of the first emperor, Akbar, the arts in India blossomed. His successor, Jahangir, boasted that he knew the style of every artist living. His son's portrait 'Shah Jahan as a Prince' is splendid – we will see that later on. It shows the prince on a flower-spattered ground and dressed richly in bejewelled clothes. No wonder this was called the Golden Age of Rajasthan. This prince became the ruler who built the glorious Taj Mahal with its heavenly garden – an earthly Paradise. Now, let us go on to see more of the riches of the palace.

Mark scheme

The mark scheme for such a question would have some marks allocated to content, style and audience (20) and some for expression and accuracy (15).

Content

There would be specific points to make.

1 The Red Fort was built in the mid-seventeenth century.
2 This was during the Mogul Empire.
3 Four rulers are named: Akbar, Jahangir, Shah Jahan and Aurangzeb.
4 Akbar started patronage of the arts.
5 Jahangir was very well informed about the quality of artistic work.
6 Shah Jahan's portrait is a particularly rich example.
7 Shah Jahan built the Taj Mahal.
8 He favoured designs of flowering plants, as in a heavenly garden.
9 The Delhi Palace was designed to be a paradise on earth.
10 Sadly, this paradise and family dynasty ended ferociously.
11 Art at court waned.
12 Jahan was captured in the Red Fort,
13 and imprisoned in the Red Fort,
14 by his son, Aurangzeb.
15 Aurangzeb was the last Mogul ruler.

This candidate would score well for content. Points 1–4, 6–7 and 11–15 have all been made. Point 5 is overstated, and Point 10 is too weakly made to score. Points 8–9 are missing. The content score would be 11 – very good.

Expression and accuracy

To score maximum marks for expression and accuracy, the work should:

- be within the specified word limit;
- be expressed in the candidate's own words;
- be accurately expressed;
- be in the first person;
- show an appropriate sense of audience;
- have an appropriate style for the purpose.

This candidate's work is only 150 words, and is very clearly and accurately expressed. It shows a few signs of copying from the text ('the arts in India blossomed'; 'a flower-spattered ground'). It is written in the first person 'We will see that later ...'. There is a sense of audience ('Now, let us go on ...') and the text is written in a suitable consultative style, relaxed but not too casual. The score here would be 8, making an overall total of 19 (grade B).

Now try the following question. Compare your answers with the mark scheme below.

First, scan the web page below, then read it more carefully to answer the questions that follow.

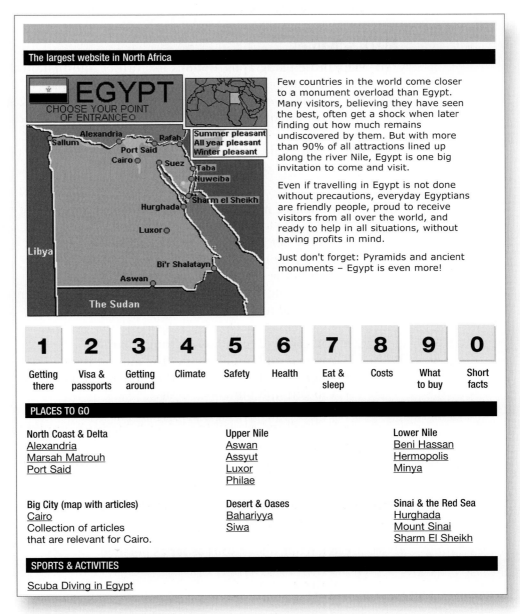

The largest website in North Africa

Summer pleasant
All year pleasant
Winter pleasant

Few countries in the world come closer to a monument overload than Egypt. Many visitors, believing they have seen the best, often get a shock when later finding out how much remains undiscovered by them. But with more than 90% of all attractions lined up along the river Nile, Egypt is one big invitation to come and visit.

Even if travelling in Egypt is not done without precautions, everyday Egyptians are friendly people, proud to receive visitors from all over the world, and ready to help in all situations, without having profits in mind.

Just don't forget: Pyramids and ancient monuments – Egypt is even more!

1	2	3	4	5	6	7	8	9	0
Getting there	Visa & passports	Getting around	Climate	Safety	Health	Eat & sleep	Costs	What to buy	Short facts

PLACES TO GO

North Coast & Delta
Alexandria
Marsah Matrouh
Port Said

Upper Nile
Aswan
Assyut
Luxor
Philae

Lower Nile
Beni Hassan
Hermopolis
Minya

Big City (map with articles)
Cairo
Collection of articles
that are relevant for Cairo.

Desert & Oases
Bahariyya
Siwa

Sinai & the Red Sea
Hurghada
Mount Sinai
Sharm El Sheikh

SPORTS & ACTIVITIES

Scuba Diving in Egypt

From website www.i-cias.com/m.s/egypt

(i) **Name four different ways information is presented on the page. (4 marks)**

(ii) **What are the main attractions Egypt has to offer, as claimed here? (4 marks)**

(ii) **What disadvantages are hinted at? (2 marks)**

(iv) **In not more than 150 words, your own as far as possible, write a paragraph of helpful information for a friend who wants to visit the North Coast, Delta and the Upper Nile.   (15 marks)**

Mark scheme

(i) Map, prose paragraphs, options for further information through choosing a number, summarised key points. (4 marks)

(ii) The pleasant weather / the vast number of archaeological monuments / the proximity of the Nile to 90 per cent of them / friendly people. (4 marks)

(iii) You are advised to take some precautions – health and personal safety, presumably. (2 marks)

Content (score 12 marks from the following points)

- There are lots of monuments to see.
- Ninety per cent of attractions are along the Nile.
- Local people are friendly and welcoming.
- Weather is pleasant at any time of year.
- You should check for passport and visa requirements.
- You need to take safety and health precautions.
- The website has further information to explore.
- You can find out about getting there.
- You can find out about getting around there.
- You can find out about eating and accommodation.
- You can find out about costs.
- You can find out about what to buy.
- You will see Alexandria, Marsah Matrouh and Port Said.
- Cairo is the main city.
- Aswan, Assyut, Luxor and Philae are towns in the Upper Nile.

Expression and accuracy (score 3 marks from the following points)

- Keep within the word limit.
- Use your own words as far as possible.
- Use a friendly, casual tone but avoid slang.
- Write accurately.

This chapter has considered the selecting of main ideas, related ideas and supporting detail. It has shown how to write about these in an orderly way, taking care to convey the ideas as exactly as possible in your own words, and making use of the words in the text when this is necessary.

The next task is to extend these skills in various ways. Firstly, there is a vast range of possible readers and most of these need to be addressed in a style suitable to their tastes. Secondly, there is also a vast range of ways of organising your ideas to make the best impact on the readers. Finally, there are issues of layout and presentation to be considered. When you can do all this you will be fully equipped to write very good answers to this type of question. You will find out what else you need to know in Chapter 5.

5 Writing in different ways for different audiences

In this chapter you will practise:

- writing in both formal and casual styles
- organising your work in a suitable way
- presenting your work appropriately

One of the tasks you will find in the examination is to write for different kinds of reader, usually known as different **audiences**. We do this all the time in life. Suppose you have to take time off from school, college or your workplace to visit a doctor. On the same day you might write a note for your teacher, lecturer or employer explaining your absence, and then send an e-mail to a friend, after the visit, telling them what happened. The different audiences would cause you to write in different styles.

Consider these three examples:

> *20 August*
>
> *Dear Mr Shah,*
>
> *I am sorry that I will be absent from class on Monday. I will be visiting a doctor about my knee problem. You know it has made it hard for me to take part in Games for some time now.*
>
> *The doctor lives some distance from here, so I will be away for the whole day.*
>
> *Here is a copy of my appointment letter for you to see.*
>
> *Best wishes,*
>
> *Abdul Khan*

> Mr K. Shah
> Depot Manager
> 20 August 2002
>
> Dear Mr Shah,
>
> I enclose my medical appointment card for the company records. It is about my visit to a doctor this coming Monday. I hope to get a specialist's advice on the cartilage problem I told you about earlier.
> As you see, the doctor's surgery is in Riyadh so I will need to take the whole day off. When I return to work I will inform you what the prognosis is.
> Yours sincerely,
>
> Abdul Khan

> From: akhan@clas.com.net
> Sent: 20 August 2002
> To: afahal@clas.com.net
> Subject: update
>
> Been to the doc at last. Says it s not too bad. Got a knee support to wear for a bit — v. hot and itchy! C U Friday.
>
> Aby

Although all three texts convey the same message, the first is quite informative in content and semi-formal in expression. It has a clear addressee, the teacher, Mr Shah. It is written fairly carefully, in major sentences (it is to his teacher, after all!) but with everyday expressions: 'knee problem', 'doctor'. A personal touch is the reference to Games, as the teacher and pupil share this reference to school sports lessons. It ends courteously but not stiffly. The writer gives his name in full, which is practical as well as polite. After all, there may well be other Abduls at school! This is called writing in **consultative style** (i.e. correspondence between the writer and someone higher in status but well known to them).

The second is the most informative in content and formal in expression. It not only has the name of the addressee but his position in the firm. This is also written in major sentences, and there is some **subject-specific vocabulary**: 'cartilage', 'specialist', 'surgery'. The signing off is correct, also.

This is called writing in **formal style** (i.e. correspondence between the writer and someone higher in status but not known by them).

The third example has its own form of address and date, but these are appropriate for e-mail. The recipient will know at once who the sender of the message is. Little information is given because the two are soon to meet. Sentences are elliptical (they have words missing) or minor. Vocabulary is simple. There are no polysyllabic words; on the contrary, there are abbreviated words and invented spelling: 'doc', 'C U'. These are characteristic features of e-mail, which is more like speech written down than other forms of writing. This is called **casual style**. Another term in use for this style is Weblish! Here grammar, punctuation and spelling are usually non-standard. It has visual features, **icons** such as :) to mean 'happy' :(to mean 'sad'; X to mean 'fingers crossed'. For speed of communication there are abbreviations which spell out a phrase: CUL8R – 'see you later'; IYSWIM – 'if you see what I mean'; NRN – 'no reply necessary'. These are fun and used in cyberspace, but are not yet acceptable in an examination paper!

Formal, consultative or casual style?

In the examination, the styles of the first two examples illustrated above are those you will most often be asked to use. Occasionally, though, you may need to write casually. The pitfall here is that there is always another audience – the examiner – so bear this in mind.

With a formal or a consultative style, you will be writing in standard English, which is the usual mode when writing examination answers. With a topic that seems to require a casual style, such as writing a letter to a friend, there is the danger that the candidate will not allow sufficiently for the examiner audience factor and will write in a way that is too relaxed, abbreviated and non-standard. Suppose the question were as follows:

Task

> Read the following passage, then imagine that you have been asked to give a talk to a local travel group. Write the text of your talk telling them about the pleasures and pains of the trip.

This seems to be even more problematic. Speech can be even more relaxed than casual writing, surely? How can the candidate write in the appropriate style and satisfy the examiner as audience, also?

In the following exercise, you will have an opportunity to practise writing for all three types of audience.

Read Text A, produced by a group of people who are concerned about the near-extinction of black rhinos in part of Africa. Next, read Text B, produced by a conservation sanctuary, and answer the three questions which follow. Check your answers against the sample answers and commentaries on pages 109–12.

Writing in different ways for different audiences

By the end of this year, black rhinos could be gone from the earth forever.

Dear Friend

The statistics are truly horrific. During the seventies, Kenya lost 90% of its black rhino population; they were brutally slaughtered by illegal poachers. Their numbers plummeted from 20,000 in 1970 to just 350 in 1983.

The rhinos were slaughtered for their precious horns. Sometimes it was because people in the Far East believed the rhino horn had medicinal value. Sometimes it was to use the horns for handles on ornamental daggers. But always, the result was just the same.

Then in 1992, WWF began funding the Kenya Wildlife Service Black Rhino Project, involving an extensive protection and management programme. Twelve sanctuaries throughout the country were established and together they have succeeded in raising the total black rhino population to its current number of 462.

Photos by Kenya Wildlife Services/WWF–UK

Kinyanjui

But while rhino horn can still fetch three times its weight in gold on the black market, these creatures remain a vulnerable target to poachers. We are doing everything we can to prevent this illegal trade and wipe out the demand for rhino horn once and for all.

Florence and Little Naomi

In the meantime, we must continue to provide protection for those magnificent creatures that still survive. But to do so, we desperately need your help.

Lilian and her family, Ejore and Emma

Please help us today by completing the enclosed Adoption Application. It could be our final chance to help save rhinos from disappearing forever.

Yours faithfully

Richard

Richard Barnwell
Head of Africa Programme, WWF–UK

Based on World Wildlife Fund pamphlet.

Let's conserve Wildlife and its Habitat

Conservation breeding

We have a vital role to play in saving endangered species. As the wild populations fall, zoos can ensure back-up populations by breeding these species in captivity. If a natural disaster like fire, drought or disease should wipe out a small wild population overnight, we should be able to save the species from complete extinction. At the same time, we support the conservation of that species in the wild.

With the help of other conservation organisations, it may be possible to re-introduce species, but only if the habitat is still there and the animals can be protected.

Animals such as Arabian oryx, Pere David's deer and some Partula snails would be extinct today were it not for conservation.

A good founder group

The animals in a breeding programme must be fit and healthy and the population as a whole must be as genetically diverse as possible. This means having lots of different genes in the captive population. Genes are passed down from parent to off-spring. If the parents are closely related, the young will inherit very similar genes. Bad genes causing disease or weakness

will crop up more often and this will lead to low survival rates in the young and reduced fertility in adults. This is known as inbreeding. It is therefore very important to retain as much genetic diversity as possible by breeding unrelated animals.

All this is done using studbooks

Computer databases help compile studbooks that record the details of each individual animal on a breeding programme (e.g. date of birth, sex and ancestry). Species co-ordinators manage individual breeding programmes in different regions around the world. It is they who decide which animals should be paired for breeding.

From Your Guide to London Zoo.

Imagine that you are a wildlife protection officer who has found a young rhino, deprived of its mother. Write to the local sanctuary offering the rhino for its conservation programme. Use ideas from both leaflets. Write in your own words, as far as possible. Do not exceed 220 words.

Look at this sample answer and the examiner's comments below.

KENYA WILDLIFE SERVICE
P.O. Box 20110
Nairobi
7 July 2002

Director
Conservation Programme
East African Wildlife Sanctuary
Nairobi

Dear Sir,

I am writing to you on behalf of the Wildlife Service to offer a young rhino for your programme, which we have heard has been very successful in protecting and breeding this species.

The young calf is no more than three months old. She was found by the side of her mother, a magnificent creature that had been cruelly shot by poachers. Her horn had been hacked off, probably for sale as medicine or for ornamental use. Rhino horn, at today's prices, as you know, can fetch three times its own weight in gold on the black market. Though we patrol nightly, poachers still get through.

The calf is fit and healthy, showing no physical weakness or abnormality and would be ideal for your breeding programme. As you may know, we hope to raise the black rhino population to well beyond its current all-time low number of 462. This is a tragic statistic, remembering that only 30 years ago numbers were around 20,000 in this part of Africa.

We will continue to provide protection for these magnificent creatures that still survive in the wild, but we desperately need your support also.

Please let us know, as soon as possible, whether you will accept this young rhino for your programme.

Yours faithfully,

Senior Game Warden

This letter has been well written in several respects:

- It is in suitably formal style.
- It is written in major sentences and standard English.
- Vocabulary is mature and precise.
- It is within the required word length.

Surprisingly, for work at this level of competence, it has some copying directly from the original texts. Sometimes this cannot be easily avoided, for example, to write out 'Kenya Wildlife Service' more expansively as 'Government backed programme to protect wildlife in Kenya' would be clumsy and unnecessary. However, the sentences copied verbatim (exactly as in the original, word for word) could easily have been put in the candidate's own words: 'Rhino horn ... can fetch three times its weight in gold on the black market', could be rewritten as 'Rhino horn can earn a huge cash reward for those selling it illegally'; 'We will continue to provide protection for these magnificent creatures that still survive in the wild, but we desperately need your help,' could be rewritten as 'Our service is committed to protecting the black rhino, and with your help, we can achieve that aim.'

However, this would be thought a very good answer overall.

Question 2

Imagine that you are an assistant game warden. Write a report on your last patrol, when you found the young rhino mentioned in the letter above, to inform your fellow wardens. Take ideas only from Text A. Use your own words as far as possible. Do not exceed a length of 200 words.

Here is one student's attempt at answering this question. The examiner's comments are given below.

Report No CXVII: Division 3
Mt. Kenya Reserve
Kenya Wildlife Service

On 20 August, I was driving early, at about 6 am, through the reserve, looking for Florence and her calf, little Naomi. I'd last seen them a week ago, near the swampy area by the big rocks.

I soon picked up their tracks – two sets of prints: one large, one small, side by side. Looking ahead through binoculars, imagine my shock; I thought I could see a large, humped shape on the ground.

I raced over in my four-wheel drive and saw a dreadful scene. There were many footprints in the dust. Florence was lying dead in a pool of blood, her magnificent horn hacked off brutally. Little Naomi was wandering close by, dazed and frightened.

We are doing all we can to prevent this type of incident, but still the poachers get through. We must act to protect these creatures, if they are to survive, but the money the poachers can expect – three times the weight of a single horn in gold – means the raids will continue.

As the calf is so young, I suggest that we offer her to the Wildlife Sanctuary for their Conservation breeding programme, which will at least help to build up the herd of black rhino from the present four hundred or so.

Signed,

Assistant Game Warden

This report is written in consultative style, appropriately. It is less successful than the first answer in content, but the style is good. Here are some of the stronger and weaker points of the answer:

- Not much information has been taken from the leaflets.
- Too much of the content is imaginative reconstruction of the night's events. There is some place for this, but if it takes up too much room it can mean that important details are left out.
- The style is semi-formal, suitable for an audience who know the writer and the situation he describes well.
- Content and style take account of the examiner. For example, some information is given (such as the need for the wardens to be vigilant against poachers) that his colleagues would be sure to know already, but it is included to fulfil the requirements made by the question to take ideas from the leaflets. Unfortunately, this information has been crammed into the final paragraph, as if the writer has only just remembered that it should be included.
- The answer exceeds the word limit, but not by very much, so that is not too much of a problem.

This is a good answer, overall.

Question 3

Suppose that you are the assistant game warden mentioned in Question 2. You have been invited to take part in a phone-in programme called 'Bush Drum' on Kenya Radio, answering listeners' questions about your work as a game warden with particular responsibility for protecting the black rhino species. Write out the transcript (the questions and answers that the listener would hear), drawing ideas from both leaflets. Do not exceed 280 words.

Presenter: *"Good evening, everyone. This is your presenter, welcoming you all once again to another phone-in on Bush Drum. Today, we are privileged to have Mr Michael Koikai, a senior game warden from Kenya Wildlife Service. The topic today is how to protect and conserve the black rhino. Now, Mike (I may call you Mike?) can you tell us the present situation with the black rhino ... I mean, I've heard that numbers are falling."*

Warden: *"That's right. Only thirty years ago there were about 20,000 rhino in our national parks. Now, numbers have dropped to about 460."*

Presenter:	*"That's terrible! But ... why is this happening, Mike?"*
Warden:	*"Well, it's because of the price that rhino horn can command in the market. It's worth three times its own weight in gold."*
Presenter:	*"Goodness! Now why is that, exactly? Could you tell the listeners?"*
Warden:	*"The horn is used ground up in oriental medicines. Some people even use the horn for dagger handles!"*
Presenter:	*"That's tragic! But what are you wardens doing to stop this?"*
Warden:	*"As a game warden, I patrol the reserve, with my colleagues each day and especially at night, on the look-out for poachers, and also to keep track of rhinos and their young. In the reserve recently we had two young families: Florence and her calf, Naomi, and Lilian with her calf. Sadly, last week while on an early morning patrol, I came across Florence, who had been shot and killed. Her horn had been brutally hacked off – her young calf was wandering bewildered. It was a wretched sight. That kind of thing makes me even more determined to stop the poachers and the illegal trade in rhino horn. We have an ongoing programme of protection and also breeding with several sanctuaries in East Africa."*
Presenter:	*"What will happen to Florence's calf? I'm sure the listeners will want to know."*
Warden:	*"Well, I'm offering her to the nearest sanctuary to raise, and if possible they can breed from suitable pairs to enlarge the herd."*
Presenter:	*"Thank you, Mike. I hope our listeners will give their support to your efforts."*
Warden:	*"Please send donations to help our work and say NO to the sale of illegal horn."*
Presenter:	*"I'm sure listeners will respect what you say. I wish you every success in your efforts – and thank you for joining our programme."*

This is a really lively piece of writing in what seems to be casual speech or **conversational style**. Notice that the writer is also aware of the examiner.

These are the good features of the answer:

- It has thorough coverage of the content of both articles.
- It has the kind of content you would expect to find in such a programme, for example friendly, welcoming remarks by the presenter, who guides the discussions throughout. All this takes up words, though, and the candidate has exceeded the word limit.
- The style is mostly major sentences. There are a few **fragments** - 'Good evening, everyone', 'Thank you, Mike' – and several exclamations– 'That's terrible!', and 'Goodness!'. There are also hesitations and **fillers** (adverbs or short phrases put in to make the talk run smoothly), for example 'Well ...'
- Words are sometimes elided ('that's', 'isn't', 'I'm') as in natural conversational exchanges.

The main weakness of the piece is that it is far too long. On balance, despite its length, this is a near-excellent piece of work.

Writing in different ways for different audiences

Writing dialogue

Many candidates are unsure about handling extended direct speech. Here are the main differences between speech and writing:

- Speech is passing, time-bound; writing is permanent.
- Speech is interactive, involves people present at the time; writing is a solo activity, involving a reader who is not present at the time of writing.
- Speech has a looser structure; writing has a fixed structure.
- Speech has repetitions; writing is edited.
- Speech has hesitations and fillers; writing is fluent.
- Speech has changes in intonation, pitch, volume; writing signals these with punctuation.
- Speech is usually more informal than writing.

When writing dialogue, care needs to be taken to make it convincingly interactive. Although it is looser in structure, speech nevertheless has a sequence of responses known as turn-taking, which those engaged in the conversation usually do automatically. In the example, though, the presenter takes control and prompts the warden from time to time:

Presenter: Goodness! Now why is that exactly? Could you tell the listeners?

Quite a few natural features of speech are included in the model answer above, but it is not advisable to overdo the realism, bearing in mind the ever-present examiner. Leaving out all punctuation, using slang or half-formed expressions that would not be clear to the reader would not be wise.

Organising your writing in a suitable way

In Chapter 4, we looked at how to select information for your answer by finding the main idea, then the related ideas, and finally the **supporting details**. The same technique applies here, but there are some more strategies which will help you to structure your work, giving you the edge, and helping you to write a good answer, rather than just a competent one.

There are several basic ways of organising an answer. These basic plans are known as **paradigms**. Consider the following examples of how to restructure the following randomly organised ideas.

Chess is a game of skill. It was invented by the Chinese fifteen centuries ago. Chess involves two players. It is said to be the world's oldest board game. You do not need creative intelligence to play chess well. It is played by millions world-wide. Chess has an opening game, a middle and an end game.

Dynamic

Who says you have to be a genius to play the oldest game in the world? Once you've mastered the skills of the opening, middle and end games, you can join the millions of people who have enjoyed the game of chess since it was invented fifteen hundred years ago.

This **dynamic** opening has an attention-catching opening statement, which is expanded by filling in details.

Classic

Chess is the world's oldest board game, which was invented by the Chinese, fifteen centuries ago. It is played by millions worldwide as a game of skill that does not need creative intelligence to get good results. It involves two players, and has an opening, a middle and an end game.

This **classic** structure has an opening, a complication/development and a conclusion.

Chronological

Chess, a game of skill but not needing creative intelligence, is the world's oldest board game. It was invented by the Chinese, fifteen centuries ago. Today, it is played by millions: two sit at a board for an opening, a middle and an end game.

A **chronological** structure has a clear time sequence leading to a conclusion.

Causal

You do not necessarily need creative intelligence in order to play chess. After all, it has been played by millions of people since it was invented fifteen centuries ago. Chess is a just a game of skill, involving opening, middle and end games.

This starts with a general statement which is followed by reasons supporting it.

Consequential

When playing chess, two opponents start with an opening game and play on until they reach the end game. Despite the skill required, the game has been played by millions of players since it was invented fifteen centuries ago, proving that you do not necessarily need creative intelligence in order to play well.

Consequential organisation is logically **progressive**, moving from supporting details to a general concluding statement.

Comparative/contrasting

> Chess is a game of skill but not one necessarily requiring creative intelligence. It is the world's oldest board game, invented by the Chinese fifteen centuries ago, but it is still popular with millions today. Two players try to outwit each other in the opening game, then again in the end game.

This picks out similarities and differences.

Task 1

Read the following article about chess and computers. Using only ideas taken from the passage, write a paragraph of about 150 words on the topic 'Does chess have a future?' Use one of the paradigms described above to organise your writing.

Supercomputer checks King Kasparov's success

New York: Deep Blue, an IBM Supercomputer, beat Garry Kasparov, the chess champion, last night in the second game of their rematch to level the series.

The Russian grandmaster resigned after Deep Blue's forty-fifth move with the white pieces after 3 hours and 42 minutes' play. It was the second time in history that a computer program had defeated a reigning champion in a classical chess format. "The computer played a terrific game," Mike Valvo, the international master said. "It squeezed Kasparov into an anaconda-type position."

On Saturday, Mr Kasparov crushed Deep Blue at the Equitable Centre, Manhattan, in the first of six games, which lasted nearly four hours. Last year the chess champion won his first series of matches against the computer.

IBM's new challenger, affectionately called "Deeper Blue" by its creators, is able to calculate 200 million moves a second. Its database includes the opening games played by every chess grandmaster in the past 100 years. Mr Kasparov by contrast calculates a mere three moves a second.

From The Times.

Here is a student's answer. Read it and see if you can match the organisation used here with one of the six types listed above.

Is it endgame for chess?
The great chess champion, Garry Kasparov, who can calculate three moves a second, has been beaten by Deep Blue, IBM's super computer, capable of reckoning two hundred million moves a second, and programmed with the games of every grandmaster of the last hundred years. The game, held in Manhattan, was a struggle over three hours and 42 minutes. This is the second defeat of a reigning great chess champion by a computer. However, as it is only the second of six games, there is hope yet for Garry, who last year won the first series against Deep Blue. After all, it was human intelligence that created the programme, so all may not be lost.

Did you see that this was a dynamic opening? It makes an effective paragraph, doesn't it?

Task 2

> Now write another version, using a different paradigm.

Organising your essays

You can use some of these paradigms in your own essay writing, also. Here is a series of essay openings. Each clearly shows a different method of organisation, and each is good because it catches the attention and interest of the reader and takes him/her to a point from which the essay can develop.

> 1   *It can be described as the new fashion which is taking place everywhere in the USA. It is the latest trend which is called 'lifestyle discrimination'.*
>
> *Employers in America have started to discriminate against people for activities such as smoking, sky diving, motorcycling, mountain climbing, which are undertaken as recreational activities, but they could, in their opinion, endanger employees' health. More often than not, this is a rather controversial issue which they do not agree with, therefore, they will fight to get their freedom back. As a girl who has been discriminated against, I say, "It is not your concern, what I do away from work, on weekends, or on my vacation."*

This is another dynamic opening. We are kept slightly in suspense about the 'new fashion' sweeping through the USA and are then introduced to a phrase for the new concept: 'lifestyle discrimination'. By the end of the first short paragraph we are alarmed. Maybe this could affect us – but whatever is it? The details which follow in the second paragraph begin to clarify the concept. There are some clumsy sentences with too many clauses to make easy reading and there is some ambiguity in the second paragraph: 'a rather controversial issue ... they will fight to get their freedom back' would be better expressed as 'a rather controversial issue which employees do not agree with, and which will cause them to fight for their freedom.' The final personal statement by the writer is a direct challenge, which picks up the dynamism of the opening.

> 2   *One night, not so long ago, I was sitting at my friend's house at four o'clock in the morning. It was after a party, and my mouth tasted like the inside of a marathon runner's shoe. All the guests were gone and my friend had passed out and was slumped in a chair. I was just sitting in the living room with his guitar and a book of music on the table in front of me. I flipped the pages of a B.B. King song, and began to try to play the song. The notes were correct but I did not have the sound of the original at all. I gave up and put the guitar down. I sat for a while and suddenly I got this lonely feeling. Here I was, no one awake. I was tired, hungry, wanting to be at*

> *home and sinking deeper into depression. I picked up the guitar, which at present was assuming a position of quiet aloofness you would expect from a guitar that is not being used, and began to play. Instead of playing the careful notes of the song, I just used it as a channel of feeling and what came out was the Blues.*

The writer starts an essay on the Blues with some attractive detail, a personal anecdote. He invites us to share his experience early one morning after a good party when he discovered for himself the meaning of the Blues. This is a consequential opening. Having caught his reader's attention, he later moves on to give a chronologically organised account of the early development of this kind of music.

> 3 *The ordinary Russian people love strong nicknames. If they present somebody with a nickname, it sticks with him and is his lot for a lifetime. He is carrying it around like luggage. He may go to the army or work in an office, he may go to Moscow or to the other end of the world. He may try cunning manoeuvres to change his nickname, like bribing a civil servant to add some unexpected and invented nobility to his family name. All this does not help; the nickname croaks like a raven in full throat and says clearly and exactly where this bird comes from. A striking name cannot be felled by any axe in this world. And how striking is everything that is growing from the heart of Russia, where there are no other types of people but only the direct, lively and fresh Russian minds, which do not ponder over a name or painfully brood over it but suddenly, and without warning, give it to someone like an eternal passport. It does not need any explanation about the nose or the lips of the person. The whole character is drawn from head to toe with one line when you hear this name.*

The organisation here is causal, the opposite of Example 2 above. It starts with a general statement, and this is the main idea of the piece, that is that strong and apt nicknames are a feature of Russian culture. This claim is then supported by details which lead to other restatements of the main claim, for example: 'it sticks with him and is his lot for a lifetime'; 'the nickname ... says clearly and exactly where this bird comes from'; the name 'cannot be felled by any axe in this world'; it is 'like an eternal passport', so reinforcing the ideas of strength and aptness. The writing has some grammatical errors, for instance he uses the continuous present tense 'he is carrying it', 'that is growing'. The sentences are short and the effect is staccato. Even so, the candidate conveys his ideas confidently and memorably, especially through the images. There are four in quite a short space, all different. This seems rather a lot, but they do seem to bear out the writer's point about the Russian character, that is, they are direct, lively and fresh. The amusing sentence 'the nickname croaks like a raven in full throat and says clearly and exactly where this bird comes from' sounds as if it might be an old Russian saying. Certainly, we want to read on, and find out more about Russian nicknames.

> 4 Let us discuss gun control. Gun control is an effort to stop the rise in violent crimes by strengthening laws on the ownership of firearms. Gun control aims to reduce the criminal use of guns without interfering with the legal use of guns. To state some facts, in the USA more people have been killed in the twentieth century by privately-owned guns than in all the wars the nation has fought. Half of all the families in the USA own guns, either for protection, hunting, target practice, or other legitimate reasons.
>
> There are many forms of gun control. Federal law prohibits the sale of firearms to drug addicts, alcoholics, the mentally ill, and people with criminal records. Federal law also prohibits the sale of guns to people under 21 years of age. At that age you can apply for a permit to purchase a firearm. The individual has to wait for a seven-day period after the purchase of his or her firearm before receiving it, in order to allow the local authorities to run checks on them.
>
> Let us put ourselves in two different situations. First, you want to buy a gun, you go the local sheriff's office and ask for a gun permit. You take it home, fill it in, tell your life story and send it off. Before this, though, you have to wait for your twenty-first birthday. Then you get clearance and pick up your permit at the sheriff's office, which is one and a half hours' drive outside the city. You then go to the gun shop, look around and choose your gun. Now you wait for the seven days before you can become the owner. One week later, you go back, get the gun and take it home.
>
> Now, let's try it another way. You get up one morning and drive out to the Bronx. You go up to some guy hanging out on the street, tell him you want a piece (slang for gun), he gives you a price and a meeting point. You go to the bank, take out the dough, go to the meeting points, pay the guy, he gives you the piece, some ammo (ammunition) and you take it home. How long did that take? Maybe two hours.
>
> So, gun laws which are set up to protect the public by allowing them to bear firearms actually make it more difficult for them to get them. The people who should not have guns, easily get them, outside the law.

This contrastive opening draws the reader in most effectively. Notice how the writer changes style. At first he writes in standard English, rather formally, giving the facts. The first example of buying a gun continues in this style. He writes in major sentences, with subject-specific vocabulary: 'gun', 'sheriff's office', 'permit'. In the second example, the style is casual, 'laid back', just like the people engaged in the criminal action. There is a long string of clauses separated by commas, which gives the impression that (unlike the first example) this is a fast-moving, slick operation. The rhetorical question 'How long did that take?' challenges us, and the answer is the conversational fragment or minor sentence: 'Maybe two hours.' The two contrasted examples lead directly to the devastating contrasts in the conclusion. This **parallelism** (putting similar or contrasted examples directly side by side) makes the candidate's point most strikingly. This is excellent writing.

---

5 In 1991, a year after my mother leapt to her death from the Oresund Bridge in Malmö, south of Sweden, I moved to Spain to begin life anew, with my father. I had just turned six years of age when my mother stopped her car on the highest point of the bridge, and looked, for the last time, at the city she loved so well. She had applied the emergency brake, opened the door of our car, then lifted herself up onto the rail of the bridge with the delicacy and grace that was always Mother's catlike gift.

On the rail, all eye-witnesses agreed that it had looked as if mother hesitated and looked out toward the sea and shipping lanes that cut past Fort Sunder, trying to compose herself for the last act of her life. Her beauty had always been such a disquieting thing about her, and as the wind from the sea caught her black hair, no one could understand why anyone so lovely would want to take her own life. It seemed that she just wanted to set the flags of all her tomorrows at half-mast …

… The flight to Spain along with my father was our attempt to place the memory of mother and Malmö permanently in the past. For my father, Malmö was baggage he could not shed, no matter how many borders he crossed; as for myself, I was still a child and my father wanted to create a new life for me. My father is the strongest man I know and the girl I am today is thanks to him. Without him I would be nothing, Mother and Malmö are just faint memories – I shall never look back.

Here we have an example of classic organisation, with a dynamic opening, also. Interestingly, there is a paradox in the opening of this powerful piece of writing: her mother's tragic death marks the beginning of a new life for her, one with her father alone. The shock opening is stark and the matter-of-fact account (almost like an official report) is punctuated by just a few haunting phrases: 'Her beauty had always been such a disquieting thing'; 'the wind from the sea caught her black hair'; 'why anyone so lovely would want to take her own life'; and the wonderful image 'she just wanted to set the flags of all her tomorrows at half-mast.' These bring out the real depth of the writer's feeling. She then reverts to her matter-of-fact style for the account of her growing up in Spain (omitted here). The piece ends starkly again, and I don't think we quite believe the final line, because the opening is so deeply felt.

6 *Free – ability to go anywhere. Spirit – the will of a person to go anywhere. My free spirit is my will to go anywhere and do anything I choose.*

Is anyone ever really free? I mean, we have to eat, you and I. We have to clothe and shelter ourselves, and to do that we need money. To get money we have to do whatever we are capable of, market our capability and pray we profit. That, to me, is not 'something with the ability or will to go anywhere' but that is something we all are and must be in this world. Therefore, with reality in mind, how can anyone become a free spirit? How can we find a way, with such limitations, to go anywhere, be anything, find our 'spirit'? I will tell you my theory, but be on your guard – my mother says I'm an idealist!

This is a consequential opening. The writer starts with a definition. This is often a good way of making your thinking clear to the reader, especially if you hammer out your own definition, instead of just copying one from a dictionary. Then she poses a question: 'Is anyone ever really free?' In answer, she moves step by step through a series of logical points, reaching a conclusion: 'Therefore ...'. This is followed by another question for the reader: 'How can we find a way, with such limitations, to go anywhere, be anything, find our "spirit"?' By the time she reaches the final sentence of the paragraph, the reader can't wait to find out her theory. How about you?

Your turn

Write one paragraph opening for an essay, trying out three of the paradigms. Here are some suggested topics:
- Betrayal
- An occasion when I performed in public
- How far do you share your parents' ambitions for you?
- The fashion industry
- Describe your favourite magazine and say why it appeals to you
- The genius

Presenting your work

You may be asked to present your work in a variety of different forms. The most usual forms requested in examination questions are:
- a personal, consultative or formal letter
- a report
- a dialogue
- a leaflet
- a newspaper article.

Letters

The layout, opening, conclusion and general style of a letter should differ, depending on the degree of informality or formality involved.

Here are the three main types of letter you need to know about.

Personal letter

Look at this letter to a friend.

80 Pond Street
Wednesday evening

Dear Nicky,

Just to let you know that I'm going to try for a place in the new athletics club – you know, the one opening in the centre of town. They only want the best, but I have high hopes.

I'll see you soon and tell you all about it.

Best wishes,

Laurie

Consultative letter

This is a letter to someone you know of, but don't know personally.

80 Pond Street
London W1A 8CD
15 May 2002

Head of Sports
Ormond High School
London W1A 8DD

Dear Mr Cox,

I expect you remember me from two years ago in school. I had a good record in athletics and I've kept up my interest, training regularly. It is hard to do that on your own, though.

I recently saw that there was a place available in the new Ajax Athletics Club and I want to join.

Would you be kind enough to give me a reference, to support my application?

Yours sincerely,

Lauren Black

Formal letter

This is the style to use when you are writing to someone you do not know or who has higher status.

80 Pond Street
London W1A 8CD
20 May 2002

The Manager
Ajax Athletics Club
London W1H 7BQ

Dear Sir,

I am writing in response to a notice in the local paper, which says that the Club is looking for new talent.

I left school two years ago and was a very good sprinter and hurdler. I enclose a reference from my sports coach there, Mr William Cox.

I am in good shape as I train regularly. I would benefit from the programme and facilities that your club can offer.

Please let me have further details. I hope to hear from you soon.
Yours faithfully,

L.R. Black

If a word limit is set when you are asked to write a letter, remember that the address, salutation and signing off aren't included in the limit.

Your turn

Imagine you are producing a play at school or college. Write inviting people to attend, giving details of the play, the date of the event, the cost of tickets and where it is to be held. Write two letters in different styles: one to other students; the other to important guests.

Reports

A report conveys essential information in a clearly planned format.

For the attention of: Police Sergeant X
Date: 2:3:02
From: Constable Y
With reference to: Collision at the crossroads on Wednesday 2.3.2002, twelve noon.

Police were called to the scene of a traffic accident at the junction between the High Street and Peace Avenue.

Two vehicles, a Toyota four-wheel drive, reg. TUY 4882 and a Land Rover, reg. PAN 2779 had collided at the junction.

The Toyota skidded on a patch of oil on the road, as it turned out from Hope Avenue, and an eyewitness, Mr Jeffrey Dabo, saw the driver lose control, hitting the side of the other vehicle. There was glass all over the road.

An ambulance was called to take the driver of the Toyota to hospital. Details of insurance were taken from both drivers. Two eyewitnesses gave accounts, leaving their names and phone numbers.

Your turn

Write a short report on one of the following:
- a local carnival;
- a sports match played away;
- the unveiling of a monument to a famous person;
- an instance of petty crime where you are the victim;
- a work experience programme you took part in;
- a school open day.

Dialogues

One advantage of dialogue is that it is easy to punctuate. The conventions for setting it out are as follows:
- Brief introductory information about the scene is given in italics or underlined.
- Each speaker is named alternately on the far left, next to the margin.
- A colon follows the speaker's name.
- Brief indications of how the speakers behave are placed in brackets after the name and before the colon.
- Each **speech act** (the remarks of one speaker) is enclosed in double inverted commas and starts on a new line.

Two men stop at the roadside to watch soldiers marching by.

Algar: "Where are these men marching?"

Lukas (*hesitantly*):   "I'm not sure..."

Algar: "The columns seem to go on and on."

Lukas: "Yes, and the men's faces show signs of strain. I think they are going to fight."

Algar (*anxiously*):   "Who could have sent them?"

Lukas: "Why, the commander, of course."

Your turn

Write a short dialogue (about 20 lines maximum) between any of the following pairs of speakers:
- an employer sacking an employee;
- a parent arguing with a teenage child;
- a quarrel between a boy and a girl about jealousy;
- a teacher and a student who hasn't done any homework;
- a grandparent and a grandchild;
- a presenter and a caller on a radio phone-in programme.

Leaflets

A leaflet has the following characteristics.
- It needs to be more or less 'seen at a glance'; that is, a reader could skim the page in a few seconds and get the main idea, plus essential supporting details.
- It is usually on one sheet of paper.
- It has a bold, centred heading.
- Essential information (such as data, statistics, dates, phone numbers, addresses) is also in bold.
- Paragraphs are clearly set out with plenty of space between them for easy reading.
- The size of the lettering may vary or it may be more spaced out than is normal, again for quick and easy reading.
- The main idea is usually in the opening paragraphs.
- Information that needs to be remembered or acted upon is usually put in bold print at the end.

Look at the example opposite.

Massive killing by Millham

80,000 animals die in vain every year at the Millham Research Laboratory. The notion that results from animal tests can be directly applied to humans has been proved false, time and time again.

by Andrea Leon

- Aspirin causes birth defects in cats but not in humans.
- Penicillin is toxic to guinea pigs and hamsters.
- Morphine sedates people but excites cats.
- Benzene causes cancer in rats but not in humans.

There are many alternatives to animal experimentation, either for cosmetics or drugs. Some of these methods, such as population and clinical studies, have been used successfully for years and some methods have been developed recently with advances in scanning and computer technology.

A great deal of research can be conducted in test tubes using human tissue cultures, which have proved to be an extremely effective means of developing drugs and producing vaccines.

Unfortunately, research to develop non-animal testing methods is seriously underfunded. To try and solve this problem, a group called BUAV (The British Union for the Abolition of Vivisection) is calling for a Government-funded strategy to promote the use and development of humane research methods.

Animal testing causes needless pain and suffering to thousands of animals each day. It is of little or no value and can, in fact, produce dangerously misleading results. Relying on animal testing drains time and resources away from the use and development of more valuable research methods. Human and superior research alternatives do exist. **For more information call BUAV 0207 700 4888**.

Your turn

Write a leaflet on one of the following:

- a new restaurant opening in your area;
- a local pressure group opposing the building of a reservoir;
- saving endangered species;
- a local auction or sale of goods;
- a local election;
- the opening of a new community centre.

Newspaper articles

Newspapers are either **broadsheets** or **tabloids**. Broadsheets usually have fewer pictures, fewer headlines and more printed text than tabloids.

All newspaper articles are concerned with conveying information immediately, often selectively or dramatically and in a way that will catch and keep the reader's attention.

Layout and presentation

- The headline is large, centred and dominant. It draws the reader's attention.
- The **strap line** is the first thing readers see at the very top of the article. This is a cue to the text.
- The sub-headings break up the text so that readers can take in the information gradually.
- Varied fonts and print sizes are meant to sustain interest. The opening is often in larger print than the rest.
- The text is arranged in columns with space between each for easy reading.

Organisation

- The main event is described first, often in a summary statement.
- Other content can be a mixture of fact and opinion, background information and continuity (if an ongoing event is being reported).
- Organisation is more complex than a straightforward chronological report.

A good method of organisation is as follows.

WHAT THIS ARTICLE IS ABOUT

- **abstract:** a summary of what happened – the main idea of the article

WHERE, WHO, WHEN?

- **orientation:** setting the scene and giving the reader important information

THEN WHAT HAPPENED?

- **complication:** this is the development of the article

WHY WE NEED TO KNOW ABOUT THIS

- **evaluation:** this gives the reporter's or commentator's view of the matter

WHAT HAPPENED FINALLY

- **resolution:** this concludes the article

RETURN TO THE PRESENT

- **coda:** sometimes there is a final comment, reminding readers that life goes on

1000 FREE
FLIGHTS TO
WIN P. 16

The News

MONA LISA IS
A FORGERY P. 5

★★★ October 30th 2003 ★★★

30 pence

French farmers dispute EC ruling

PARIS BURNS AS FARMERS RUN RIOT

The city of Paris was ablaze last night due to a night of violence and rioting by 2000 farmers protesting against the EC decision to suspend all French farm exports.

The largely peaceful march exploded into violence at around 9pm when the farmers arrived outside the French Ministry of Agriculture to protest at the decision by the French government not to challenge the EC ruling which banned the exportation of all French farm produce in an attempt to increase home consumption of all crops.

Police fought for two hours

by Jason Hazell

to contain the crowd outside the ministry, but the violent mob overpowered the small force of law protectors.

The chief of police Henri Taussaud said: "We were expecting a quiet march so police presence was kept to a minimum, but these animals have proved they are prepared to go to any length to make there point."

The farmers ran riot through the centre of Paris, smashing and looting stores and setting fires at every opportunity. Cars were rolled onto their roofs and set alight by the rampaging crowds. Firefighters drafted in to douse the flames, were

attacked and there efforts to bring the blazes under control were abandoned shortly after midnight.

Jacques Piccard of the Farmers' Union said: "Last night events were regrettable but it shows that we will not sit down at let these politicians ride roughshod over us."

Extra police were put onto the streets and by dawn the crowds had been dispursed and peace once again reigned over the city. As the clean-up operation began a government spokesman said: "Those responsible for the abhorrant violence will be severly punished and any attempt of a repeat performance by these thugs will be crushed."

City News p. 23 • Today's T.V. p. 34 • Last Night's Soccer p. 45

This is an attractively set out article. It has a number of errors, though. Can you find five spelling errors and three errors of phrasing? (They are: 'there point' (their point); 'there efforts' (their efforts); 'dispursed' (dispersed); 'abhorrant' (abhorrent); 'severly' (severely). Errors of phrasing are 'setting fires' (setting fire to); 'down at let' (down and let); 'attempt of' (attempt at). Did you get them all right?

Before attempting the exam questions on pages 130–3, read the following article and write a leaflet to hand out to tourists visiting Egypt's Valley of the Kings. Your leaflet should set out essential information clearly and directly in not more than 220 words, your own as far as possible. Compare your response with the sample answer and commentary provided on pages 129–30.

Before attempting the exam questions on pages 130–3

Text A

SHAME
OF THE
PHARAOHS

Pawing mobs and filthy air and water are fast destroying the irreplaceable wonders of Egypt

The Pharaoh's curse is not what it used to be. In the old stories, archeologists who penetrated Egypt's inner sanctums died of strange wasting diseases. Now the tombs are in trouble. The polluted air of Cairo bathes the pyramids at Giza in nitric and sulphuric acid. Sewage and detergents percolate up through the desert floor, poisoning the Sphinx. Within the Egyptian Museum of Cairo, itself a period piece, the antiquities shed gold leaf and wood chips in a priceless scurf. In the Nile Delta, thousands of monuments moulder in neglect. Upstream, sewage leaves filthy rings on the Temple of Luxor. In the Valley of the Queens, a salty pox has disfigured the tomb of Queen Nefertari. And in the Valley of the Kings, a brown fungus is eating away at the walls of King Tutankhamen's tomb.

The past 70 years of excavation and development have worked more damage on the wonders of ancient Egypt than the 4,000 years that came before. The country's population, 1.6 million at the time of the Old Kingdom (2573–2134 BC), had

TOURISM

A constant procession of sightseers inevitably leaves its mark on the tombs, temples and treasures of the past. Even tour guides absently nick away at the walls with the sticks they use as pointers.

swollen to more than 50 million. New villages cling to ancient temple grounds and rivers of sewage suck at columns as old as time. With roaring vibrations and a belch of grey exhaust, planes, buses and river steamers disgorge their mobs of tourists to gawk and paw at an entire country turned theme park. Touch the blue or red on an old wall painting in Luxor and 3,000 years of loveliness may come off on your hand. They're still talking about the athletic German caught doing handstands against the temple of Amenhotep II and III.

Egypt has perhaps one third of all the world's ancient monuments. "This heritage is vanishing before our eyes", says Prof. Peter Dorman of the University of Chicago. The old wreckers were armies intent on pillage and grave robbers out for gold and jewels. The new are bureaucrats lusting after tourists' dollars, marks and yen.

From Newsweek.

Writing in different ways for different audiences

Here is the sample answer. The examiner's comments are given on the next page.

THIS HERITAGE IS VANISHING

We have to face it: tombs and temples with their precious hieroglyphics, ranks of sculpture, and wall paintings are now decaying faster than archaeologists can study them.

Egypt has perhaps one third of all the world's ancient monuments, but the Pharaoh's curse is not what it used to be. In the old stories archaeologists who penetrated Egypt's inner sanctums died of strange wasting diseases.

NOW THE TOMBS ARE IN TROUBLE

- Within the Egyptian Museum of Cairo, itself a period piece, the antiquities shed gold leaf and wood chips in a priceless scurf.
- In the Nile Delta, thousands of monuments moulder in neglect.
- Upstream, sewage leaves filthy rings on the Temple of Luxor.
- In the Valley of the Queens, a salty pox has disfigured the tomb of Queen Nefertari.
- In the Valley of the Kings, a brown fungus is eating away at the walls of King Tutankhamen's tomb.
- Touch the blue or red on an old wall painting in Luxor and 3,000 years of loveliness may come off on your hand.
- A tourist was caught doing handstands against the temple of Amenhotep II and III.

Roaring vibrations and a belch of grey exhaust fumes from planes, buses and river steamers disgorge their mobs of tourists to view and touch an entire country turned theme park.

Please take care when walking around these monuments and respect the historical value.

This has very good presentation aspects. It can be 'seen at a glance' and is boldly set out, with large type in varying sizes and plenty of space between headlines and paragraphs.

The opening paragraphs give the essential problems. Then, supporting detail is listed with bullet points for rapid and easy reading. The last piece of advice is italicised so that, as the final thing the tourist will read, it will stay in the mind.

The text has some weak and some good aspects. The weak aspect is the amount of direct copying from the original text that this candidate has done: 'The Pharaoh's curse is not what it used to be'; 'the tombs are in trouble'; 'roaring vibrations and a belch of grey exhaust'; 'buses and steamers disgorge their mobs of tourists.' These are all striking phrases and they have been well arranged throughout the leaflet, but they are not the candidate's own words. The good aspect, apart from the presentation and organisation, is the quality of writing in the bullet points, where the detail of what may have been going on to damage the tombs is vivid. However, because of the copying, this would only get a low grade.

Sample exam questions and answers

Questions 1 and 2 are similar to those you would find in Sections A and B of the exam paper. Section A gives you 30% of your total mark; Section B gives you 35%.

Question 1

Glance at the pages of a brochure on pages 131–3. It was produced by a tourist company to persuade people to visit Egypt. Now read it carefully. Answer the following questions.

 (i) **Give six reasons stated for taking a Nile cruise. (6 marks)**
(ii) **Pick out four words or phrases which describe Egypt in a way that would attract visitors. (4 marks)**

Now read Text A on page 128 and answer the following question.

(iii) **Imagine you are an official employed to protect Egypt's monuments. In one paragraph of not more than fifteen lines, write a short report which explains what damage has been done so far. (15 marks)**

Now consider both texts together.

(iv) **Compare these two leaflets, giving five reasons why you think one to be more successful than the other. (You may consider design, layout, argument, ease of reading.) (5 marks)**

Writing in different ways for different audiences

River Nile

Egypt has so often been described as the gift of the Nile and a cruise along the river is for many the experience of a lifetime. Few places in the world can compete with the magical atmosphere and grandeur of this spectacular waterway, dotted with ancient temples and sites which have stood for thousands of years.

The sense of permanence and duration makes Egypt the land of the past – names of her pharaohs, ancient kings and temples echoing throughout time. Her modern-day people are warm, friendly, generous, intelligent and fiercely proud of everything this wonderful country has to offer.

Cairo, Egypt's capital, is an exploding metropolis which somehow preserves within it one of the finest medieval cities in the world. It is, however, the Museum of Antiquities, and the Pyramids at Giza with the enigmatic Sphinx which hold visitors spellbound. Luxor was known in pharaonic times as 'the city of a thousand gates' and was the site of Egypt's capital during its most glorious period in history. Vast fortunes were expended on building temples such as Karnak and Luxor.

Across the river is the starkly desolate Valley of the Kings, burial ground for many of the New Kingdom pharaohs.

FLYING TIME
Luxor, 5½ hours
LANGUAGE
Arabic, English and French
CURRENCY
Egyptian Pound
LOCAL TIME
GMT +2hrs
VISA
Required
HEALTH
Recommended: Polio, Typhoid, Hepatitis A
TOURIST OFFICE

From Goldenjoy Holidays brochure.

THE NILE AND UPPER EGYPT

Thebes

The entire west bank opposite Luxor is a giant necropolis, riddled with tombs and mortuary temples. Not only kings were buried here – princes, queens and nobles found a resting place for all eternity. Difficult to see everything on offer in one visit, we recommend visiting the highlights – Valley of the Kings, temple of Queen Hatchepsut and perhaps either the tombs of the Nobles or the Valley of the Queens on a first visit, returning to savour the other sites at a later date.

Edfu temple

Dedicated to the falcon headed Horus – son of Isis and Osiris – the inner walls tell the story of Horus's epic battle and ultimate triumph over the evil Seth. The temple is in an excellent state of preservation and much of the roof is still intact, casting deep pools of shadow over the dark and mysterious interior. The great hall of columns was built by Ptolemy VII, known as 'Fatty' to his friends.

Karnak Temple

One of the greatest – and largest – temples in the world, the 250 acre site of Karnak is, quite simply, astonishing. Dedicated to the supreme god Amun, the site and its priests were all-powerful during the New Kingdom era, one of the richest and most lavish periods of pharaonic history. No expense was spared in decorating the various chapels and halls – lapis lazuli from Afghanistan, cedar wood from Lebanon, gold from Nubia. Neglected and abandoned at the end of the New Kingdom, enough remains to strike awe into any visitor.

Feluccas

These traditional river boats can be seen depicted on the walls of many temples and tombs – the hull may now be made of steel instead of wood, but the design has remained the same and they are still in use upon the river today.

NB: Not all sites shown are visited during a Nile cruise – please see individual itineraries for further details.

Writing in different ways for different audiences

Hieroglyphs

This mysterious form of writing, dating from about 3200 BC, is found on virtually every temple in Egypt and Nubia. Unreadable until Champollion made the first translations in the 1820s, the temple walls finally yielded their secrets and we began to understand the history of the pharaohs who ruled ancient Egypt.

Lake Nasser

One of the largest man-made lakes in the world, Lake Nasser and the Aswan High Dam are essential to controlling the Nile floods and hence the prosperity of Egypt. Almost a kilometre thick at its base, the dam took eleven years to build and Lake Nasser stretches for over 500km, deep into Sudan.

Abu Simbel

Regarded as one of the finest temples in Egypt, this bold temple was intended by Ramses II to confront invaders sailing up the Nile to Egypt. Twice a year, on the birth and coronation dates of Ramses, the rays of the rising sun pierce into the inner depths and illuminate a statue of Ramses.

The river Nile

Herodotus described Egypt as being 'the gift of the Nile' and without it, the country would be desert. The pharaohs were well aware of the importance of the annual floods and many inscriptions describe the dire events which resulted if they failed to appear.

Temple of Isis, Philae

This romantic island temple is dedicated to the goddess Isis – during Roman times, worshippers travelled from the furthest corners of the Empire to make offerings at the temple.

NB: Not all sites shown are visited during a Nile cruise – please see individual itineraries for further details.

Imagine you are a tourist guide taking visitors around some of the ancient sites in Egypt. In not more than 220 words, your own as far as possible, write your speech of welcome and advice to the group. Using material from Text B choose one of the sites mentioned: Thebes, Edfu or Abu Simbel. Look again also at Text A. (35 marks)

Your speech should include:

• some introductory information about the chosen site;
• some information about the local transport used to get there;
• advice about how to behave so that the place is not damaged during your visit.

Question 3 is an essay question, such as you would find in Section C in the exam paper. This offers 35% of the total mark.

Write EITHER
a leaflet inviting tourists to come to visit a famous historic place in your country,
OR
an essay contrasting the benefits brought by tourism with the disadvantages involved,
OR
a story entitled 'The Pharaoh's Curse'.
(35 marks)

Though these questions are generally related in theme to the text, you should not take any material directly from them.

Mark scheme

This mark scheme is very similar to the one the examiner would use to assess your work. You may find it helpful to measure your work against how the examiner would assess it.

Section A (30 marks)

1(i) The six reasons are:
- A cruise is the experience of a lifetime.
- Egypt's waterway is outstanding in atmosphere and grandeur.
- There are thousands of ancient monuments.
- Egypt is the land of the past.
- Cairo has a great deal to offer the tourist.
- The Valley of the Kings is across the river.

(6 marks)

(ii) Four words or phrases from the following:

gift/ experience of a lifetime/ magical atmosphere / grandeur/ spectacular waterway/ land of the past/ wonderful country/ glorious period in history.

(4 marks)

(iii)

Content

The following ten marks may be scored for content:
- Rapid decay before we know all they can teach us.
- The tombs seem to be cursed/fated.
- The monuments decay through neglect.
- Gold leaf and wood chips fall off the exhibits in Cairo Museum.
- Sewage marks the Temple of Luxor.
- Queen Nefartari's tomb has been badly marked by salt deposits.
- King Tutankhamen's tomb has fungus decaying the walls.
- Old wall paintings are damaged by hand contact.
- Tourists' thoughtless actions damage monuments.
- Transport with its fumes and vibrations causes deterioration.

(10 marks)

Expression and accuracy

The following marks may be scored for expression and accuracy (+ 2 marks for form and style):

3 marks for consistently good expression;
2 marks for fluent expression with some errors;
1 mark for disjointed and inaccurate expression;
0 marks for verbatim copying or incoherent expression.

(5 marks)

(iv) The five reasons should be plausible and relate to:
- Design/layout: the use of photographs, maps, graphics.
- Argument/readability: personal and emotive appeals, persuasive words and phrases, rhetorical style.

Any plausible reasons will be accepted.
(5 marks)

Section B (35 marks)

Content
2 20 marks are allocated to content, style and audience.
Information about the site:
THEBES
- This is on the west bank.
- Opposite Luxor.
- Many tombs and temples of the dead.
- Kings and other nobles are buried here.
  Highlights: • Valley of the Kings;
  - Temple of Queen Hatchepsut;
  - Tomb of the Nobles;
  - Valley of the Queens.

EDFU
- This is dedicated to the falcon-headed Horus.
- Horus was the son of Isis and Osiris.
- The story of the battle and defeat over Seth.
- is told on inner walls of temple.
- The temple is well preserved.
- The roof is still intact.
- The great hall of columns may be seen.
- This was built by Ptolemy VII.

ABU SIMBEL
- This is one of the best temples in Egypt.
- It was built by Ramses II
- and is boldly designed
- to confront invaders sailing up the Nile.
- Twice a year the rays of the sun pierce its depths
- and illuminate a statue of Ramses
- on the dates of his birth
- and on that of his coronation.
  (8 marks from the points above)

Writing in different ways for different audiences

Information about the local transport:
- This is by felucca
- which are traditional river boats.
- They were often drawn on walls of the tombs
- and also on temples.
- The hull is now made of steel
- but once was made of wood.
- However, the design has remained unchanged
- and they are still used as river craft. (8 marks)

Advice on how to behave:
- Don't touch the walls of monuments as you may damage wall paintings.
- Take care not to handle or push roughly into monuments.
- Don't park too near to monuments as this will cause vibrations.
- Don't belch exhaust fumes near them. (4 marks)

Expression and accuracy
15 marks are allocated to expression and accuracy.

Assessment
The mark for content is decided without reference to expression and accuracy. The mark for expression and accuracy is not affected by the mark for content, but reflects the quality (or lack of it) of such aspects as:
- sentence structure;
- range of vocabulary;
- control of grammar;
- spelling;
- punctuation.

Count each answer to ensure that the word limit is right. Cross through extra words. At the foot of each answer indicate the marks for content (C) and expression and accuracy (E/A) as follows:

$$\frac{C}{10} + \frac{E/A}{8} = 18$$

This section has shown that a variety of different styles and techniques are called for when answering exam questions. The following chapter will give you more practice at handling different kinds of essay titles and response, and will look at some techniques you could use to improve your range of styles.

6 Writing creatively in a range of styles

In this chapter you will practise:

- describing places
- describing people
- writing narrative
- writing personally
- writing discursively

Choosing which essay title to write on needs careful thought. Examiners sometimes see candidates' scripts with openings for three different essays, occasionally even several paragraphs crossed out and a new topic started. Apart from being a waste of valuable time, it must be very disheartening to run out of ideas and have to start again from scratch.

This can be avoided in two ways in the examination. Spend a few minutes jotting down ideas for one or more topics – it should then become clearer which one to choose. Organise your points into a rough plan, but do not spend too long on this, as your ideas may develop as you write. The second idea is to experiment in advance with different kinds of writing, to discover which you enjoy and are best at.

In this chapter we'll look at different kinds of essay title and response, with techniques you could use to improve your range of styles. After examining extracts from published work, you can read some examples of other students' responses to a selection of titles, with examiners' comments and some contrasting versions on the same themes.

Writing descriptively

Your purpose in a piece of descriptive writing is to make it come alive for the reader, to make it credible, by painting a picture with words. The best descriptions are usually based on your own experience, at least as a starting point. If you come across a title such as 'Describe a place that has had a great impact on you', how do you choose what to describe? This will be connected with what makes it special to you. If you can convey the individual nature of your choice, the reader will be able to picture it, will want to know more and will enjoy reading your essay.

Describing places

A place doesn't have to be picturesque or pretty to be interesting, and your writing doesn't have to be a purely visual account. A vivid description may use other senses, such as smell or sound, to convey a sense of place. What is absent can also be very important. Read the following extract, which uses sound, texture, movement and simple colour names to create a dramatic picture.

> There are few more barren places on earth than the plains surrounding a volcano in the aftermath of its eruption. Black tides of lava lie spilt over its flanks like slag from a furnace. The momentum has gone but they still creak and boulders still tumble as the flow settles. Steam hisses between the blocks of lava, caking the mouths of the vents with yellow sulphur. Pools of liquid mud, grey, yellow or blue, boiled by the subsiding heat from far below, bubble creamily. Otherwise all is still. No bush grows to give shelter from the scouring wind; no speck of green relieves the black surface of the empty ash plains.

From Life on Earth: a Natural History *by David Attenborough.*

It would seem inappropriate to use 'flowery' language to describe such a desolate scene. The impact here is made by simple, concrete images and a few well chosen verbs: 'creak', 'tumble', 'hisses', 'caking', 'boiled', 'bubble'. There are some alliterative echoes, in words such as 'creak' and 'creamily'; 'boiled' and 'bubble', and the writer uses a variety of sentence lengths and structures, which add to the drama. The last sentence, with the two negative constructions balanced by the semi-colon, gives an air of finality to the paragraph.

Task

Try to write a paragraph about a scene that is similarly bleak, which you have observed. Note the absence of human or animal life.

It may be difficult to find a place as unpopulated in your experience. Maybe a scene in the early morning or at night might be effective; you could then try a contrasting account at a different time of day. Share your account with someone who also knows the place and discuss whether you have the same feelings about it. How have you revealed those feelings? Was it through colours, verbs, adverbs, or by describing what was missing? Could you imagine an incident which might happen at the scene you have described?

Many descriptions, whether of a place or a person, set the scene for a narrative, as in the start of a short story or a novel. Here the picture needs to be set quickly, so the readers can involve themselves in the thought or action, believing in it and wanting to know the outcome.

Your turn

Could you develop your description of the bleak place you have written about with a dramatic incident?

Describing people

A description of a person contains far more than just a physical picture, though that may be a clear starting point. You could also include comparisons – what certain aspects remind you of, including mannerisms, movement or stillness. Clothes can tell us about character, peer group, fashion, musical tastes, wealth, hobbies, constraints the person is under or the image they want to project. There may be hidden or sometimes altered aspects of behaviour, changes in speech to different audiences. Above all a description of a person may convey opinions – yours, other commentators' or the character's own – and relationships between writer and subject.

Authenticity is often created by well-chosen, sharply observed details, rather than pretended emotional reactions. Look at these three descriptions of the same person. What does each of them tell you about the relationship between the writer and the boy?

This person is 1.75 metres tall.
He wears black clothes.
His hair is short.
He has an earring in his left ear.
His lip is pierced, which affects his speech.

Hugo is tall and thin like a giraffe. His clothes always look the same, dirty black T shirt, jeans, boots.
His earring is the only bright element in his appearance.
His crew cut is as short as school rules allow.

He's everything I'd like to be – tall, slim, moves like a panther. His murky black gear suggests conformity but with anarchic touches, emphasised by his matching earring and cool lip stud. His cropped hair reveals an amazingly shaped skull and in the school holidays it's adorned with sculpted symbols. My idol – a pity I'm his sister!

Writing creatively in a range of styles

Task 1

Compare these descriptions.

- Start with the verbs – what is conveyed by the choice of 'wears', 'is', 'has' as opposed to 'adorned', 'reveals', 'suggests', 'emphasised'?
- What attitude is suggested by the adjectives – 'dirty' or 'murky', 'thin' or 'slim'?
- Examine the **similes** – 'giraffe', 'panther' – both wild animals, but what image does each bring to mind? Would you want to be compared to either of them?

Personal descriptions often convey attitudes. Even the first one, which could be described as factual, objective, neutral or unbiased, has selected certain details, which could tell us what the writer considers important, maybe the reason for the description. It could be notes for an identification parade, an audition or an interview.

Task 2

What impression do you have of the relationship between the second writer and the boy?

We learn something of the writer as well as the subject in this kind of writing. The second description might have been written by a schoolteacher or a critical parent, as it implies some disapproval. The third conveys admiration, even hero worship. Both the second and third are subjective, giving a clear opinion or bias, which may result in criticism or praise.

Your turn

Try writing descriptions of someone you know well, from different viewpoints; then try a similar exercise about someone who is in the public eye, such as a sports star, a singer or a politician. What types of details are missing from the second set of descriptions?

If you want to make a character come alive, you stand a better chance if you base your writing on observation, including small details, even if the character is partly fictitious.

Writing narrative

Descriptions often include narrative, the action that takes place in the scene portrayed, which in turn adds atmosphere to what happens.

The chapter of *Life on Earth* that opens with the paragraph on volcanoes, in the previous section, continues with an account of millennia of evolution condensed into a few lines.

> The first volcanoes to appear on the surface of the cooling planet erupted on a far greater scale than any that we know today, building entire mountain ranges of lava and ash. Over the millennia, the wind and rain destroyed them. Their rocks weathered and turned to clay and mud. Streams transported the debris, particle by particle, and strewed it over the sea floor beyond the margins of the land. The continents were not stationary, but drifted slowly over the earth's surface, driven by the convection currents moving deep in the earth's mantle. When they collided, the sedimentary deposits around them were squeezed and rucked up to form new mountain ranges.

From Life on Earth: a Natural History *by David Attenborough.*

The action is conveyed, as was the description in the opening paragraph, mainly by very explicit verbs: 'erupted', 'building', 'destroyed', 'weathered', 'transported', 'strewed', 'drifted', 'driven', 'collided', 'squeezed' and 'rucked'.

Task 1

Try writing a paragraph describing an activity which you know very well, using ten varied verbs to convey different stages or aspects. Do you think you could convince a reader that your chosen activity is special?

Once again, language choices can make an impact on the reader by their clarity, whether they define or carry connotations. Maybe you could write an incident in the life of the boy described by three different people earlier in this chapter. Could you involve the writers as characters in the drama and develop a conflict and a resolution to their differences? As an alternative, you could develop your own contrasting personal descriptions in the same way.

Now read the following extract from a short story by Ernest Hemingway. There is only one character and not a great deal happens in this extract, but we learn a great deal. Note the style: many short sentences, with understated description. Hemingway was originally a journalist, and his spare, unadorned writing style was a real challenge to literary critics of the time. Many have since tried to imitate him – maybe you can learn about the effective use of simple language by reading some of his short stories and novels.

Big Two-Hearted River: II

In the morning the sun was up and the tent was starting to get hot. Nick crawled out under the mosquito netting stretched across the mouth of the tent, to look at the morning. The grass was wet on his hands as he came out. He held his trousers and his shoes in his hands. The sun was just up over the hill. There was the meadow, the river and the swamp. There were birch trees in the green of the swamp on the other side of the river.

The river was clear and smoothly fast in the early morning. Down about two hundred yards were three logs all the way across the stream. They made the river smooth and deep above them. As Nick watched, a mink crossed the river on the logs and went into the swamp. Nick was excited. He was excited by the early morning and the river. He was really too hurried to eat breakfast, but he knew he must. He built a little fire and put on the coffee pot.

Rapidly he mixed some buckwheat flour with water and stirred it smooth, one cup of flour, one cup of water. He put a handful of coffee in the pot and dipped a lump of grease out of a can and slid it sputtering across the hot skillet. On the smoking skillet he poured smoothly the buckwheat batter. It spread like lava, the grease spitting sharply. Around the edges the buckwheat cake began to firm, then brown, then crisp. The surface was bubbling slowly to porousness. Nick pushed under the browned under surface with a fresh pine chip. He shook the skillet sideways and the cake was loose on the surface. I won't try to flop it, he thought. He slid the chip of clean wood all the way under the cake, and flopped it over on to its face. It sputtered in the pan. When it was cooked Nick regreased the skillet. He used all the batter. It made another big flapjack and one smaller one.

Nick ate a big flapjack and a smaller one, covered with apple butter. He put apple butter on the third cake, folded it over twice, wrapped it in oiled paper and put it in his shirt pocket. He put the apple-butter jar back in the pack and cut bread for two sandwiches.

In the pack he found a big onion. He sliced it in two and peeled the silky outer skin. Then he cut one half into slices and made onion sandwiches. He wrapped them in oiled paper and buttoned them in the other pocket of his khaki shirt. He turned the skillet upside down on the grill, drank the coffee, sweetened and yellow brown with the condensed milk in it, and tidied up the camp.

From Big Two-Hearted River: II *by Ernest Hemingway.*

The style is deceptively simple. Look at how he builds the picture, making us feel the excitement growing, from 'the grass was wet on his hands' to the reinforcement through repetition of features, feelings and activities: 'smoothly fast', 'smooth and deep'; 'Nick was excited. He was excited by the early morning and the river.'

And then the detailed, methodical account of making breakfast and packed lunch, through to clearing up, which tells us a great deal about his character. We can see, hear and smell the pancakes cooking. Picture him drinking the coffee, 'sweetened and yellow brown with the condensed milk in it', all the time wanting to start fishing.

Task 2

How would you describe preparing a meal? Could you describe sound, smell, taste as well as action and sight? Try it, then read it to someone and ask if it makes them hungry.

The carefully observed details make all the difference to the reader's belief in the account. We really feel that Hemingway must have lived like Nick, that the story is based on experience.

Your turn

Focus on something in your life that you now do almost automatically, maybe riding a bike, practising a craft or skill or playing an instrument, and write an account of it for someone who knows nothing about it. It's a bit like teaching, in that you have to break it down into components and really think back to when you learned how to do it yourself.

Narrative doesn't have to be an adventure, as an account of everyday activities can reveal a great deal about a lifestyle or a personality. Remember, what is normal to you may be fascinating to another reader. On the other hand, a flat account of everyday activities is not likely to impress an examiner, so try to vary your action verbs and avoid a list-like approach. Compare these two versions of a morning which started badly.

I got up, got dressed, went to the bathroom, went downstairs and found there was no milk for my coffee. I put on my jacket, went to the bus stop and got on the bus. It had a puncture so I was late for school.

I fell out of bed, flung on my uniform, splashed my face with cold water and fell down the stairs. As I raced into the kitchen I remembered that I had forgotten to call into the shop the night before, so there was nothing for breakfast. More cold water! Grabbing my jacket from the chair and trying to brush away the cat's hairs, I didn't notice the cat herself, who also wanted breakfast. As I tripped over her, she protested loudly and scratched my bare leg. It was a relief to escape from the house and collapse onto the bus. Unfortunately my relief was short-lived as the bus screeched to a halt with one tyre in tatters.
My teacher would never believe it!

Which of these versions creates a personality you can 'hear' talking and would find interesting to meet?

Writing dramatically

Dramatic writing can be part of a story, as dialogue during the narrative, a playscript or an oral task such as a speech or a debate. These are all different from real speech, which, if taped and transcribed, would be full of hesitations, repetitions, false starts, interruptions and other natural elements. So to achieve credibility in a piece of dramatic writing you need to have an ear for dialogue, but do not try to imitate real speech exactly.

Conversation is used either to establish a relationship between characters or to move the action on, maybe by filling in the gaps the reader or viewer has missed. If you are keen to write dialogue it is a good idea to try the following tasks.

Task 1

First, attempt to write ten exchanges between two characters, using only 'he said' or 'she said' as the speech verbs.

> "I'm going to the pictures," she said.
> "What's on?" he said.
> "*Dinosaur*," she said.

Are you already bored? This may seem extreme, but many people feel they have to establish that each speech item is spoken, although the punctuation does it for them.

Task 2

Now try to vary the speech verbs, using the conversation above as a starting point. Your version might go something like this:

> "I'm going to the pictures," she announced.
> "What's on?" he muttered.
> "*Dinosaur*!" was her excited reply. "Do you want to come?"
> "Saw it last night."
> "Oh!"

We learn more about the possible relationship between the two characters in this version. You can also try to use evocative adverbs to expand the range of feelings in the speech.

Task 3

Try to write a list of twenty speech verbs and twenty adverbials that might accompany a dialogue. Be as imaginative and varied as you can. A thesaurus might help. Here are a few to start you off:

yelped	emphatically
cried	pensively
whispered	aggressively
howled	with menace
stuttered	in a croaking voice
	bashfully

Think about what you can't hear in a written version of speech – emphasis, tone, emotion, pauses, etc. You can try to convey them by the dialogue itself, but your choice of speech verbs and adverbials, plus appropriate punctuation, such as question marks, exclamation marks, dashes and leader dots to indicate pauses, will increase the feeling of hearing the conversation. We can also learn a great deal about personality by what is said and the interaction between the speakers. Even the length of each person's contribution can add to our knowledge of character or relationships. Who dominates? Who interrupts? Who wins an argument?

Task 4

Try to write a narrative just through dialogue, without speech verbs.

Conversational exchanges can be established purely through the layout conventions of direct speech, with inverted commas and a new paragraph for each speaker, but it can become confusing if there are more than two speakers.

Task 5

Now try rewriting your narrative as a scene from a play, with stage directions and advice to the actors. Read the following extract to give you an idea of layout and the conventions of script writing.

Writing creatively in a range of styles

Mrs Avon:	"Yes, well as I say ..."
	(*Avon eats*)
	"... and then there's the children. One of them cut his head open today. That meant a plaster. And it all has to come out of the housekeeping."
Avon:	"Which one?"
Mrs Avon:	"Which one what?"
Avon:	"Which one of the children?"
Mrs Avon:	"Which one of the children?"
Avon:	"Yes."
Mrs Avon:	"Well – how do I know?"
Avon:	"Oh."
Mrs Avon:	"My concern was with the wound. You don't ask for names in an emergency like that."
Avon:	"But didn't you recognise him?"
Mrs Avon:	"You're so tiresome, Avon. Of course I recognised him. How else would I know it was one of ours? I can't afford to go sticking plaster all over other people's children you know."
Avon:	"Are they all in bed?"
Mrs Avon:	"Yes. Washed, dried – "
Avon:	(*To himself*) "– And polished."
Mrs Avon:	"Clean clothes ready for school as usual and I changed the sheets this morning. That's besides everything else."
Avon:	"You're working too hard, my little darling."
Mrs Avon:	"Hm!"
Avon:	"Perhaps we can get a daily – next year say."
Mrs Avon:	"That means somebody else to clean up after."
Avon:	"No, no, a daily is supposed to clean up after you."
Mrs Avon:	"Me? *Me*, Avon? I need cleaning up after? You're not home five minutes before the insults start."
Avon:	"I didn't mean ... I mean clear up before you ... that is – I wouldn't dream of ... everything's so tidy and lovely because of you –"
Mrs Avon:	"Oh, get on with your fish."
	(*He eats quietly*)
	"Besides, you don't earn enough for a daily."
Avon:	"I could ask for a rise."
Mrs Avon:	"Ten pence? Fifty? ... Don't be ridiculous. Perhaps if you'd had a bit of ambition and drive in the past, changed your job, I wouldn't need to slave like this now."

From Made in Heaven
by Andrew Sachs.

Note how the punctuation, such as dashes and leader dots, gives clues as to pauses, incomplete sentences and interruptions. Italics are used both for stage directions and to show emphasis in speech (you could use underlining in your work).

What does this dialogue tell us about the relationship between the characters? Is there deliberate misunderstanding of the questions? The outcome, which is only possible through the medium of radio, is Avon's fantasy about murdering his wife, with stage directions such as the following:

*(A vicious thumping sound, and heavy breathing from Avon ...
Her voice recedes quickly to an echo into the distance as she falls. There is a sickening squelch as the body impales itself below. Avon giggles gleefully. Sound back to normal. Mrs Avon is quite unperturbed.)*

The opening dialogue establishes the relationship and the imagined violent deaths could be described as wish fulfilment, made more humorous because of Mrs Avon's complete obliviousness to her husband's fantasy.

Your turn

Conveying humour is very difficult, but it is a good exercise to try to write a short sketch and perform it in front of a group, to see if it works. Another possibility is to record a radio programme, with some scripted and some authentic dialogues, to become more aware of what sounds realistic. This could show you whether you have a skill for this type of writing.

Writing personally

Although many titles may give you an opportunity to write from experience, there are some that allow you no choice other than to do so. Obviously, you could create or exaggerate your answers to any of these topics, but the ring of truth will probably create a better essay than trying to impress. The details of other people's lives or opinions can be fascinating – think of the number of biographies and autobiographies which are published and the magazine articles about the lives of famous people. Some television companies give video recorders to members of the public to record their lives, or allow access to booths for them to give their opinions on issues of the day.

What will be important, as in most types of writing, will be the freshness, in vocabulary, style, material and its organisation, which you bring to the subject. Try to avoid the temptation to repeat the title throughout the essay – as long as there is a clear focus on the topic, this should not be necessary. You could think of the essay as talking to someone about your life, or writing to a friend who has moved away. Obviously your language will be more formal than speech, but the sense of audience should keep your writing lively.

Task 1

Write about a radio or television programme which had a powerful impact on you. Explain the effects in your essay.

It is important also to focus on all aspects of a question, to maximise your content and relevance marks. Here, the question is not just asking for a summary of a programme, or even a review, but an explanation of why you have chosen to write about it, what made it special. This could be because of the plot, the acting, certain artistic features, because of your mood at the time, those you shared the experience with, what it reminded you of, the issues it raised. There is far more depth here than maybe it seemed at first, with more potential for thoughtful writing. It is very important to be aware of such possibilities when you choose your title.

Task 2

Write an essay about the musicians you most admire.

If you choose to write, for example, about a singer or group whom you admire, give a variety of reasons for your choice. This could include appearance, musical range, empathy with your age group, originality of material, stage presence, approachability. Think about their unique qualities and choose the words to express these. Try to vary your verbs as well, to convey special aspects of the performance, including your feelings, physical and emotional. What lengths would you go to for a personal interview? Would you change your appearance to be more like them? Has being a fan influenced your clothes, friends or lifestyle?

Maybe a sporting hero or event has had more influence on you, or reading about or meeting someone else has changed your career plans or your ambitions. Whatever or whoever the stimulus, it could make a strong piece of personal writing through which you can reveal something of your own character or motivation. You may need to extend your vocabulary and powers of expression to make such an essay effective, but it could be very rewarding. You could even practise in the form of an argument with a friend about the merits of your respective choices or role models!

The format you choose may also be more varied in personal writing. Some examples include:
- a diary;
- an exchange of letters (maybe between generations);
- a conversation;
- an advice column;
- a talk;
- an autobiographical piece in a magazine;
- an obituary.

Remember above all that you are writing to convey your own feelings or opinion, or your reaction, so you can be honest, even adventurous. Examiners respond very positively to the expression of genuine feelings, even if your feelings differ from the examiner's!

Writing discursively

A discursive essay can ask you to look at both sides of a topic, such as the advantages and disadvantages of, for instance, different forms of energy, transport or ways of life. With such a title you have to decide on a structure which allows you to balance both sides without too much repetition and to come to a reasoned conclusion. Try to avoid the 'catch-all' approach of 'There are advantages and disadvantages in all kinds of energy. I shall outline the advantages and the disadvantages and come to a conclusion.' Even in such an essay it is possible to have a dramatic opening, such as a brief account, maybe with a headline, of an explosion at a nuclear power plant or an oil leak from a tanker. A petrol shortage or a storm that brings down power lines could also be an effective introduction to the topic. It is worth spending a few minutes thinking of a striking opening when planning such a topic, and maybe using some skills of rhetoric to convince your reader. It is possible to convey a passionately held opinion very effectively in writing and your examiner will appreciate the effort.

Another type of discursive essay asks you to focus on one side of a topic, but maybe to give personal preferences.

Oral debates or discussions can form the basis of a realistic structure for a discursive or argumentative piece of writing. Not everyone has the opportunity to practise formal debating techniques, but it is possible to listen to or watch politicians or others in the news arguing or defending their opinions and decisions. Newspapers often present contrasting opinions, through choice of topic, language and viewpoint in editorials, cartoons, etc. Some try to influence their readers to vote a certain way in referenda or elections. They may try to do this through obviously biased language or photographs, often claiming a responsibility to inform the public. It may be done through more subtle use of language, through innuendo or irony, or by omission of relevant facts. You can learn a great deal about the language of argument through studying the media, for instance by examining articles on the same topic in contrasting newspapers.

Some magazines and newspapers, even radio and television programmes, invite different points of view from the public, sometimes giving them the opportunity to confront spokespeople from organisations in the news. The format could be a question and answer session to a panel with contrasting opinions, a phone-in on the radio on a current topic, a public exchange of views between two people with strongly opposing opinions, the letters page of a newspaper or other means of feedback.

Look at this extract from a newspaper column called 'Private Lives' in which readers, instead of writing to an agony column which will be answered by one person, or a team writing with one voice, write a problem letter which is published in advance, inviting the public to offer comments and suggestions. The topics and age range vary widely, as do the number and length of the replies.

Should I try to win back the friends scared off by my disability?

A few years ago, at the age of 43, I was diagnosed with a progressive neuro-muscular condition.

Unable to continue my previous occupation, I have started voluntary work, and hope that eventually I will find new opportunities in life. My partner and family have given me a lot of support, but several of my friends have withdrawn from my life, apparently 'scared by and unable to deal with' disability. This is hurtful to me, as I supported them through traumas in their lives, and I thought our friendship was unbreakable. My partner says that, if they can't see that I'm still the same person, their friendship is worthless. I miss them terribly and feel hurt by their rejection. Should I try to 'educate' them about disability, or just move on?"

From The Guardian.

Here are two answers written by readers with contrasting viewpoints:

Clear the air

When I was in my early twenties, a close friend of mine became severely ill. As in your case, her family offered support whilst most of her friends let her down, myself included. She was furious that the world kept turning round whilst her life had stopped. I felt guilty for carrying on with my life and resented her for this guilt.

I now judge my behaviour as at worst selfish and insensitive, and at best desperately out of touch. Sadly, most of us are not equipped to handle illness in others. Most problems in other people's lives enable us to give advice and thus feel useful. Illness is unfair and unexplainable, and leaves us feeling powerless. Your friends might feel that their good health is an insult to you. Perhaps they need to hear how disappointed you are with them and how much you miss them. If they don't respond, at least you will have let them know what terrible friends they are.

Time will tell

I have been disabled from birth but have managed to lead a normal life. I have made many friends over the years but I am sure I must have met many people who couldn't cope with my disability and dropped the acquaintance at an early stage.

I have never found it much use trying to 'educate' people about my disability as, if you give them too much information, some people come to see you as a symbol of your condition rather than the unique individual that you are. Perhaps it is better to ask for help when the need arises, have a laugh over clumsy mishaps and hope people get the picture eventually. However, you obviously can't do this with friends who won't see you.

Meeting new friends through voluntary work has helped a little. When your old friends get over the shock and hear how well you are coping, maybe they will come back to you.

Note how each of the replies, while answering the original letter, has stated the perspective and experience of the writer, thus providing alternative solutions to the problem. What makes this column fascinating is the range of opinions on each situation. Maybe you could try a similar exercise in your class, with a letter as stimulus taken from a problem page, to which each of you could write a real or fictional answer. You could then read all of them and decide which is the most useful and which combination would make the most interesting feature.

Task 1

Try writing a series of letters or short articles giving contrasting viewpoints on an issue.

It is very good preparation for a debate or meeting to assemble ideas on both sides, as this can help you to prepare points to counter the opposition's arguments. It will also help if you choose to write an essay in which you have to consider opposing views. You may also be able to use some of the techniques of rhetoric from Chapter 2.

Here is part of a published debate on the topic of UFOs, between a former government sky watcher and an astronomer from the Greenwich Observatory in London.

Dear Robin,
I first became involved in UFO watching in 1991, as part of my government work. I confess to being initially sceptical. I believed UFOs were vague lights in the sky seen by people out late walking their dogs – perhaps on their way back from the pub! I was wrong.

I received between two and three hundred UFO reports each year, and carried out detailed investigations in attempts to correlate sightings with aircraft activity, astronomical phenomena, etc. After a rigorous investigation, between 90 and 95 per cent of sightings could be explained as misidentifications of known objects and phenomena – anything from aircraft lights to weather balloons. This left what I called the *real* UFOs.

From The Guardian.

The real UFOs are structured craft of unknown origin, capable of penetrating our sophisticated air defence network with impunity. Sometimes they show up on radar; sometimes not. They have been seen by civil and military pilots, and on occasions jets have been scrambled to try and intercept these mystery craft; we have not been able to catch them.

I accept that just because a UFO sighting remains unexplained, it is not unexplainable. But these craft display technology which goes beyond the cutting edge of anything in our terrestrial inventories (including prototype craft), both in terms of speed and manoeuvrability. I am convinced this technology can only be extraterrestrial.
Yours sincerely,
Nick Pope

Writing creatively in a range of styles

Note some of the techniques used here:
- the reference to government work to establish credibility;
- the original scepticism which has been replaced by belief;
- the statistics, the repetition of the 'real UFOs' at the end and beginning of paragraphs;
- the balance between 'unexplained' and 'unexplainable' and 'terrestrial' and 'extraterrestrial';
- above all the absolute belief in his claim, ('I am convinced').

Now read the reply to this letter.

Dear Nick,

I am an astronomer, and in my 35 years of observation and research I have never come across anything I would describe as a UFO, although I did once call off a police car from pursuing Venus setting beneath a thunder cloud.

As a scientist, I respect observations and particularly your claim that between 1991 and 1994 there were between ten and 30 reports per year, made by qualified observers, for which you had no explanation. This is, of course, a valuable body of data that should be published and made available to the scientific community. Until this is done, I cannot accept your deductive jump from the observations to the existence of craft that go beyond our existing technology.

I would like to open the debate wider, and at the risk of blemishing my position as a narrow-minded scientist, indulge in a little speculation that suggests it is unlikely that we will ever make contact with another civilisation. The Earth is an ideal place for intelligent life to develop. Nevertheless it took 4,500 million years for it to appear in a form capable of communication. When the Earth was born the Universe was already at least 6,000 million years old. Clearly, there has been enough time for a civilisation like ours to develop and spread its radio signals, at the speed of light, throughout our galaxy and far beyond. As we listen with some of the world's most powerful telescopes, we hear nothing. How much less probable it is that they are flying silently around us.

From The Guardian.

The reply uses irony, even sarcasm, to mock the claims in the first letter. The writer also establishes his credentials, challenges Nick Pope to publish details of unexplained sightings and uses his own statistics to refute the possibility of alien life forms. In acknowledged debating style, he picks up points from the first writer/speaker (to show he has read/listened to them) and belittles the 'deductive jump' which he says was used.

The point of including such correspondence is to show you a range of ways in which opinions can be discussed, other than in a purely discursive essay. Of course, that also has its place in your exam repertoire and needs practice.

Task 2

Take any of the following sample essay titles and plan a response; some will require a balanced approach, others a more argumentative or opinionated one, or persuasive techniques. Make sure you understand the requirements of each type so your structure and approach match the title. Hints are given below some of the questions.

Question 1

How important do you think it is to prepare young people to share the responsibilities of parenthood?

Answers to this question could follow the hint which is maybe implied in the phrasing of the question, or challenge it, with a personal or cultural perspective. Whichever is chosen, the topic must be kept in focus throughout the essay.

Question 2

Do we take sports events too seriously? Give your views, using examples from recent sports events to support your ideas.

This question is structured rather differently, suggesting the type of material needed to justify the opinion. If you felt that sport was taken too seriously, but did not follow sport yourself, you might have problems in answering this question in the way required.

Question 3

The best way to prevent crime.

This question (and Question 5) could be answered in an objective way, without giving your perspective. You could write your answer as an impersonal report, weighing up the alternatives and coming to a balanced conclusion.

People behave towards animals in different ways: give your opinions about some of these ways.

This title has a different structure: it asserts a fact and asks for your viewpoint. An efficient way of covering a number of attitudes and avoiding repetition would be to write under subheadings, such as 'animal lover', 'hunter', 'farmer', and maybe end with a question to the reader.

The advantages and disadvantages of being an adult.

See Question 3.

The television service in my country – what I enjoy and the improvements I should like to introduce.

This title offers the chance to describe some of your favourite programmes, not forgetting the reasons for your choices, and to make suggestions for changes. It could be tackled in the form of a report with recommendations.

Traveller or tourist – which would you rather be and why?

You need to be aware of the distinction between 'traveller' and 'tourist', and to be able to develop a range of reasons for your personal choice. This could be for a website or an article for a magazine.

Describe the skills needed by an effective teacher or lecturer. Which do you think are the most important?

In an essay such as this, try to avoid a list approach. Use lively examples to illustrate your points and be prepared to justify your priorities.

Not all arguments come to a satisfactory conclusion – sometimes the opponents have to agree to disagree, but the process of stating and defending a position can help to clarify a viewpoint and is very satisfying, especially if you have managed to use language and structure in an effective and stylish manner.

Pictures as a stimulus for writing

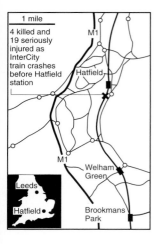

In the new syllabus there will be the opportunity to use material from the first two sections as a stimulus for writing in Section C, rather than separate pictures. The items could include photographs, cartoons, diagrams or other illustrative material which could be a focus for your writing. The titles will extend the theme of the extracts in Sections A and B, as we saw in Chapter 3.

If you respond to a picture by giving a straight description, it can be really flat. For example, beginning an essay, based on the picture on page 173 with the sentence 'On the right there are eleven hands, some small, some incomplete,' is a very basic response. A vivid description can, however, make us re-examine our response to even an apparently well-known image (look, for example, at the account of Van Gogh's *Sunflowers* in Chapter 7).

To discover a range of possible responses to pictures/images on the same theme, look at these photographs from a newspaper the day after a fatal train crash in England.

Writing creatively in a range of styles

There were seven different articles about the accident. We have chosen just three. Look at the differences between them in terms of language, purpose, content and style.

Disaster strikes at 115mph

Rail safety under scrutiny again as four are killed as London–Leeds train is derailed

The safety of Britain's rail system has been thrown into question yet again after the third serious accident in three years left four people dead and 33 injured yesterday.

The tragedy happened shortly after midday yesterday when a high-speed train derailed and broke up at more than 100mph, hurling some passengers onto the track.

The cause of the crash is still being investigated but police ruled out terrorism as the cause last night, despite receiving a bomb threat just two days ago.

Many expressed a sense of disbelief that the death toll had not been higher. The train literally came apart as it took a right-hand bend on one of the busiest stretches of line in Britain. The timing of the accident has jarred emotions; it comes less than two weeks after the first anniversary of the crash at Paddington.

The 12.10pm GNER London to Leeds service left the track barely 20 minutes into its journey.

The train split in two and a giant hole was torn in the buffet car. Some passengers reported that a loud bang was heard seconds before the carriages skewed off the track. Three ended up on their side, with four others derailed.

The dead and most severely injured came from the middle section of the train.

Two first-class carriages and the rear locomotive separated from the main section of the train and screeched to a halt; the buffet car, six standard class coaches and the front locomotive careered a few hundred yards further up the track. The buffet car then toppled over and smashed into a trackside pylon which tore off its roof.

Of the 200 passengers on board the train, four were pronounced dead at the scene and 33 were taken to local hospitals.

Witnesses described scenes of 'mayhem', with bodies by the track and people weeping.

In June 1998, another high-speed GNER train derailed on the same track, just 20 miles away, injuring nine people.

The chief executive of GNER said the train, built in 1990, would have been serviced every night. He added: "We are investigating all the reasons; we do not know the cause of the accident at this stage."

From The Guardian.

This was written by a team of journalists whose task was to investigate and write a report for the front page. It is a combination of factual information, comment, historical references, quotations and reported speech. The sentence and paragraph lengths are varied to a certain extent.

The next text is a first person account by a passenger, with details of injuries, snatches of speech and a sense of shape and emotion.

Text B

Eyewitness

Passenger tells of shock and relief

The wail of sirens pierced the silence as the police helicopter came into view, dipping and ducking to examine the twisted trunk of the train.

Fifteen long minutes earlier, the 12.10 GNER London to Leeds train had juddered, screeched and jumped around in a gruesome parody of a rollercoaster to a topsy-turvy, silent halt.

"Nobody move," screamed a guard. "Stay in the carriage. I repeat, nobody move."

Nobody was listening. Amid strangled cries of relief and uncontrolled sobbing, the passengers of Coach D scrabbled under seats for missing laptops, handbags and phones before clambering up along the aisle, now at 45 degrees, and helped each other over a pile of suitcases 6ft high.

An elderly man banged frantically on the door release button. I smelled and saw smoke rising above the blackened window; eventually the door creaked slowly ajar.

One by one we leapt on to the tracks and huddled, like refugees, on the stony side of a steep and thorny-hedged embankment.

From our vantage point, we could see the locomotive and first two carriages, still upright in the sunshine. The tilt started with the first carriage, while the back of the train lay smashed and broken across the rails.

Behind me, a woman in a pressed white shirt, now blackened with grease and mud, cradled a member of the train's crew. The attendant had lost several layers of skin on her right hand; her forearm was seared and raw.

Behind her, a portly man in an expensive suit, tie still impeccably knotted, clutched a mobile phone to his black and bleeding ear.

Next to him, a young shaven-headed chef sucked on an unlit cigarette. His hand was swathed in a makeshift bandage and his chequered pants were spattered with blood and soot.

Murmurs of dialogue got louder and louder as we were herded off the tracks to the far bank. "I'm fine thank goodness." – "The third derailment in two days." – "At least two, I heard."

We were taken to a conference centre, where there was tea and coffee. Over the loudspeaker came a voice, asking repeatedly for a passenger to come forward. Everyone looked at each other, silently relieved they were not asking for us.

From The Guardian.

Look at the differences between these accounts. The first is more detached, putting the accident into context and discussing responses and possible causes. The second contains such acutely observed detail that it could only have been written by someone who was there at the time. This account is full of well chosen language, which adds to the atmosphere. Look back at the section on descriptive writing to review how to make writing credible. The verbs are apt and pile on the tension, with movement and sound: 'juddered, screeched and jumped around in a gruesome parody of a roller coaster to a topsy-turvy, silent halt' uses a vivid contrast between a ride at an amusement park and the devastation of the accident to emphasise the unreality of the scene. Neither of the accounts is melodramatic in the sense of using excessive descriptions of horror, but each contains images, visual details, sounds, smells, feelings, which add depth to the impression of the illustrations.

The third extract is from a reaction by the editor to the issues raised by the crash.

Text C

Less safe than it should be
Rising concern over railway safety

These are boom times for the railways. People complain about high fares and trains running late but they still take the train where a year or two back they might have relied on the car. Passenger numbers are up 30 per cent.

This increase is bound to be jeopardised if the sense begins to spread that the railway is less safe than it should be. The circumstances in which a GNER train travelling from London to Leeds at a speed of around 115mph left the rails yesterday, leaving six people dead and 24 in need of hospital treatment, are still far from clear. Terrorist involvement is not entirely ruled out. A broken wheel or axle is one possibility. Another is a broken rail: should that prove to have been the case it would be deeply ominous.

But whatever explanation emerges, this is the third major crash in three years. The overwhelming majority of railway journeys are still completed safely, if not always on time. But after this sequence the confidence with which passengers settle into their seats at the start of a journey is bound to be undermined.

There will of course be an exhaustive enquiry. Yet the time these exercises take to come up with the answers is a further source of unease. The findings on the Paddington disaster are expected at the end of the year – 14 months after the crash which killed 31 people. In the interests of travellers' confidence the enquiry into what happened yesterday will need to work to a tighter time scale than that.

Adapted from The Guardian.

This editorial is more detached from the drama, but has a clear focus on the issues raised by the incident. The language chosen is more considered, more weighty, with multi-syllabic words and longer paragraphs. The verbs are less varied, with little description or sense of drama, a less personal style, but the language is still strong and wanting to affect public opinion.

All of these are valid responses to pictures of an accident, and writing in similar styles would gain credit in an examination. They illustrate styles of writing and approaches which you could use. The fact that they are all about a real accident does make a difference to the quality and immediacy of the writing, but you can learn to improve your style by looking at techniques used, such as the selection and combination of details, the use of speech, the choice of emotive or neutral language, the sense of rhetoric in the editorial, the shaping of each piece according to its purpose and viewpoint.

It is important that you convince the examiner that there is a valid link between the picture and your writing, that the picture has inspired the essay. The hackneyed account of a photograph in an album or a picture in a loft or an exhibition, which could be any photo or picture, will not gain you much credit for originality and is unlikely to inspire you to write with freshness or feeling.

Your turn

Look at the next picture, which is of students protesting.

Give it a headline and write two contrasting articles to accompany it in a newspaper or magazine. Each article should be from a different viewpoint (for example, a student involved in the riot, a reporter, or a policeman). Compare your articles with those written by others in your class. How many other responses are there to it? What other types of writing could validly be inspired by the picture?

Sample exam questions and answers

Now we'll look at some student responses to a range of exam essay titles. There are some errors in the exam scripts, but we are mainly examining the ways in which the candidates have approached the topics, with comments and criticisms by examiners.

Descriptive and narrative essays

The first example is an imaginative response which combines elements of the descriptive and narrative skills analysed earlier. (The underlined words are spelling or grammatical mistakes.)

'As the sun rose on a changed landscape ...' Use this as the beginning of a story or description.

As the sun rose on a changed landscape, only dry, dead branches shivered in the early morning wind. No birds were perched to welcome the daily visitor. No flies danced in the cool, damp air. No beetles scuttled out of their earthen beds to bathe in the golden rays of light. The lonely star stood alone <u>on</u> the pale-blue sky, <u>weaping</u> tears of light for her dearly departed Earth.

The wind glided smoothly over the barren field, <u>carressing</u> the frigid stones and the withered yellow blades of grass. Roaming through this place it once knew, it raced to find its old friends. Leaving streamers of faded foliage behind its tail, the wind hunted in haste for the baby badger it had tickled last spring. Where was the sparkling spring it had whispered to last fall? Where have the robin chicks it taught to fly gone? Finding nothing but death as it <u>sweeped</u> over the still world, it slowly drifted close to an ancient, barren tree, curled up around the firm trunk and breathed its last breath of sadness.

Now the sun was truly alone. It glared upon an empty planet wondering what had changed the land, once so abundant in life and love into a desert, devoid of happiness and harmony. Man was the answer. The sun knew that the human race was the only one capable of such destruction.

Overcome with rage the sun glared upon the wasteland. Why had such a horrible creature <u>have been</u> allowed to play with such a precious <u>jewl</u>? Like a little child he was bound to drop and destroy it one day. This time the sun searched, not for the friend, but for the foe.

The ball of fire exploded into every crack and crevice on the Earth's surface. Where had it all begun? What would drive such a stupid creature to such a heinous crime? As the sun scrambled over the death <u>he</u> finally found <u>its</u> answer. Illuminating a large, <u>ranck</u> hole, he knew that the humans, who had tried to raise themselves to the seats of the Gods, only succeeded in blowing <u>himself</u> to the bowels of Hell.

This writer has a real feeling for language, using rhetorical and literary devices to create a picture and mood. The story is a valid development of the title and is well shaped and structured, with clear paragraphing. In places the alliteration is overdone and the personification becomes confused. There are occasional verb and agreement errors and a few spelling mistakes. These errors, however, do not detract from the strong images and feelings, the confident and evocative writing which deserves an A grade.

Look at the ideas described in the first section which are exemplified here – the varied verbs, the noting of the absent features, the alliteration, the variety of sentence structures (although present participle/-ing constructions are rather over-used in the second paragraph).

Compare this with the answer to the following question, which also receives a descriptive/narrative treatment, but in the first person.

Write an essay entitled 'The Fateful Flight'.

Travelling by air wasn't a new experience for me. I had been in aeroplanes since I had turned two years of age, but <u>todays</u> flight was to be special. I was travelling alone from Bermuda to Florida – my parents were there for some business.

It was hot and I wished I could take off my matching green cotton jacket.

Waiting in the airport lounge was like watching the ten o'clock news – boring. The place smelt of smoke and alcohol, and a hint of aftershave. Soon an announcement was heard, instructing us to board the plane. I looked around and made my way through the stuffy room to fight my way through to the boarding gate. I was surrounded by people mostly of ages between twenty and thirty.

Seated on my seat, next to the window, I finally felt calm, as calm as an oyster in its shell at Whitstable <u>bay</u>. Next to me was a tall girl of nineteen, very friendly. We immediately became friends. She had warm brown eyes and hair which was similar to a tail of a pampered poodle.

What do you think of the writing so far? There is an impression that the candidate is confident in the use of English, with keen observational skills (note the effective mention of aftershave in the atmosphere). There are, however, some rather forced comparisons (for example, the oyster and the poodle's tail) and some repetitious expression – 'seated … seat'; 'calm … calm'; 'friendly … friend' – which slow down the account. The mention of the matching cotton jacket is intrusive and unexplained. A suggested improvement, conveying the same relevant information could be:

Seated next to the window, I finally felt relaxed, as calm and protected against the elements as an oyster in its shell. Next to me was a tall, pleasant girl of nineteen. She had warm brown eyes and hair which somehow made me think of the tail of a pampered poodle. In spite of that, we soon started talking and found that we had a great deal in common.

Apart from a few punctuation errors, the writing is quite accurate. The essay continues:

We were in the air. We were served dinner and drinks and most of the passengers fell asleep. I found it much more <u>intresting</u> to talk to my new friend, Cheryl.

After a while, I noticed it was dark and I felt drowsy. The atmosphere was calm. Suddenly a noise started, it was very disturbing and it grew louder as time went by. Finally it set my teeth on edge and was a terrible <u>assult</u> on my cringing eardrums! Silence.

People around me, were obviously disturbed. The noise had stopped leaving my ears little ability to fully comprehend sounds.

The darkly opaque world outside my window showed me nothing but the useless battle my window was fighting with the fierce weather.

> *The lights went out. People panicked – chaos, noise, screaming! My heart did a double somersault and landed with a thud on its back. The plane was in a full nose-dive.*
>
> *It was the end. Goodbye Florida, goodbye parents and goodbye Cheryl.*
>
> *At this point my memory faded away and I remember nothing – except being with my parents. They spoke to me, telling me that I could make it. I remember the doctors and nurses. Most important, I remember surviving.*
>
> *Later I found out that the plane had crashed in the sea and luckily for us had been caught in the rocks. Many had died, many survived. We had been rescued when conditions had improved. We were lucky to be near an island. Cheryl had risked her life for me that night. I can never forget that.*
>
> *The flight had been a fateful flight – for those who were aboard.*

Again, there are some varied images, but the sentence structure becomes abrupt and monotonous. There is also a feeling that the account is curtailed to fit the time remaining in the exam. There are gaps and unanswered questions. We do not learn how Cheryl had risked her life or how others had survived. The sense of immediacy, of credible details established earlier, is lost and the ending is weak. The impression given to the examiners was that this candidate had limited his/her mark by over-reliance on a prepared script. The potential to achieve a higher mark is visible in some fluent passages and a reasonable level of technical accuracy, but the writing seems to lack spontaneity, balance and a real sense of drama, as opposed to melodrama. More emphasis on the developing friendship would add poignancy to the implied loss.

The next example is one that most of us can relate to, although our experiences may have been very different. This concentrates on remembered feelings; for others the first day at school may evoke memories of smells, tastes, tears or other emotions.

| Question 3 |

Write an essay about something from the past which has made a major impact on you, such as an important person, building or event.

An event to remember

> *I remember it as if it were yesterday. I had stayed at home most of my life until now. I did not think I was ready for the harsh society but I had no choice. My mother had already enrolled me in school. Even though everybody kept telling me not to worry, I was still petrified. This would be the first time I would be away from my mother.*
>
> *I was always a quiet child, not too quick to reveal my emotions, but this time it was very different. I brought up many excuses, which seemed to me as very clever ideas, to avoid going to school but my mother knew otherwise. I could never fool my parents: they always read me like a book. I have no idea now why I was so scared then. Maybe at the age of six I thought I would be lost forever.*

As my mother drove up to the immense black gates of what seemed to be my school, I became more scared and nervous than I had ever felt before. At first, I did everything I could to stop my mother taking me out from the car but as time went by I saw more cars come up the driveway and little children, my age at that time, coming out of the car with no worries. I felt very embarrassed as everybody glared at me while they passed by.

After a little more <u>advise</u> given to me by my mother I decided to come out of the car. My bag seemed very heavy to me at the time. Some final words were said to me by my mother which ended with "I love you" and some kisses and I was sent to my class. I found myself in a big room filled with unfamiliar faces all staring at me. At that moment I would have preferred to be swallowed by the ground than stay there. The teacher came to me and asked me to say my name and age, she seemed very nice. Soon I made friends with a lot of the children there and I guess I became a little more independent than before.

At the end of the day when I came out of the school I found my mother waiting for me with a worried expression on her face. She ran towards me and asked how my day had passed. I told her it <u>was</u> great and I started talking for hours on end about my entire day and the people I had met. That day will always remain in my memory as an unforgettable event.

Although this account is told in a fairly simple style, and there is a feeling of events being condensed or glossed over, the writer has good control of retrospective time and tense and the experience is believable to the reader. There are some clichés but most of the writing has a freshness which adds interest. There is also a variety of sentence structure – a personal account in which every sentence starts with 'I' can become monotonous. This writer changes the subjects ('My mother', 'This', 'My bag'); the constructions ('Even though', 'Maybe', 'As', 'At first') and uses the passive ('Some final words were said to me') which all help to change the perspective slightly. There is also a twist in the final paragraph – the mother has the worried expression; the child is now relaxed and happy.

Another type of imaginative response might ask you to put yourself in an unrealistic or unusual position, maybe drawing on and developing information or themes from texts in the exam paper. A title asking for a letter to an alien, a sentient being from another galaxy, requires empathy, understanding of what would be interesting to such a being, as well as an imaginative leap. Here is an extract from such a letter.

Write a letter to an alien from another planet, describing life on Earth.

Dear Alien,

About two days ago I received a letter from you. You asked me if I could give you information about the places of interest and the value about life here on Earth. About the description you gave me of your planet, Mars, I could tell you that planet Earth is too different from your planet. The population on the planet Earth is a million times bigger than your planet, so the relationship between you and the other aliens are more familiar. First of all, to communicate with other persons, outside our country, we have to know many different languages. Languages here on Earth are one of the major problems. Languages were invented because almost every country is independent on this planet. If you are thinking of coming to live on Earth, I could guaranty you a happy and enjoyable life with us.

The human body depends on water and food. We get water from the fresh water rivers, coming down from the mountains. Rain falls down on several countries, according to the angle and rotation of our planet round the sun, at a particular season of the year. Rain is formed from water vapour in the skies. As I told you before, the human body depends a lot on food for chemical energy. Without food the human body will be ill and dies. The inhabitants of this planet get food from animals and plants. Many types of animals are found around us and from prehistoric times man used to hunt for these animals.

The reproduction of life on Earth is one of the major problems, because the population is increasing and the number of food materials are decreasing.

One can find happiness on Earth, but if two countries do not agree on something serious, there will be a chance that war occurs. One of the most cruel deaths on Earth is to be shot by a gun.

I think that life on Earth is very interesting, but I think it is not suitable to live here, because it is too hard to work and get money to survive and after all the human life is too short.

Gordon

In spite of its weaknesses and errors, this does manage to sound thoughtful and convincing, although there is some contradiction between the advice in the first paragraph and the tone of the conclusion.

What would you choose to describe in a letter to a visitor from another part of this or another world? Would your choices reflect your interests or theirs, similarities or differences? Whatever you choose to write about in a description or narrative, remember to plan and structure the material so you do not repeat or contradict yourself. Try to write in an interesting style, using clear, maybe unusual images, and really concentrating on what makes your selected features special – after all, you have chosen them, so try to convey the impact they have had on you.

Personal essays

Some titles which ask for a personal response seem to be wide enough for you to write about almost anything, so it is very interesting for examiners to read a variety of responses. Read the following candidates' scripts and examiner's comments, and think about how you might have tackled the essays.

Write about something which fascinates you.

If there is something I am fascinated about it is food. Not only because the whole world's population depends on it for survival. Eating for me is not only a necessity, but also a pleasure and a source of happiness.

I have a very personal point of view about food. It is something very psychological I would say. When I am very depressed, I eat a lot of chocolate. Just thinking about such a sweet taste melting slowly in your mouth is already a motive for happiness. I don't need any therapist and I have never been on Prozac. I also do not need to go shopping in the most fancy and expensive shop in town to boost my self-esteem in order to feel happier. Doing that, you only escape from the old problem and get another one. The bill. So why not try eating therapy?

Eating therapy is certainly the most <u>economic</u> way to cure your psychological problems. The first thing you have to do is write down all your favorite kind of food. Without hesitating run to buy it all. Then enjoy every bite you take not caring about how many calories it contains. Just let it melt inside your mouth and slowly it will melt your heart too. So open up your heart and mouth to food as if it <u>would be</u> your best friend. To me food is definitely my best friend.

I actually prefer to solve my problems with food's help instead of <u>friend's</u> help. I know food will always keep my secrets, understand me, comfort me, make me happy and never reject me as men sometimes do.

Nobody is perfect and nobody is always 100% happy. Life can be mean sometimes making us face problems and overcome difficulties. However we are all supposed to make the best of it. I try hard to be the best I can, but without food there would be no life. Therefore I am fascinated about food.

This is a lively and unusual response, with some genuine feelings, humour and sadness, a vivid description of the voluptuous sense of savouring mouthfuls and a philosophical note which lifts the content above food as enjoyment. There is some variety of style, with direct address to the reader, a minor sentence, a challenging question, personal and impersonal statements and some effective use of repetition. There are some weaknesses of idiom and syntax, but the writing makes an impact on the reader.

Compare the next essay. This seems to reproduce a learned story, with clichés and some stilted expression, but does include some vivid phrases. Does it strike you as genuine in the same way as the previous essay?

Write an essay entitled 'Facing up to something you feared.'

As all the thoughts and memories created so far drift into my mind, about all of the beautiful incidents and sheer surprises I experienced in each stage of growth, I cannot <u>help to</u> forget one particular incident in which I had faced up to something I feared. I remember very clearly that it was reaching the end of the summer season, and all of us I particularly were waiting with anxiety written across our faces for the first torrential monsoon rains to arrive. It was the twenty-third of September, and that day gave promise of a glorious day.

The first morning rays had just emerged from behind the horizon, and the bright glare of the sun was at its full penetrating our eyes. That morning my parents left home for work as usual and I had stayed home looking after my baby brother, who at that time was only three years old. Everything was going perfectly well, until the sky was submerged with clouds. At about four o'clock in the afternoon, I was brewing <u>up</u> some coffee. All of a sudden rain had started pattering onto the window pane and in a few minutes time it started pouring down in buckets. That afternoon my baby brother fell from his bed and had bumped his head onto a bedroom cabinet. Hearing my brother crying, I left hold of what I was doing and ran errands for him. What I did not know was that I had left the knob of the stove <u>accidently</u> turned on. Due to this, all the kitchen smelt like a gas mine.

When I was upstairs in my brother's bedroom, I <u>dosed</u> off and soon I was <u>to</u> the land of dreams. When I was sleeping, a huge <u>thunder</u> had struck the kitchen window. Due to this, all the room was on fire. My brother and I suddenly woke <u>unexpectedly</u>. The acrid smell of the burning had jolted us <u>up</u>. Soon we <u>had</u> realised that there was fire. When I saw what was happening, my legs <u>rattled</u> on the floor. Great was my horror. I tried to turn off the knob of the stove. But my <u>try</u> was useless. Back home from work, my parents soon realised what was in the wind. While my mother phoned for <u>rescue</u>, my father, cool, calm and collected as ever, dived into the hungry flames and turned off the knob. Brave as lions and dominant as kings, the fire-fighters stopped the fire and rescued us. All is well, that ends well. Thank God my family and I were saved, and we were ever so grateful.

(So far, 420 words, with no reference to the title.)

That night, even though I was worn to a shadow, I could not sleep. That time and still nowadays, I regarded fire as a good servant but also as a bad enemy. The incident allowed me to view my life objectively. The incident in which I had to face up to something I feared, cannot be skimmed of my conscious. It has fed my imagination and has stimulated my inner self. It has also taught me that in such cases, I would face problems like this with great boldness, and to what can occur in life, to take the bull by the horns.

This is a writer who has some confidence and ability, but is limited by apparently reproducing someone else's words, maybe even combining elements of two prepared accounts, about a storm and a fire, which are unconvincing. There is an over-reliance on clichés, ('cool, calm and collected', 'Brave as lions and dominant as kings', 'All is well, that ends well', 'worn to a shadow'), which makes the writing stale. The last paragraph does not ring true. It would have been far better to choose a real, if simple, situation, such as starting school, going for a job interview, or taking a driving test, and develop the dread and the experience as a response to the title. Remember, writing does not have to be melodramatic to be dramatic.

The title 'My view of the future' could be interpreted as a discursive essay or personal account. 'My plans for the future' or 'My ideal career' must be written from the writer's viewpoint. Such essay titles have, however, produced a wide variety of responses, detailed or general, sad or humorous. Some give great insight into the preoccupations and ambitions of the writers, whether they want to help the world, be famous or follow in someone's footsteps. Here are some extracts from such essays, to show some of the variety possible. After reading them, maybe you would like to write your own response?

Question 7

Write an essay about your ideal career.

As a modern world citizen having had all kinds of fun a normal teenager would have and now having to think about an ideal career would be tough. Though it is tough every human being in this world will have a career suited for them, like this I have chosen an ideal career for myself.

My ideal career would be having to work in a big company as a senior accountant. I chose this career because I am living in an Asian country where the cultures and customs are totally different from other European and Western countries. I would like to live a simple life with family and friends.

Working in a company is advantageous because I will have to work only for eight to ten hours. Work would be easy as what I will have to do is just sit in a comfortable air-conditioned room with a computer and prepare the accounts for the company. I don't need to face any difficulties in life as I am receiving a fixed amount of salary and not a penny less.

As I am working for only eight to ten hours I can have more time for leisure, like engaging in sporting activities, social activities, getting around with family and friends and so on. I could live a happy life because I won't need to work in diplorable conditions.

If I would have started a business or something like this I would face the miseries like tention, worries, etc. This is because when doing a business you wouldn't know what will happen next, a business can become bankrupt or something bad might happen like robberies, destruction of the building, etc.

Due to the following reasons I had to choose a career that would suit me so I chose to become an accountant.

It is not clear whether the humour in this essay was intentional. We certainly didn't learn much about being an accountant; the career could have been any well-paid office-based job with a good income and time to relax. There are also errors of spelling and punctuation which affect the style and contradict the confident assertions of the writer.

Compare this with the opening of an essay on 'My plans for the future'.

Just imagine me as a 26 year old! I will be taller. There will also be a great leap in my maturity – from a teenager to an adult.

My job will be standing up in front of a magistrate and a whole court full of people, fighting for people's rights. Being one of the best lawyers I will have to control my telephone calls, telling people "I can't reach the phone right now" or leaving messages with my secretary that I was absent from work. Having a lot of clients makes me keen of my kind of work but I will have to dive into books and files in order to prove that my client is right.

I will have a Mercedez Benz and a BMW parked infront of my house. I will have a pool and a large garden including a lot of plants and beautiful types of cactus from South America and South Africa.

Hopefully I will get married and have a couple of kids. The money that I save from not going out with my friends I'll have to spend on buying gifts for my kids and wife.

This essay also gives little detail of how the money is to be earned to pay for the lifestyle, after an opening which gave promise of more detail on the career. It is lively, however, and the personality of the writer comes through. In fact, the writer acknowledges the tongue-in-cheek approach in the last paragraph, which rounds the essay off well.

Just meet me in ten years time and you will see how I have changed! But I will still remain the same in character and still the joker of the day. So now I must end my portrait of my plans for the future and continue to be a teenager.

The final example of this type of writing is very different. Study it and see what aspects you might want to adapt for your own version.

"Be a lawyer," sounds interesting, were the first thoughts that popped into my mind when I was five years old.

I believe that everybody and everything has some aim in life. We study and educate ourselves in schools and institutions to face the social circle at one point or the other.

Different people opt for different professions and thus go their own ways. Some choose careers for their benefits, then there are others who choose for humanitarian love.

I grew up hearing the word 'lawyer' from the day I was born. My father was a lawyer and so was my grandmother. I guess I was so influenced and inspired by them that this became my choice.

"The duties of a lawyer are immense," I was told and that proved itself. A lawyer means maintaining justice in one's life, and in others. Helping people in need to prove justice is one of the most difficult tasks in the world.

This world is full of corrupted people. Evil manslaughter, robbery, rape, murder are all so common words to us. There are not enough lawyers to fight all of these. At the age of fourteen, when I had to decide in what path I should go in future life, there were no second thoughts. I was totally inspired by my father to become a lawyer and serve the community. I was touched by his deeds to prove justice to innocent victims. I decided to fight for women's rights and rape victims and child labourers.

My school life finished, and what was a dream at one stage was about to become reality. I entered law college. The syllabus for law was vast and the many speeches and debates sometimes gave me second thoughts about giving up. But a lawyer never gives up, not until he is finished with what he wants. Thus I distilled many notes and excelled in debates. The dream of becoming an excellent lawyer, a helper to the needy, being recognised, was all I dreamt, but the truth was yet to come. After my graduation specialising in criminal law, my first case is something that still lingers in my mind.

An innocent seventeen-year-old girl was brutally raped and murdered. I was to put the rapist in jail but I failed. I did not have enough evidence to prove him guilty. Then I realised that it takes hard work, courage and a fearless heart to become a good lawyer. Life became disgusting as I could not prove what was wrong, right. But thereafter, I worked very hard on each case, stayed up nights, skipped meals and this is worth just the smile on the victim's face or the victim's relations once the verdict is given and the accused is punished.

The dream which I had once at the tender age of five has now become a reality. It has been my life for the past several years and will be practically for the rest of my life till I die. Words can't express the <u>fullfillment</u> I feel inside me. I now know that there couldn't have been a better profession for me than being a lawyer. However many obstacles and difficulties I face, from the bottom of my heart I can say that this is my ideal career; I couldn't have asked for more.

This essay has an interesting shape: the twist comes in the detail about the first case, when idealism hits realism. This could of course be based on fiction or observation, but there is a feeling of facing the hard facts rather than the dream which rings true and makes the account credible. There are errors of spelling, syntax and repetition, but the writing is effective and the meaning is conveyed clearly. The sentence and paragraph structures are varied; the account is shaped and relevant, with a general introduction, a personal development and a conclusion. Altogether an appropriate and rewarding response to the topic.

Discursive essays

Look at the following extracts to consider different ways of approaching a discursive essay.

Question 8

Describe the skills needed by an effective teacher or lecturer. Which do you think are the most important?

Teachers are probably the most important people in <u>the</u> society because without them none of us <u>will</u> be educated. There <u>will</u> be no doctors, lawyers, engineers or any kind of workmanship as most of them graduate from university taught by teachers or lecturers.

Many of us do not realise the importance of teachers. Not anyone can be teachers<u>,</u> only selected people with great skills and good personality can be chosen. Being a teacher has no work boundaries or proper work time. To be an ideal teacher, a lot of sacrifices have to be made. Teachers have to commit themselves fully and most of the time they cannot differentiate working time <u>with</u> personal time. Once you have become a teacher it is a 24 hou<u>rs</u> job, seven days a week and 365 days a year.

There are certain skills that a teacher must possess. Most important of all is patience. An ideal teacher must have great patience when teaching a child or children, especially younger children as they are young and need more concentration. Some students might be quite slow in picking up things, so the teachers must have the patience and time to find every means to educate the children and make them understand, one way or another.

Being a teacher, we do not always get good students. Once in a while a problem child will come along. A teacher must be prepared to face any difficulties which <u>comes</u> along the way. The teacher must understand the student's position and problems which might affect their falling grades.

With today's societies, a lot of parents, usually both husband and wife, are working. In these cases the teacher must be the parent as well. A teacher must be hardworking, intelligent, attentive and willing to work even at odd hours or after working time. They must be fully trained and always looking for new materials and aim at different angles to educate students and bring out the best in them.

Teachers are the role models for students. Therefore teachers must always carry themselves in the right way in order to set a good example to their students. Since the students are still growing up in between <u>the</u> childhood and adulthood, it is very easy for them to adopt bad <u>behaviours</u> as well as good.

A teacher must also be fair, always seeking for the best solution <u>in</u> each problem. Since teachers educate the next generation of <u>the</u> society, it is very important that they are conveying the right message in order to determine we have a mature and intelligent group of leaders.

Lastly, teachers are the most dedicated people in <u>the</u> society. Without them, there <u>will</u> be no society. Teaching is one of the most professional jobs around. There will be no progress and no future without educated leaders. Therefore teachers must have important skills and personality to do the job.

Although this essay has some repetition, and could have been improved by clearer planning, it does in the main focus on the question with a range of skills and qualities related to the needs of society. There is some over-reliance on lists, such as 'hardworking, intelligent, attentive and willing to work even at odd hours or after working time.' This could have been used to emphasise the number of qualities needed, but it is oddly placed in a paragraph about family relationships. In a discursive essay there is always a temptation to use lists, but they can make the writing rather flat.

The paragraphing is also inconsistent, again suggesting the need for better organisation of ideas, which tend to follow in a less than logical sequence. There are also inconsistencies in agreement, changing singular and plural forms and pronouns within and between paragraphs. Some of the phrasing is clumsy, but it does communicate reasonably and is relevant throughout. This places it in the top of the adequate band; with greater technical accuracy it would be competent.

The next essay is an example of a good script. Look at how the writer has a sense of audience, with direct address to the reader after a more theoretical and impersonal opening.

Certainly, this is not an easy task. Thus let us first examine the purpose and the aim of a teacher or lecturer. Teachers and lecturers are needed in spreading and passing on knowledge. This knowledge may be based on personal experience, gathered from books or gained in any other way. Anyway, the major purpose of a teacher or lecturer could be described as the replacement of books and other information sources. For the audience, and for most individuals, a human being will be more interesting than a dead particle like a book, for example, whatever the subject or topic being taught. A person will always be more qualified in describing or even answering questions than a written text.

Now, the problems a teacher or lecturer might be faced with in class or in front of a huge audience are various and not easy. He or she has to take care that all listeners are kept happy, e.g. they must not be or feel offended; e.g. the audience must be kept willing and able to continue listening and the standard or the level of the speech has to be appropriate. If somebody cannot understand you, because the choice of your words or expressions is too simple or, worse, far too demanding, this person will not enjoy listening and paying attention to what you say, as it will inevitably become too boring or tiring. To overcome these problems a concerned teacher or lecturer has got to possess many skills. He or she should have a certain sense and a feeling for the thoughts and opinions of the audience. Never let the topic or even the subject appear boring; try to captivate and fascinate, if possible, every single member of the audience. Anticipate how your listeners might find your opinion before you present it. Imagine yourself in place of one of them: how would you like to be addressed, be talked to, be entertained, because in the end, that is what you are really doing. Sure, the aim is to pass on as much knowledge and information as possible, but if the speech is witty and the lecturing fascinating, the response of the audience will be greater and participation will be the reward.

One visible contrast between these two essays is the length of the paragraphs. The second essay could have benefited from splitting the second paragraph, but the ideas are developed, they flow and the content is cohesive. The first essay is rather jerky, with a large number of short paragraphs which could be extended or linked to make the writing flow more smoothly. The second essay goes straight into the topic, without an introduction: this catches our attention but could be seen as rather abrupt. The candidate has plenty of ideas and does not need to reiterate the title, which can prove rather monotonous in weaker essays.

Response to a picture

We end this chapter with a response to the photograph entitled 'Hands at the window.' This produced an enormous range of writing, covering topics such as street children and orphans, the experiences of being a film, pop or sports star, a politician or a tourist and a few from the perspective of the children themselves. *A picture such as this would not appear in isolation in the new syllabus, so the context would be more clearly defined.*

This essay is felt to be an excellent example of writing in examination conditions. We hope you enjoy reading it.

Question 9

Write an essay in response to the following picture.

"Cin-Jun! Cin-Jun!"

All the voices of the village were shouting this name. From the sky, if a bird had been passing over this usually quiet little village, he would have seen an agitated crowd shouting around an enormous and modern black car, which was trying to reach the dusty road with difficulty. All the way behind and ahead, and also on the sides of the car, were excited, euphoric children and young people shouting that name, hitting the windows with their hands, squeezing their faces against it.

"What is going on?"

This was exactly what Cin-Jun was wondering. He couldn't hear what they were saying: the windows of his car were protecting him from occasional bullets – and also from noise. He could only see the smiley faces and the hands against the car. The silence, inside of the car, seemed unreal, compared to the agitation outside.

"What are they saying?" Cin-Jun asked the driver.

"They're shouting your name, master," he answered.

"So that's it," Cin-Jun thought. It was his name that they were shouting. It was him that they were expecting. He could already see them, kissing his hands and feet, touching his clothes with admiration, serving him like a king, defending him with a fierce adoration.

In fact, he could already feel his shame in front of those humble, innocent children for whom he had been an example for years.

"If they knew ... If they knew what I've become," he thought.

When he had left the village ten years ago, he was a child, just like the rest of them. He had left to America, and they all hoped he would come back with money. He WAS coming with money: his pockets were full, full of money, he had become richer than the whole village.

But what they didn't know and what he was also bringing back was the blood on his hands, the blood of dozens of innocents he had had to kill at the beginning, forced by the mafia's chiefs. He was bringing back money from corruption, drugs and murder. And during those years he had only written one letter, telling them he was a successful businessman.

"I'm not worth the half of one of the children there," he thought.

And as the crowd was calming down, ready to let him come out of the car, as the way ahead was finally free, Cin-Jun said to the driver:

"Paul, I want you to leave this place now."

"But, master ..."

"Now."

The driver pressed the pedal with his feet and the car rushed towards the dusty road, far away from the little village, which fell into desperation.

Cin-Jun had understood that the window would separate him from those hands forever.

Writing creatively in a range of styles

This essay is a very imaginative response which is impressive in its narrative variety, crisp dialogue, with limited verbs to speed up the action, appropriately used minor sentences and the twist. The use of the image of the bird as an observer is a clever device to focus on the scene. The multiple adjectives and echoing present participles in the first paragraph of narrative increase the sense of anticipation. The ending is particularly effective in its spare and factual account, leaving the emotions to be sensed, rather than over-dramatised. This candidate shows not only a control and command of English, but an ability to pace a narrative; the understatement reveals a feeling for plot and character which stays with the reader. In all, it is a sophisticated piece of writing, in spite of some errors.

We hope that this chapter has given you confidence in your ability to tackle essays in a variety of different styles. Just to pull all the strands together and to give you even more confidence, in the next chapter we will consider how to write accurately in standard English, looking at common problems with grammar and spelling.

7 Writing accurately in standard English

Standard and non-standard English

At the present time about eight hundred million people worldwide have some knowledge of English. It has status as a universal language. In this context, 'English' could be very widely defined. Countries where English is the national language, such as the United Kingdom, United States of America, Canada and Australia each have their own slightly different varieties. Similarly, countries where English is the language of commerce, of instruction in schools, and occasionally of government, have it as a 'lingua franca' (language shared by all for certain purposes) while also preserving their own languages and dialects. These countries also have their own varieties of English, now called 'New Englishes'. All these English varieties have their value and are appropriate in context.

For the purposes of GCE examinations, standard British English will be most relevant. It may be used with different degrees of formality or informality, but essentially it is the variety that is used for official communication in the United Kingdom, and in many other countries.

Standard English has a fixed word order – SVO (subject–verb–object) or SVC (subject–verb–complement). When it is written formally these patterns are the norm and they appear as five basic sentence structures:

subject + verb

Ella dances.

subject + verb + object

Ella loves parties.

subject + verb + indirect object + direct object

Ella gives her guests refreshments.

subject + linking verb + subject complement

Ella is a pleasure-seeker.

subject + verb + direct object + object complement

Ella calls her guests her friends.

Now we can put all five patterns together to form a short paragraph.

Ella is a pleasure-seeker and she loves parties. She dances and sings. She orders good food and gives her guests refreshments. She calls all her guests her friends.

This is correct, but very basic. It can be built up into quite an interesting and sophisticated short paragraph, though.

Ella is a pleasure-seeker! She loves parties. Walking around on tiny strap sandals, not quite able to balance herself, she looks elegant and amusing. Her eyes are dark and flashing. The long lashes look like spider legs stuck on her eyelids. She dances; she sings. She orders luscious refreshments for everyone to enjoy, handing them to her guests. Ella calls all her guests her friends. She talks earnestly to them. She likes to give the impression that she is very intellectual. She stands there talking, smiling, doing what she loves best – seeking pleasure for others.

This still has a simple structure – all the sentences are on the basic pattern and all five patterns are here. Notice the introduction of a few well-observed details, for example the 'tiny strap sandals' and the fact that she is 'not quite able to balance herself.' Notice, too, the one entertaining image: her 'long lashes look like spider legs' which is a **simile** or comparison which makes you smile. It also sounds attractive because of the **alliteration** (here the repetition of the letter 'l'). The cleverest idea here, though, is the way that the paragraph turns around your impression of Ella. At first you think she is only concerned with enjoying herself. By repeating the first sentence in the final phrase, but with a slight variation, the writer shows that you were wrong. So you see that you can write very simply, with short, basic sentences, and still write well.

Your turn

Now try writing a paragraph of your own, including the five basic word order patterns above.

Here is another paragraph about a lovely and intellectual girl, which is written in quite a different way.

Girl with knotted hair of lightning bolts, skin sweetened by frankincense, trying to centre my power on lips painted raspberry brown. A well-established mind, different points in a galaxy, making me wonder as I move in circles like the moon seeing different sections of the earth. Keeps me in the dark, grasping at new understanding where A is for Ah!, B for Black Magic. To be plain and simple ... like you a lot, a lot, a lot times seven minus zero.

It is vivid. You may grasp at the meaning – the images are very rich and evocative. None of these sentences is standard, though. This writing has more in common with poetry. Most of us experiment with using language sketchily to convey thought and feeling as in this example, sometimes with very attractive results, but it is not appropriate to write in this non-standard style in the examination.

Minor sentences

Another form of non-standard English is writing in minor sentences or fragments. These have no place in formal writing. Here are some examples of minor sentences which are misused. Each is only a part of a sentence. A minor sentence may omit the subject, the predicate, or it may omit both.

These minor sentences lack a subject:

Always looked for pleasure.
Acts without thinking of others.

These minor sentences lack a predicate:

Pleasure-seekers pure and simple.
The party-loving person.

These minor sentences lack a subject and a predicate:

On Friday night at nine.
With a radiant smile.

There are places in your examination paper where you may find it appropriate to use minor sentences. Occasionally, you will use them when you are writing speech.

"What would you like to eat? Would you like sweet or savoury biscuits?" she asked, smiling.
"Savoury, please," I replied. (minor sentence)

To reply "I would like savoury rather than sweet biscuits, please" would be very formal, even pompous, and quite unsuitable for chat at a party. You would be 'talking like a book' (as the saying goes).

Alternatively, you may wish to express someone's train of thought.

> *When I arrived, a man came straight up to me. I thought I half recognised him. What was his name? ... Hars ... yes ... something like that ... Harsha Ranjeera.*

Here the writer has made it quite plain, both explicitly (using 'I thought') and by punctuation (the **ellipsis** shows that words are deliberately left out) that what is being conveyed is someone puzzling over something. The minor sentences are correctly used.

A range of sentence structures

Standard English has a range of sentence structures. So far we have looked at several word order patterns in one type of sentence only. This structure is known as a simple sentence. This has only one subject and one predicate. It is a **main clause**.

> *The party starts at ten.*

Here are the other basic structures.

Compound sentences

A compound sentence has the main subject and predicate and another added on as a co-ordinate clause. These co-ordinate clauses are introduced by 'and', 'but', 'for', 'yet', 'so', 'or', 'nor', as well as by some pairs 'both ... and ...', 'either ... or ...', 'neither ... nor ...', 'not only ... but also ...'.

> *The party starts at ten **and** it will be in Paceville.*
> *The party starts at ten **but** dancing will be later.*
> *We could **either** go to the party **or** stay at home watching TV.*

Complex sentences

A complex sentence has one main clause and at least one subordinate clause. These are introduced by such words as 'after', 'although', 'as', 'because', 'before', 'how', 'if', 'once', 'since', 'then', 'though', 'unless'; and also by phrases: 'even though', 'in case', 'no matter how', 'now that'. A group of relative terms also introduce subordinate clauses: 'that', 'what', 'which', 'who', 'whoever', 'whom', 'when', 'whenever', 'whose'.

> *The party starts at ten **because** people can't come earlier.*
> *The party starts at ten, **although** that seems rather late.*
> *The party **that** I told you about starts at ten.*

Compound–complex

A compound–complex sentence has a main clause, a co-ordinate clause and at least one subordinate clause.

> *The party is in Paceville **and** it starts at ten, **unless** the arrangements have been changed.*
> *The party starts at ten **and** it should be very good **because** Ella is hosting it.*

Sentence types

There are four main purposes for sentences.

- statements/declaratives

  I will come to the party

- commands/orders/imperatives

  Come to the party. (without a subject)
  Come to the party, Ella. (with a subject)
  Come to the party, everyone. (with a general subject)

- questions/interrogatives

  Are you coming to the party? (positive question)
  Aren't you coming to the party? (negative question)
  What time is the party? (information-seeking question)
  Is it at nine or ten? (alternative question)
  It is at ten, isn't it? (tag question)

- exclamations

  It was a great party!

Here are some examples of how students have used each type of sentence in writing really effectively. Each has written about a sporting action.

Simple sentences in composition

- Roller-blading

  I enthusiastically buckle on my roller-blades. I hook my Walkman onto the loop of my jeans. I tune it to 104.8 Fm. They are playing the top 40 Countdown. I start pacing myself to the rhythm. I zigzag down the path, zooming past the ice-cream truck. The people's faces pass by in a blur, like flashes of colour at the corners of my eyes. The shrieks of the children, the cries of the hot-dog vendor, the calls of the birds are all mingled in the background with the music in my ear. I feel vibrant. I feel reckless.

Compound sentences in composition

- Football

  I emerged from the tunnel and found the lights blinding and the noise from the crowd deafening. With a blast on his whistle, the referee signalled the start of the second half of the game. Within a few seconds, my muscles were relaxed and mind focused on the game. Shortly afterwards, the ball was there and with a few expert touches I passed it on. Now someone else had his turn to work his magic. I could see the determination on his face. Support from the crowd urged him on and, with a few deft touches, the ball moved along, but a bone-crunching tackle came from nowhere.

Complex sentences in composition

- High dive

    All was quiet as the diver removed the towel, then started walking to the diving board. She had the waiting crowd's attention. Slowly, she climbed the spiral stair, tread by tread, continuing until she was ten metres above the pool. When she arrived at the top, she stood still, listening carefully. She could not hear a sound. She paced to the front edge of the board, then, standing poised as she pressed downwards with all her strength, she lifted her arms, launching upward and forward. Splash!

Compound–complex sentences in composition

- The Japanese wrestler

    When he enters the ring, the enormous wrestler first claps to attract the gods' attention and to indicate his own purity of heart. Having done that, he shakes his apron to drive away evil spirits, then raises his arms to show he carries no weapons and means to play fair.

Your turn

Try writing four paragraphs, each using predominantly one of these types of sentence.

Choosing the right words

Using words appropriately is the essence of good writing. Sometimes in the examination students think that good writing requires many important-sounding words, complex in structure or Latinate in origin. Examiners recognise sympathetically that the candidates are trying to show their vocabulary, trying to impress, but they call this style over-writing, that is, you are drawing attention to the words themselves rather than to the ideas behind them. You are also trying the patience of your reader by making them struggle through a mass of verbiage to get at your meaning. It is not a good idea to try the patience of the examiner! Look at this sentence:

> *The concretisation of the project is our primary objective before we address the issue of promulgation of our concepts to a wider forum.*

This would be better expressed as follows:

> *We need to plan the project clearly before it is made public.*

Avoid polysyllabic words. If there is a simple term which will express your meaning just as well, choose it.

The extreme opposite in style would be very casual vocabulary:

> *You guys had better wise up and firm up what we have going for us before we take it to Joe Public.*

Vocabulary and phrasing: things to avoid

Ambiguity

Here your message has more than one meaning. Sometimes you can use this very effectively if it is deliberate:

> *Turning on the pursuing policeman, the gang leader shouted to the youth with the gun,* **"Let him have it, Chris!"**

This can mean either 'Give the gun to the policeman, Chris' or 'Shoot the policeman, Chris.' A celebrated legal defence turned on the meaning of this sentence.

More often, the writer is unaware of the confusion created in the reader's mind:

> *After changes had been made to the document, the chairman was asked to **resign**.*

This would have been clear if a hyphen had been inserted: 're-sign'.

Clichés

These are over-used metaphors which have consequently lost their impact on the reader.

> *My heart skipped a beat, butterflies swarmed in my stomach and a shiver careered down my spine when I heard the news.*

> *A crowd of people gathered like a pack of agitated birds. Curiosity was working overtime and adrenalin was pumping when, with my heart in my mouth it sank to my boots as I yelled, "We haven't a hope in Hell!"*

Here the one good image – that of the agitated birds – is forgotten in the banality of the rest.

Mixed metaphors

Here ideas are drawn from too wide a range of materials. The images collide in the mind of the reader, leaving only confusion, and sometimes causing laughter.

> *I'd bitten off more than I could chew. It was hard cheese but, on my return, my family killed the fatted calf. People say you can't have your cake and eat it, but I proved them wrong.*

> *We must take steps to stamp out football hooliganism before it overwhelms us like a cataract or a hurricane of violence, swamping our civilised values in a heap of broken dreams and shattered expectations.*

There is something particularly inappropriate in referring to 'stamping out' hooliganism, that is, the remedy seems as violent as the problem to be solved.

Ornate or 'flowery' style

Here the candidate is over-writing, straining for effect and to show off vocabulary, but the result is lack of clarity.

> *When I visited, I was eager to begin splitting hairs of mere cutaneous profundity with them. With much candour, I voiced my anxiety, which was a prerequisite to work towards a subjective goal. I found them faint yet quite distinguishable oxymorons of themselves.*

The examiners spent quite a while trying to work this out. What do you think this ornate language means?

Redundant phrasing

If you use redundant phrasing, you are saying the same thing over and over again.

> *The **tardily presented** project was **not on time** and was **too late** to be accepted.*

Wordiness

Here you are taking too many words to say something that could be more simply expressed.

> *Chess is a board game in which two players pit their wits against one another until the cleverer wins, whereas bridge is a card game which requires good luck, no matter how much the players know.*

This would be better expressed more simply. Wordiness can be eliminated with a tighter sentence structure:

> *Chess is a game of skill, bridge of chance.*

Vocabulary and phrasing: getting it right

To write well you should try to use words which express your thoughts and feelings exactly, drawing on your own vocabulary, so that it appears like your own natural style of expression. Of course, you can always increase your vocabulary through reading, but do not strain for grand effects when writing. Try to keep the following points in mind.

Precise denotation: nouns

Precise denotation is the exact meaning of a word – what you would find if you looked it up in a dictionary. For example, 'youth' means the period between childhood and maturity.

Consider the following extract from a piece of writing on Lebanese cuisine.

> *Appetizers include Hommos, which is made of chick peas. Hommos Bel Lahme is hommos topped with spiced ground meat, pine nuts and almonds, sprinkled with olive oil; Kibbeh, that is ground beef and crushed wheat shells, stuffed with lamb, beef, pine nuts and almonds; Sambosek, which is a dish of light pastry, stuffed with spiced meat, almonds and pine nuts. Makenek is home-made spiced beef and lamb sausages, sautéed in lemon butter; Sojok is*

beef and lamb sausages served with spicy tomato sauce, and of course Kibbeh, which is Lebanese steak tartar - fresh, raw lamb mixed with crushed wheat, herbs and spices, served with an assortment of pickled vegetables, olive oil and garlic paste on the side. Then there are also hommos with pine nuts, hommos with simmered fava beans flavoured with garlic and lemon, baked eggplant pureed with tahini, vegetable patties made from chick peas, fava beans, onions, garlic and spices, roasted eggplant mixed with garlic, lemon and olive oil, eggplant and chickpeas baked with tomatoes, onions and garlic, creamy dip made from strained yoghurt topped with a dash of olive oil, grape leaves rolled with rice, chick peas, tomatoes, mint and parsley, and poached halloum cheese served with tomatoes and olives.

I don't think I could ever get tired of the dishes that are served in Lebanese restaurants, since in order to try everything that is offered on the menu, I would probably have to eat Lebanese food almost every single day.

Your turn

Try writing a paragraph of your own which is noun-based, on one of the following topics:

- a safari
- your room
- a spice market
- your hobby
- a department store
- a car rally.

Precise denotation: adjectives

The second example, about Van Gogh's painting *Sunflowers*, uses adjectives with great precision.

In Van Gogh's painting called Sunflowers, one immediately notices a thin blue line that separates the dark yellow table from the pale yellow wall. Yellow, to Van Gogh, represented the sun, so when he was painting Sunflowers he mostly used different tones of yellow, with a bit of blue and green. There are fifteen sunflowers in the vase; however, each of them has its own shape, shade, and size. Some of the flowers look fresh and ready to burst with life and vitality; for these, Van Gogh used dark yellow, ochre paint. A couple of the sunflowers are losing their petals, and look dead, even though their tendrils still have their dark green colour. The painter needed paler shades of yellow in order to express their end. The rest of the flowers appear to be in a constant motion: these animate the entire bouquet, making it look real, as if you are seeing an actual vase with a bunch of flowers in it, and not a painting. The top of the vase is bright yellow, which is painted against the pale, lemony wall, whereas the vase's base is a paler shade of yellow, which stands out, for it is painted against the dark golden table-top.

Writing accurately in standard English

Your turn

Try to write a paragraph, using adjectives precisely, about something in nature which you have carefully observed.

Precise connotation

The **connotation** of a word is what it suggests or implies. This time 'youth' suggests happiness, energy, beauty, hope, a bright future, idealism, Springtime, and so on. Context helps to limit the range of connotation, for instance, a youth club is a place where young people enjoy sport, entertainment and get together to chat and dance. Compare with a youth hostel – a spartan place for walkers which suggests different things. Association with the first might bring to mind fun, laughter, friendship, pleasure, exercise; the associations with the second are more likely to bring to mind meals, rest, work, packing, comradeship.

This piece of writing is rich in connotation which we can all share, though possibly our personal associations might differ a little.

> ### Composition with Grey, Black, Red, Yellow and Blue
>
> *Mixtures of colours show a perfect harmony and balance; in their own way they complement each other. Grey, black, yellow, blue and red – all of these colours are not used together very often.*
>
> *I see this painting as a representation of life: each square, each colour has its own significance.*
>
> *Grey is our everyday colour, when nothing exciting is happening; red is for passion, blue is loneliness, black for tragedy, yellow is warmth and happiness.*
>
> *All the colours are mixed, just as the events in our lives are. It is like a game where you stand on one square and you have to choose in which direction to take your next step.*
>
> *This painting could be called The Game of Life.*

Your turn

Choose a picture that you like and write a paragraph, using words with strong connotation to bring out its theme and mood.

Imagery

Most candidates who use imagery in the examination do so in the form of similes (a comparison introduced by 'like' or 'as'):

*The welcome was **like a warm rug wrapped around me**.*

*She smiled suddenly, and it seemed **as if the sun had lit up a stormy sky**.*

or as metaphors (a direct comparison without 'like' or 'as'):

> The **wrap-around welcome** warmed my heart.
> Give me **the sunshine of your smile**.

Sometimes an extended image continues throughout a paragraph.

> The pouncing fire leaps on its prey like an angry lion. It slowly slinks on its paws and then, with a gigantic leap, falls like a shower of sparks on its kill, its jaws thrust open wide. With a long sigh it is gone, sliding among the jungle trees and then, with a sudden spurt of anger, it sidles around a trunk again and quivers into life, as it rears up high and destroys.

Occasionally, the image continues throughout the whole piece of writing (an extended metaphor). When this happens it often takes a simple narrative form and is seen to be a correlative (or equal in meaning or value) for a more complex idea. Such a parallel image, often told as a parable or fable, can take on particular or deep significance for the reader).

Why the sky is so high

> A certain man, living in a small town with his mother, was very much blessed by the Lord of creation. He was happy and rich, and his mother was happy. They lived contentedly together.
>
> Now one day, this man decided to find himself a wife. He and his mother looked all around the whole town and surrounding districts, and at last they found a young and very pretty girl for him to marry.
>
> The young wife came to live with him in the house, but unfortunately she did not turn out to be a very good wife. She did not respect her mother-in-law. In fact, she did not seem to respect anybody at all, even her husband. She would never do what her mother-in-law asked her to do and sometimes, even when the mother-in-law was speaking, she would laugh out loud and mock the older woman.
>
> This wife got worse and worse and could get along with no one. Very often when all the women were together and cooking the day's meal in the kitchen this young wife would take her coal pot, and her cooking utensils and her food and move outside on her own and start cooking there. The mother-in-law tried to reason with her and pleaded with her to be civil and sociable.
>
> She told the young wife, "You must not cook outside; it is simply not done. We have always cooked inside the kitchen, and that is the way cooking is meant to be done." But this young and pretty girl would not listen. She just went right on cooking outside.
>
> Now, in those days, the Lord of creation lived in the sky and the sky was much closer to the earth. In fact, the sky was just about the roof of the kitchen. A very tall man could almost touch it, in fact. The Lord of creation, who sees everything, used to like to watch the women cooking, and He smiled upon them. But when the young wife started cooking and pounding her fufu* she raised her pestle higher than the roof of the kitchen, and her elbow hit Him right on the chin. So He frowned. Then the young woman pounded again, and hit Him a second time, now on the cheek bone, so He frowned and got angry. Then the girl pounded a third time and hit Him with the pestle in the eye. Now He became so

angry that he pulled Himself far, far up and away from the vain, selfish and stubborn girl. He took the sky with him, too. He was so far away now that He could never be seen again by his people. And that is why the sky is so far away.

*fufu – one of the staple foods of Ghana, made from cooked plantain and cassava, pounded together in a mortar with a pestle.

Your turn

Try a short paragraph of your own, using an extended image. Here are some suggested topics:

- drought
- torrential rain
- tornado (twister)
- earthquake
- ocean
- pain
- laughter.

Originality of expression

Finally, use expressions that are original, inventive, have a fresh impact on your reader, if you can. For example:

***Inaction** speaks louder than words.*

*If a thing is worth doing, it's worth doing **badly**.*

*She went through every passion from A to **B**.*

*A problem shared is a problem **doubled**.*

They make you stop and think, don't they?

Some problems of grammar

As this is a book about how to improve your performance in an exam, rather than a grammar textbook, let's look at some of the common errors which candidates make in exams, so you can try to avoid them in your writing. The types of mistakes you make may vary depending on what other languages you speak, whether you use English at home or every day at school or work, and how carefully you check your work. All of us make mistakes when writing under pressure of time, even examiners! Some errors, however, are more avoidable than others, so here are some to watch out for in your work.

Verb tenses

Using the wrong tense, or wrong sequence of tenses, may lead to confusion for the reader. Languages have varying tense or time structures; English has various ways of expressing the present, future and past.

The most common error in students' writing is to start writing in one tense and to change to another for no apparent reason. Of course, you can consciously change tenses within a piece of work, in speech, when directly addressing a reader, for flashbacks or to bring an account up-to-date, with a present conclusion or a future possibility. These changes would be deliberate and have a purpose. Confusion arises, however, when candidates, especially in narrative or discursive essays, jump about between the past and the present.

Read the following extract from an exam essay to see such confusion.

> Every village _had_ a person who looked after the people like a leader. But this village _had_ no leader. Their leader _was_ a statue who they _believed is_ everything for them. There _is_ always water coming out of the mouth of the statue and it never _finishes_. The statues _seemed_ so natural as if they _have_ human spirits inside them.

We can understand the possibility that the account is set in the past and the statue might still exist, but the verb changes halt the flow of the story.

Science fiction, which is often set in the future, creates special problems with tenses. This story was progressing quite well, but the writer developed some thoughts and was unable to control the tense structures needed.

> The world was undergoing changes. Everyone was fighting for power and almost every country wanted supremacy. People with a huge machine threatened my party. We struck its leg with a missile, so the machine couldn't balance itself, but, once we (had) fired the first missile, it destroyed the huge truck we had. Then an idea struck me. If that machine _is_ able to aim at huge objects, that implies that it _has_ vision.

By contrast, read the introduction and conclusion from a piece on Genghis Khan, which uses a variety of tense structures appropriately and with control.

> I have always been captivated by the life and deeds of Genghis Khan, the Mongol ruler who conquered most of Asia. His story has the feeling of an epic fairy tale, yet it is real. The legacy left by the ancient Mongol Empire can still be felt in most of Asia.
>
> One of the things which fascinates me most about Genghis Khan is the casual way he carried out his campaigns. Back then, weapons of mass destruction did not exist, and warfare depended much more on cunning and tactics than it does today. Commanders of his calibre were, and still are, few. He shared every hardship with his troops; they were devoted to him.
>
> Perhaps the most important lesson learned from his, and other large empires preceding and following his, is that virtually everything is temporary, and no matter what it is, it will eventually decline and disappear.

If you are unsure about changing tenses, the best advice is to be consistent, but certain structures, such as 'used to', become very monotonous, so even if you are writing an account in the past, try to vary your range of past tenses.

Agreement

The other main confusion with verbs is their agreement with singular or plural subjects. When the structure is subject + verb + object/complement, it is quite easy to identify such errors:

> The _roads_ in Colombo _was_ very narrow and _was_ heavily congested with traffic.
>
> If _someone ask_ me what do I want to be in future ...
>
> I _am_ a _taxonomists_.

Other structures may be more confusing:

> _Challenges? Is_ this what keeps the human mind awake?
>
> _Various types of abuse_ – physical, mental and sexual – _are_ what mainly _surrounds_ many women and children today.
>
> I still think I want to be a fireman as my life is insignificant to the number of lives _I saves_ in the line of duty.

Your turn

Read the following piece and identify the mistakes of agreement, then rewrite it. Remember, there may be more than one accurate version.

> During the cast meeting we were given the script and the character which every actor had to be. The rehearsals took about three month and finally the performance day had arrived. All the members of the cast was nervous and excited. This was our first experiences on the stage for most of us. Finally the play started and each actor were performing well. It was a real success for all the members of the cast.
> I am sure that in the next years I will not hesitate to accept the invitations to take part.

Singular/plural forms

Singular and plural forms can be confusing in other ways. Is 'money' singular or plural? Coins or notes are plural, but 'money' is singular, so 'There's few money for research' is wrong, but 'There are too few dollars' is right. Whether you can count something as individual items is also important in grammar. 'The beach is less sandy than last summer; there are fewer grains of sand.' This is like the distinction between amount and number. The amount of sand has reduced; the number of grains (if we could count them) is smaller.

There are some words which remain the same in English whether they represent one or more – 'sheep', 'fish' ('fishes' is old-fashioned), 'deer', 'cod', for example. Others, such as 'physics' (and 'mathematics'), the names of some diseases, such as 'mumps', and games, such as 'billiards', are used only as singular. Others are always plural, especially those we think of as 'two-part' items, such as 'scissors', 'jeans' and 'binoculars', but to form a singular we say 'pair of'. We could write 'My jeans are in the wash' or 'That pair of jeans has shrunk.'

Misrelated participles

Other errors often commented on by examiners can sometimes be unintentionally funny. They include the misrelated participle. A misrelated participle leads to confusion about the subject of a clause, especially when it is omitted or assumed. For example:

Walking along the cliff-top, the flowers looked beautiful.

After boiling it, the baby should be given the clean bottle when it has cooled down.

Over-use of pronouns can lead to similar confusion.

Articles

Your turn

To what does each 'it' refer in the previous example?

Articles can also cause confusion, either when used to excess or omitted. Remember that in English, as well as the definite and indefinite articles, there is also the zero article, as in 'go to bed', 'in winter', 'come to supper', 'I caught chickenpox.' We can say, 'I have plans' or, 'I have a plan' or, 'The plan won't work', depending on our meaning.

Task 1

The following introduction to an essay on 'My ideal career' shows several errors in the use of articles. How many can you find?

If someone asks me what do I want to be in future, I take ten minutes to think about it. Even though it is the one of the common question I receive as high schooler I don't have well prepared answer. I have great future plan. Most of the times I find myself comfortable writing the diary every night. Even though I'm not very active person I wanted to experience some other kind of the world. I do not hope to be a finest writer but I want to be the writer who is always on reader's side.

There are eleven places in this paragraph where articles are used wrongly (and some other errors too), which interfere with the reader's understanding and enjoyment of the writing.

Prepositions

Read the following extract from an essay entitled, 'My ideal career'. The writer has some excellent ideas and a confident style, but the use of prepositions is often faulty, which affects the fluency and impact of the writing.

Women of all ages suffer through many disastrous tortures but at many a times nothing is done to prevent their tortures. People in the community we live today tend to ignore and close their ears upon to many of these happenings. The cries for help by these unfortunate souls are often left unheard.

Compare this with the following version, only slightly altered.

Women of all ages suffer many disastrous tortures, but many times nothing is done to prevent this torture. People in the community in which we live today tend to ignore these happenings and close their ears to many of them. The cries for help from many of these unfortunate souls are often left unheard.

Faulty prepositional structures may reflect translating from other languages which you speak, so affect the reader's overall impression of your ability to think and write in English.

Your turn

Find the faulty prepositions in the next extract. Can you change six prepositions to make the paragraph more accurate?

These two people are both in my class of school but they are very different from each other. When I talk at Joseph I feel free. To him I talk around my girlfriend, homework, activities and all my life. When I need help in homework, he is always able to help me. When Peter needs help he always comes after me and if I don't help to him he does not leave me behind.

Faulty idioms and 'borrowings'

These also remind the reader that you may be translating from another language. Compare the following:

They emplaned back home. / They boarded the flight home.

as many informations as possible / as much information as possible

She unpacked her bagages. / She unpacked her luggage.

The abbitants of this planet ... / The inhabitants of this planet ...

On reaching the sixteen years of age ... / On reaching sixteen (years of age)

the next plate / the next course

The last one was used in a comedy series, when a request to 'bring a plate' to a supper party was interpreted as an item of crockery, rather than something to eat!

Comparative/superlative forms

The comparative is used when two adjectives or adverbs are being compared; the superlative for three or more. Avoid doubling up on these – 'the most loudest music' or 'a more cleverer student' say the same thing twice. In regular structures you need, 'more' or -er, 'most' or -est, but not both. Try to learn the irregular forms of adjectives and adverbs, such as 'bad, worse, worst' and 'well, better, best'. Longer adjectives, of three or more syllables, often use 'more' or 'most' for their comparisons, as in 'more/most musical' or 'less/least reliable'. Confident use of these structures will improve your written style.

Some problems of spelling

Most of us make occasional spelling errors, and examiners understand that. An essay can receive full marks even if there are some errors, especially if they are in adventurous or unusual words. You will definitely lose marks, however, if you make mistakes in common words or mistakes which make it difficult to understand what you are writing. We will look at some of the common types of spelling error so you can try hard to avoid them.

Mistakes in copying words from the text or questions can and should be avoided, as they are a sign of carelessness. Recent examples include 'heater' for 'heather' and 'heard' for 'heart'.

Homophones

Words which sound the same but have different spellings and meanings are amongst the most common errors which will be penalised in Sections B and C. It is fun in an end-of-term quiz to see how many pairs, triples and even foursomes you can find in English, but in an exam you must make sure you distinguish between them. By being clear about meaning you can avoid common ones such as 'wear'/'where'; 'there'/'their'/'they're'; 'new'/'knew'; 'you'/'ewe'/'yew'; 'taught'/'taut'; and 'one'/'won'. However, there are others such as 'cue'/'queue' or 'I'll'/'isle'/'aisle' which may need more thought. Although there is a use for such errors in jokes or puns, choosing the wrong word in a formal situation can make your writing unintentionally amusing. Here are some other similar words which sometimes confuse students, with explanations.

• Past/passed

'Past' is about time, but can also mean 'on' or 'onwards'; 'passed' is an action, what someone did.

He hurried past the school gates, anxious to find out whether he had passed his exam.

• Lose/loose

'Why did I have to lose my penknife?' he thought as he tried to loose the ties that bound his friend.

- Dye/die

'Dye' means to change the colour of something; 'die' means to cease to live – an important distinction.

> *When she phoned the salon to make an appointment to have her hair dyed, she was horrified to learn that her hairdresser had died the week before.*

- Probably/properly

> *If you check your work properly, it will probably have few errors.*

- Course/cause

> *You are studying an English course book; the cause of your confusion is that two words sound similar.*

Of course, there are many more examples – you need to identify the ones you tend to confuse and work on them, so you understand the distinctions and can use the correct one with confidence.

There are rules which may help you to learn, for instance, the spellings which represent different sounds in plurals or the difference between verb and noun forms. Listening to the correct pronunciation can often help the correct spelling to stick in your mind.

-ise/-ice endings

There are some words in British English, such as 'practise'/'practice', which sound the same but alter their spelling when they are used as verbs or nouns or adjectives. There are two ways to remember which to use. You could tell yourself that the noun form has 'ice' in it; and think of words with a similar structure which have varying pronunciation, such as 'devise'/'device'; 'advise'/'advice'.

> *I went to an advice centre to ask for advice about my noisy neighbour. I was advised to ask her to turn the volume down when she was practising on the keyboard after 11 pm. In practice, I'm not sure whether this will help.*

The same rule of 's' for the verb and 'c' for the noun also applies to pairs such as 'license'/'licence' and 'prophesy'/'prophecy'.

Tips to help your spellings

Some spellings cause problems for even the most fluent writers – we all have words which make us stop and think! As you can't use a dictionary to check in an exam, it may be helpful to have some of your own ways of remembering your most frequently confused spellings.

Useful techniques include mnemonics, which stick in your mind to help you remember. Ones which make you smile are best – you may wish to adapt some of these to make them more appropriate for you. Examples of mnemonics are:

> *necessary: never eat cake, eat salad sandwiches and remain young*
> *their: ten huge elephants invaded Russia*

Other memory tips often take a section of a word, maybe a syllable such as 'cess' in 'necessity', to help the correct spelling to stick in your mind. Once again, you need to identify your common errors, but here are a few ideas.

> necessity: 'There is a cess pit in the middle of necessity.'
> secretary: 'Trust the secret to your secretary.'
> separate: 'I found a rat in the separated section.'
> friend: 'There's an end in friend.'
> business: 'Take a bus to business.'

Often breaking a word down into syllables can help you to fix the spelling in your mind so that it becomes automatic.

Your turn

Make up some mnemonics or phrases to help you remember words you find difficult to spell.

Some problems of punctuation

Sentence structure is covered earlier in this chapter, but it is very important to be clear about sentence boundaries and punctuation.

Sentence boundaries

The most common punctuation error is caused by not knowing where to end a sentence, which can lead to a really breathless style, galloping through a paragraph with only commas for pauses. Jamming ideas together may also confuse the reader or can lead to ambiguity. You need to develop an 'ear' when writing or reading to judge where to end sentences. Try reading some prose aloud to improve this listening skill. Punctuation is used in English to add stress, variety in pace and colour to written work, often as an alternative to underlining or italics.

Task 1

Read the following extract, which has deliberately been printed with missing full stops and capital letters, and try to make sense of it.

> My father left the decision to me although he says it's not valuable to be a fireman I have to convince him of my dedication even though I have a long way to go before I can be what I desire I took the first step by joining my school's safety patrol my parents appreciated my determination however I was impatient to become a fireman.

Words such as 'although' and 'however' can be important links, but the meaning alters according to which part of the paragraph they belong to. 'My father left the decision to me, although he says it's not valuable to be a fireman', means something different from, 'Although he says it's not valuable to be a fireman, I have to convince him of my dedication.' Similarly, 'My parents appreciated my determination, however', is different from, 'However, I was impatient to become a fireman.' 'However' and 'although' can each only belong to one clause; they cannot join two separate statements, and the punctuation helps the reader to know where they belong.

The other common error with sentence boundaries is writing in incomplete structures, such as omitting a finite verb by mistake (rather than for effect, as in a minor sentence or speech) or using the wrong pause indicator. Types of sentences are dealt with more fully earlier in this chapter, and referring to the section 'A range of sentence structures' on page 179 will help you to check the punctuation for your writing. What is most important, to you and the examiner, is whether you are writing in complete 'units' of sense. Should you be indicating the end of a sequence with a full stop, question mark, exclamation mark or semi-colon? Would the sense be improved by a conjunction or a relative pronoun, or is a comma the appropriate pause?

Here is part of an essay entitled 'Panic', which loses its momentum because the reader is unsure of which ideas belong together.

> One day after a dinner party at my friend's home, we heard a big blast. People were confused some were screaming others ran and the whole place was in chaos because people were seeking refuge all over. My friend's father went to find out what was going on. While he was gone one of my friends came up with a suggestion and it was Faith. She said that we should occupy ourselves by a game or dance. After a while the tension started to disappear when suddenly we heard another blast this time it was stronger than the first one. Every one of us stood still like statues no one knew what to do next.
>
> Suddenly we heard the door banging, and we thought that, that was the end of our lives when we saw Ann's father come in the house laughing. He explained that it was a bang from the mine four miles away it was blowing up the stones. Removing them from the ground producing that noise. After that we all felt a sigh of relief, everyone rejoiced and thanked God.

Compare this with a more clearly expressed and punctuated version.

> ... People were confused; some were screaming, while others ran. The whole place was in chaos as they sought refuge. While my friend's father went to find out what was going on, Faith, one of my other friends, suggested that we should occupy ourselves with a game or dance. After a while the tension had started to disappear until suddenly we heard another blast, this time stronger than the first. Each one of us stood as still as a statue, no one knowing what to do next.

Suddenly a bang at the door made us think the end of our lives had come, but no! It was only Ann's father, who was laughing. He explained that it had been a machine at the mine four miles away which had produced the blast while blowing up the stones to remove them from the ground. Sighing with relief, we all rejoiced and thanked God.

This version varies the sentence lengths and structures, using conjunctions, relative clauses and correctly placed participles to avoid unnecessary repetition and make the account tauter. The content is the same, but the organisation is clearer and the sense easier to follow.

Apostrophes

A commonly confused mark of punctuation is the apostrophe. It has two uses, the first to indicate omission of letters or contractions, as in 'wasn't', 'she's', 'I'll'. Although this is less formal, you will want to use it in speech, such as a radio script, a dialogue or maybe direct address to the reader. It is important to remember that there is only one apostrophe in a word, even if there is more than one contraction, and if the word is negative, the apostrophe goes between the 'n' and 't', as in 'shan't' for 'shall not' or 'can't' for 'cannot'.

The other use of the apostrophe is to show possession or belonging to something or someone. The main rule to remember is that regular singular names or nouns take, 's: 'the girl's laugh', 'Helena's bedroom', 'a star's brightness'. Regular plurals take s': 'the boys' team', 'the planets' sequence', 'the books' authors'. When dealing with words with irregular plurals, those where the singular ends in 's', and multi-syllabic words, it may be simpler to express the plural by changing the structure to, for example, 'the length of the radii' or 'the horns of the rhinoceros'. What is important is that you make clear in your writing who or what is the owner of the feature you are writing about.

Possessive pronouns ('yours', 'hers', 'his', 'ours', 'theirs') do not take an apostrophe. The only time you write 'it's' is to indicate an omission or contraction, such as 'it is' or more rarely 'it has', as in 'it's broken down'. Straightforward plurals do not take an apostrophe, so only put one in if you are sure that the sense demands it.

Inverted commas

Double inverted commas are needed for speech or quotation. If you insert a title or quotation within speech, you should use single inverted commas. Single inverted commas are also used for words used in a special sense. Make sure you always have an equal number.

"Thank you for my copy of 'Huckleberry Finn'," she gasped as we ran for the departure gates. "I'll read it on the plane." The indicator was flashing 'Flight delayed', so we had time for coffee after all.

"We've earned this after the panic!" I said. "Who's going to pay?"

"I've got no currency left," was her feeble excuse.

Remember that reported or indirect speech does not have inverted commas, but titles or quotations will still need single inverted commas. Look at this slightly altered version of the dialogue above to clarify this.

She thanked me for the copy of 'Huckleberry Finn' as we ran for the departure gates, promising to read it on the plane. As the indicator was flashing 'Flight delayed', we had time for coffee after all. We thought we'd earned it after the panic, but argued about the bill. I was the only one with currency, so it was my turn, again!

This chapter has reminded you of some important details which can really help to improve your writing. Hopefully, you should now feel quite confident about the exam, but there's just one more thing to consider, which can really make a difference to your result: checking and correcting your work.

8 Checking and correcting your examination paper

You should feel quite well prepared for the examination after completing this course and it would be a pity to spoil your chance of success by failing to correct errors made while you were sitting the final paper. A small proportion of people become extra alert when facing test conditions; it is more common, though, to feel nervous and ill at ease, which makes you liable to make mistakes. Many of us have left at least one examination, discussed it with others and then had a sense of shock: "Oh no! I left out this, or I thought that meant something else!" At the time it seems a disaster. Don't let such occasions worry you too much; things are rarely as disastrous as they seem. Examiners are told to take a positive view of any paper in front of them, giving candidates as much credit as possible for their work.

Here are some of the things you can do to help yourself before you hand in your paper.

Look carefully at instructions

Instructions about how to complete the paper (known as rubrics and always printed in **bold letters like this**) should be carefully considered before you start writing, as has been pointed out earlier (see Chapter 1). It is worth checking, though, to see if you can put right anything you have overlooked.

• Have you answered the correct number of questions in each section?

It is not uncommon for candidates to find a question they cannot answer, panic, and skim down the page looking for something manageable, missing out some questions they could attempt and get partly right, in order to gain a few more marks.

• Have you numbered the questions answered correctly?

Examiners accept the candidate's numbering, which usually matches that on the question paper. It can happen, though, that a candidate misses out a difficult question, then continues with the number sequence as if this hadn't been done.

• Have you taken into account the number of marks awarded for each question?

After each question, the number of marks awarded is given in brackets, for example (6 marks). It makes sense to check that you have included all the relevant ideas if the number suggests that there are several to be scored. It also makes sense to take more time doing questions which will give you most marks and, should you have the misfortune to run short of time, concentrate on completing the questions where you could score the higher number of potential marks.

- **Have you put the sections attempted at the top of the page and on the front cover?**

Examiners can do this for you, but it saves time and possible confusion if you do it for yourself.

- **Have you made it clear where you have written continuations?**

When a candidate decides to write more for an answer and finds there is no room left, he or she will usually put it at the end of the paper. Sometimes, though, continuation answers are scattered throughout where the examiner is not expecting to find them. The safest method is to write boldly:

CONTINUED ON PAGE 3

then turn to page three and write

CONTINUED FROM PAGE 1

or whatever numbering of pages is appropriate.

- **Have you taken care not to exceed word limits?**

If you have exceeded them, there may just be time for you to cross through the excess writing and rewrite it more concisely, so keeping within the word limit. Remember that writing too much on one question may mean that you run short of time for the rest, or even fail to complete the paper. Very lengthy answers are usually rambling, and candidates make more mistakes in expression and accuracy, so guard against this problem.

- **Have you missed out any sections?**

This happens sometimes if candidates forget to turn a page.

- **Have you answered too many questions?**

Some candidates write two or three essays! You may be surprised, thinking it is hard enough to write one. What happens in such a case is that the examiner marks ALL of them, and records the highest mark. If you spot your mistake you can cross through the work you do not want the examiner to mark.

- **Have you run out of time, leaving draft work uncopied?**

This sometimes happens with essay or summary questions. In such a case, the examiner will look back over the draft work, to see if you are entitled to any extra credit.

Check your paper for relevance

Candidates often spot for themselves that they have included the wrong information in a comprehension answer, cross it through and add something better.

Sometimes it seems that the situation cannot be saved. Suppose, for example, that you are asked in a summary question to select some material from a text and rewrite it for a different type of reader, for instance as an official report. If you realise, within a few minutes of the end of the examination, that you have just shortened the original passage and not made it like a report, you have no time to change the style. You could, though, write at the top of your answer:

Report re. oil spill off the coast of Java.
October 2002

and then add, at the end

Signed......................
Environmental Officer

or whatever fitted the text. That would signal to the examiner that you were trying at least to offer your work in the correct form, and it would gain you some marks.

When one considers an irrelevant essay, what can be done? Suppose that you have been asked to write about an occasion when you had a stroke of luck. You write an account about a day when you were caught speeding. A police car gave chase, flagged you down and you were very frightened, especially when a policeman with a gun in his holster came up to your car and ordered you out. You get caught up in the drama and tension of the incident, as you are writing. You conclude the incident by putting down that you were glad when the policeman let you off with a caution. You write a final sentence and sit back with a sigh of satisfaction. Just a minute! You haven't said anything about luck. You add a further sentence: 'So I got off, and that was a stroke of luck.' This makes some attempt at relevance, but you can do better than that. A student in this situation had a good idea. He wrote a title at the top of the essay: 'I spick no England.' Then he added the information at the end of the first paragraph that he had been brought up bilingual, and spoke English fluently. Later, when the policeman is interrogating him, he slipped in his reply, 'Sorry! I spick no England,' and the officer sighs and comments 'He doesn't understand a word I'm saying,' so letting him off lightly. That was certainly a stroke of luck, and the ingenuity of the writer amused the examiner.

Check your paper for accuracy of expression

On the front cover of the examination paper you will find the following statement printed:

Write your answers neatly and in good English.

'Good English' here means all the aspects of your work that were discussed in Chapter 7:

- your ability to write most of your answers in standard English;
- your ability to choose a suitable style to match a given audience;
- your acquaintance with a range of grammatical structures;

- your ability to use words appropriately and with precision;
- your knowledge of the 'conventions of written English' – that is, spelling and punctuation.

In the final check of your answer paper you should scan what you have written quickly, to pick up any mistakes of this kind that you can see at a glance. When you look back at your work as 'editor' rather than 'author' you see it rather differently. You are more detached, and can sometimes see errors that you made when your mind was preoccupied with getting ideas down on paper. When composing, people often leave out words or repeat them – check for this and correct it. Not everyone can spell well, or recognise that mistakes have been made. Most people make some mistakes, especially with words that they do not often see written down, or use in writing, for example 'psychic' or 'paradigm'. Concentrate on getting right words that commonly recur, or that you are going to use a lot in a piece of work. Everyone, for instance, can spell words which are actually printed on the paper. Remember that you have a large word bank that is all correct, right in front of you. There can be no excuse for candidates working on a themed paper who misspell key words which are printed in the texts under their noses! It does make a bad impression if you have spelt the word 'millennium' or 'environment' wrongly (the usual wrong versions are 'millenium' or 'enviroment'). One candidate persistently wrote the name 'Frankenstein' (which was correctly printed five times on the examination paper) as 'Frank N. Stein'!

Finally ...

Before you hand your paper to the invigilator, do four more things.

- **Check** that your name, examination and centre number are clear and correct on the front cover of your answer book.
- **Check** that the number of sections and questions are listed on the front cover of the answer book in the order that you have answered them, and are also written above the relevant piece of writing inside the answer book.
- **Check** that you have crossed through all rough work, drafts and false starts that you do not want the examiner to assess. Do not obliterate these too heavily, though, because remember that the examiner will look over them and give you credit if you run out of time copying up draft answers.
- **Check** that any extra sheets you have used are firmly attached to your answer book.

Then you can hand your paper in with the feeling that you have done your best. We wish you good luck in the examination!

Exemplar examination paper

Read the following pieces and answer the questions which follow. Make sure that you answer the starred questions (*) in your own words.

Text 1

Modified Man

Scientific developments have led some prophets to foresee the emergence of a new relationship between man and machines, a relationship in which the two become so intermixed as to be virtually indistinguishable. The word 'cyborg' (an abbreviation of 'cybernetic organism') has been coined for such hybrids. The essential difference between them is two-way. The machine not only receives instructions from the man, but also informs the man of the conditions it is encountering, just as his own hands or feet do.

Another development, for space purposes, is 'slaves' or robot doubles. The idea is simply to establish a radio link between a robot and its operator. This link would carry sound and television signals, instructions from the operator to the slave and feedback from the slave to the operator. In this way, an astronaut could sit within his spacecraft, while his slave went out into space to make a repair or link up equipment – the advantage being that the slave requires no oxygen supply, heating or other maintenance while it is there, and is impervious to radiation, while danger to the astronaut is minimised. Equally, slaves could be sent out on the surface of the moon; if one dropped into a crevasse it could be replaced by another.

Adapted from The Biological Time Bomb *by Gordon Rattray Taylor.*

Text 2

Robot raiders of the red planet

Tim Radford reports on the new wave of intelligent machines about to start exploring the surface of Mars.

Mars is about to be invaded by another wave of robots. The first will land violently in a crude attempt to get under the planet's skin. The second will bounce down to end up perching daintily on its surface. But in future missions others will crawl, fly and drift across the planet and even one day arrive as floating 'personal assistants' to the first space-suited human invaders.

Two bits of metal the size of basketballs will detach themselves from a freshly-arrived spacecraft and crash at the edge of the Martian south polar icecap at 200 metres a second. As they hit the frozen carbon dioxide and soil of the red planet, they will shatter and release two small probes which will punch up to two metres into the planet's rock.

Then, little antennae will pop up to establish communication with scientists back on earth. Tiny sensors will 'feel' for evidence of water buried under the Martian soil, then they will spend 50 hours measuring soil temperature and sending back weather reports from Mars.

They will land 200km from another robot, the Mars polar lander, which will transmit back to Earth both pictures and sounds of stormy weather on a cold, hostile planet. The two tiny spaceprobes will be fitted with delicate instruments but will hit the planet at 400mph. "Imagine requiring a computer to work after being hit by a truck at 400mph," says Nasa. But even if things do go wrong, Russian, European and US scientists and engineers will go on sending robot probes to Mars for years.

The ultimate ambition, decades away, is a human landing. There could be tiny robot helicopters buzzing ahead to survey dangerous terrain. And they could be accompanied by a new kind of 'hands-free' nanny and secretary designed to keep an eye on future human space travellers.

The robot personal assistant will be about as big as a softball, but it will act as 'another set of ears, eyes and nose' for the crew. Like something out of science fiction, the autonomous intelligent globule will float alongside a spacecraft crew member but keep out of his way.

It will monitor gases and bacteria in the air, keep a check on oxygen levels, serve as a personal radio link, act as a navigator and even open channels for video-conferencing with other astronauts or mission control back on earth.

From The Guardian.

Innovations: Guards and gastrobots

• Thai scientists have just unveiled Roboguard. It totes a laser-sighted gun and can track suspects via infra-red sensors. It can fire at will, or it can check with a human via the Internet before it attacks. So far the fire command is protected by a password.

• A Brussels consortium is working on a full-size, autonomous walking robot dinosaur which will stroll round European museums. The creation of the automaton, based on an iguanadon, has involved an expert on dinosaur biomechanics. But the robot engineers behind the project are after a bigger prize: a 'walking' rescue machine that could step through minefields, over avalanches or collapsed buildings looking for human survivors.

• A flesh-eating robot called Chew-Chew could be the first automaton to be completely powered by food. The 12-wheeled 'gastrobot' was unveiled in Hawaii. It uses bacteria to convert food into chemical energy. Meat is the most efficient fuel, but a gastrobot could even mow lawns and use the clippings for fuel. Another  team has designed a slug-eating robot, and suggested that a fish-eating robot could monitor beaches for sharks.

• Scientists from New York and Israel have co-operated on a robot surgeon which performs human knee replacement operations. They argue that a human-monitored robot hand would always be steadier, would work in finer detail, and would never get tired.

• Los Alamos scientists have built tiny little four-legged robots which have been tested on fields of unexploded mines. If a leg gets blown off, the robot carries on with only three, or two, or one.

From The Guardian.

Sony predicts decade of the robot

The creator of Sony's robot pet Aibo says his toy will be the companion of the future, but its days as a guide dog for the blind are still far off.

"The 1980s was the decade of the PC, the 90s of the Internet, but I believe the decade just starting will be the decade of the robot," a spokesperson said in Tokyo.

A version of the robot pet has a camera in its nose to capture those special moments and can better express anger or joy. The makers believe that in ten years' time most households will keep two or three personal robots and their performance will increase 100 times.

From The Guardian.

SECTION A Comprehension
You are advised to spend about 40 minutes answering the questions in this section.

Read Text 1.

1 In your own words, what information would the radio link between a robot slave and its operator carry? **(4 marks)**

2 Give a word or short phrase (**maximum 5 words**) for the following as used in the passage:
   coined
   impervious
   minimise
   crevasse **(4 marks)**

Read Text 2.

3 The writer uses several verbs to describe the motion of robots. In your own words, can you explain the difference between 'crawl', 'drift' and 'float' as used in the passage? **(3 marks)**

4 There is information in the first and second paragraphs about the landing of the first robot in this experiment. Using both paragraphs, explain in your own words:
   (i) why it will 'land violently';
   (ii) what scientists hope it will do immediately after landing. **(4 marks)**

5 Identify three names for future robot helpers in space. **(3 marks)**

Read Text 3.

6 What are:

(i) the similarities between the 'walking' rescue machine in the second section and the robots in the fifth section?

(ii) the major differences between these two machines? **(6 marks)**

7 From information given in this extract, identify the robot which seems to be the most independent and the one which is the least independent.

(2 marks)

From Texts 1 and 2.

8 Both writers describe the work of robots in space. They seem to have very different attitudes to these machines. If you were a robot, which writer would you prefer to work for? Refer to key words or phrases in the text to justify your choice. **(4 marks)**

TOTAL FOR SECTION A: 30 MARKS

SECTION B Summary and directed writing
You are advised to spend about one hour on this section.

You have been asked to contribute to a discussion on the value of using robots instead of people in dangerous situations. **Using information from these four passages**, write the text of your speech, referring to as many different uses of robots as you can to support your viewpoint.

Although you may have to use some technical terms, **try to choose your own words as far as possible**. Marks will be given for content, style and accuracy, and will be deducted for excess copying. Do not write more than 200 words. **(35 marks)**

TOTAL FOR SECTION B: 35 MARKS

SECTION C Essay
You are advised to spend about one hour on this section

Choose one of the following topics on which to write between 350 and 400 words. You may take ideas from the texts you have read for the other parts of the paper, and the illustrations, but you will receive no credit for copying from them.

1 Do you think humans should try to explore more of space or concentrate on this planet? Give details to justify your choice.

2 Write the opening or ending of a science fiction story which includes robots.

3 'The 1980s was the decade of the PC, the 90s of the Internet, but I believe the decade just starting will be the decade of the robot.' (Quotation from manufacturer of robot pet illustrated in Text 4.) How far do you think this prediction will come true? **(35 marks)**

TOTAL FOR SECTION C: 35 MARKS

END

Answers to exemplar examination paper

Finally, let's look at some sample answers to the exemplar comprehension questions. A candidate's answers and the examiner's comments are given below.

Section A Comprehension (30 marks)

Question 1

In your own words, what information would the radio link between a robot slave and its operator carry? **(4 marks)**

The radio link would carry television and sound signals, instructions to the slave from the operator and feedback the other way. (1 mark)

Although the information is correct, this candidate has made minimal attempt to express the ideas in his own words, merely altering the order slightly.

Question 2

Give a word or short phrase (maximum 5 words) for the following as used in the passage: **(4 marks)**
coined

faked

The candidate has been misled by the mention of 'coin'. Better answers would be 'invented' or 'made up'.

impervious

impermeable

Although this definition is correct, it relies on the same structure as the word in the question. A better way of expressing it would be 'not permeable', to show understanding of the prefix im-. 'Not able to be penetrated' would be excellent and within the five word allowance.

minimised

lessened

This is on the right lines, but not specific enough. 'Reduced to the least possible' or 'made as small as possible' would be better.

crevasse

crack

This answer is acceptable. 'A deep crack' or 'fissure' or 'deep split in ice' would be more precise.

(total of 2 marks)

Question 3

The writer uses several verbs to describe the motion of robots. In your own words, can you explain the difference between 'crawl', 'drift' and 'float' as used in the passage? **(3 marks)**

'Crawl' is on the ground, 'drift' and 'float' are in the air. (1 mark)

This distinguishes where the actions take place, but doesn't distinguish between 'drift' and 'float'.

Question 4

There is information in the first and second paragraphs about the landing of the first robot in this experiment. Using both paragraphs, explain in your own words:

i) why it will 'land violently';

ii) what scientists hope it will do immediately after landing. **(4 marks)**

(i) *The aim is that the missiles will land with such force that they will break through the surface of the planet.*

(ii) *The containers will break open and a sharp tube will strike two metres beneath the ground; small aerials will relay messages; feelers will search for proof of water under the ground, measure the temperature of the land for 50 hours and communicate meteorological information.* (4 marks)

This is an excellent answer; although some of the words reflect the language of the passage, they are used in such a way as to show understanding. Some of the ideas, such as 'water' and 'temperature' could not easily be expressed in other ways. Five points are made: full marks would be given for four of the possible points, clearly made, with an attempt to use the candidate's own expression. No marks would be given for completely copied ideas.

Question 5

Identify three names for future robot helpers in space. **(3 marks)**

personal assistant(s), nanny, secretary (3 marks)

All correct ('globule' would not score, as it is not a name for a helper).

What are:
(i) the similarities between the 'walking' rescue machine in the second section and the robots in the fifth section?
(ii) the major differences between these two machines? **(6 marks)**

(i) *They could each be used in minefields; they each have legs/ could walk.*

(ii) *The first is large, the second small; the first could also be used in snow or rubble. The second has already been tested in minefields; it can operate even after losing up to three of its legs.* (6 marks)

This candidate shows clear understanding of the question and the text. The answer is organised and thoughtful. It avoids discussion of pseudo-sentimental issues such as seeing the robot losing legs. It also shows awareness of the mark allocation: six separate points are made. This question did not ask for the candidate's own words, but to gain full marks you must be able to recognise synonyms and alternative phrasing, such as 'minefields' and 'fields of unexploded mines'; and antonyms, such as 'full-size' and 'tiny'.

Here are some ideas on how to answer the remaining questions.

From information given in this extract, identify the robot which seems to be the most independent and the one which is the least independent. **(2 marks)**

The walking robot dinosaur is described as 'autonomous', suggesting independence; the robot hand is described as 'human-monitored', so cannot work on its own.

Both writers describe the work of robots in space. They seem to have very different attitudes to these machines. If you were a robot, which writer would you prefer to work for? Refer to key words or phrases in the text to justify your choice. **(4 marks)**

The first writer calls the robots 'slaves', which would take the risks, protecting the astronaut. They could also be easily replaced, emphasising that they are only machines. The second writer uses anthropomorphic names, such as 'personal assistant' and 'nanny', with more human attributes and senses. The terms 'small' and 'tiny' are also friendlier. I should therefore prefer to work for the second writer.

Section B Summary and directed writing (35 marks)

The marks are divided between content, style and audience, and expression and accuracy.

Content, style and audience

The following list of points refers to the value of using robots instead of people in dangerous situations. The answer as a whole is assessed out of 20 for content, style and audience.

- In space, an astronaut could stay inside the spacecraft.
- The 'slave' could carry out repairs ...
- ... or link equipment.
- There is no need for air ...
- ... or warmth ...
- ... or other support.
- The robot is not at risk of damage from radiation.
- Any robots which disappeared could be replaced.
- Equipment could be sent in containers which can crash land.
- Robots could be used to view possible dangers ...
- ... they could monitor air quality ...
- ... and oxygen levels.
- On land, robots could go through minefields...
- ... search in avalanches ...
- ... or damaged buildings, where it would be dangerous for people to explore.
- Robots can continue working even if they are damaged ...
- ... unlike an injured person.
- In water, they could patrol for sharks.

Expression and accuracy

The 15 marks available for expression and accuracy take account of how well you have used your own words. To score well, you should:

- use standard English grammar and idioms;
- use a range of sentence structures;
- organise and structure your text well;
- use a good range of vocabulary;
- express your ideas clearly and precisely;
- use accurate spelling and punctuation;
- use an appropriate style;
- use your own words;
- sustain the theme and tone throughout your writing.

Section C Essay (35 marks)

The examiner will identify the strengths and weaknesses of your essay, and will place your answer in one of five mark ranges. To score well, you will need to:

- write using the standard grammatical forms and idioms of English;
- write effectively, with confidence and a sense of style;
- sustain a topic with conviction;
- organise a range of ideas coherently;
- demonstrate an impressive range of vocabulary and variety of syntax;
- show fluency in expression, with few errors of grammar or syntax;
- write very accurately with regard to spelling and punctuation.

Glossary

abstract	main points of a text
alliteration	repetition of a consonant at the beginning of a word
ambiguous	confusing because there is more than one meaning
assertion	statement with no supporting evidence
audience	readers to whom a text is addressed
balanced statement	two ideas separated by a conjunction and phrased alike
broadsheet	newspaper which is formal in style
casual style	relaxed style, used when writing to / speaking for a known audience
chronological organisation	writing organised along a time sequence
classic organisation	writing organised with a beginning, a middle and an end
cliché	an overused phrase, often a metaphor or a simile
coda	a final comment in a text, added on to the conclusion
compare	show how two ideas are alike
complex sentence	a sentence with more than one clause joined by a subordinate conjunction
complication	the development of a text
compound sentence	a sentence with more than one clause joined by a co-ordinate conjunction
compound–complex sentence	a sentence with a main clause and a clause joined by both co-ordinate and subordinate conjunctions
conflation	two ideas with one verb which seem related but may not be
connotation	the related meaning of a word/phrase
consequential organisation	writing organised in a logically progressive way
consultative style	used when writing/speaking to someone you know, but not personally
contrast	two ideas which are opposite
conversational style	see *casual style*

co-ordinate clause	two equal clauses with a conjunction
correlative	ideas which are mutually related
denotation	the precise meaning of a word or phrase
dynamic	style of opening which attracts a reader's attention
elided	with a syllable omitted
ellipsis	omission of words from a sentence which are needed to complete the sense
evaluation	part of a text giving the writer's view
explicit comprehension	understanding ideas in a text which are clearly stated
extended metaphor	implied comparison or contrast throughout a text
fable	story involving the supernatural
filler	word or phrase put in to ease speech
first draft	initial written sketch of an idea
formal style	used when writing/speaking to someone of higher status or not known to you
fragment	a partial sentence, which may omit the subject, the predicate, or both
generalisation	something lacking precise details
headline–punchline	a technique whereby the key initial idea is repeated at the end
icon	an image standing for an idea
inference	an idea which is not stated directly
inferential reading	reading between the lines
intensive reading	careful, slow reading
interrogative	a question
imperative	a command
jargon	terms that obscure meaning, unlike subject-specific terms
key idea	an idea which is central to theme of a text
ladder statement	a sentence which builds step by step to a conclusion
literal meaning	the exact, explicit meaning
loaded word	a word with a bias or covert meaning
main clause	clause which is central to theme of a sentence
metaphor	stated comparison which is not literally exact
minor sentence	see *fragment*
mixed metaphor	text using different images which collide and confuse
orientation	a scene-setting introduction

ornate language	language which is too elaborate, often with too many adjectives
over-writing	straining to impress with vocabulary
parable	see *fable* – usually with a moral, also
paradigm	basic pattern of organising writing
parallelism	putting similar or different ideas side by side
paraphrase	to write in your own words but keeping close to a text
persuader words	adverbs to make a reader agree
progressive	building on each idea to establish the next
redundant phrasing	when the same idea is repeated in different words
reflective reading	thoughtful reading, drawing on life experience
related idea	idea which supports the main (key) idea of a text
resolution	the conclusion of a text
rhetorical question	a question to be answered in the mind
rubric	instructions for how to answer questions
scanning	steady reading, glancing along the lines
search reading	reading to gather information
simile	a comparison introduced by 'like' or 'as'
simple sentence	a sentence with one subject and predicate
skimming	reading by glancing through the text quickly
speech act	the remark(s) of one speaker
statement	sentence asserting a fact
strap line	line of text above a headline
sub-heading	minor heading within a text
subject-specific vocabulary	terms needed to define a topic not commonly known
subordinate clause	a clause which is dependent on another clause
sub-topic	point supporting the main idea
supporting details	minor points expanding an idea
tabloid	a newspaper which is popular in style
tag question	a statement which ends with a question
verbatim copying	reproducing a text word for word
wordiness	when too many words are used
word limit	maximum number of words which may be written